175VEGETABLE
CURRIES

175 VEGETABLE CURRIES

Deliciously hot and spicy recipes from round the world, shown in 190 beautiful photographs

MRIDULA BALJEKAR

southwater

This edition is published by Southwater, an imprint of Anness Publishing Ltd
Blaby Road, Wigston, Leicestershire LE18 4SE; info@anness.com

www.southwaterbooks.com; www.annesspublishing.com

If you like the images in this book and would like to investigate using them for publishing, promotions or advertising,
please visit our website www.practicalpictures.com for more information.

© Anness Publishing Ltd 2013

A CIP catalogue record for this book is available from the British Library.

Publisher: Joanna Lorenz
Editor: Joy Wotton
Jacket Design: Nigel Partridge
Production Controller: Mai-Ling Collyer

Previously published as part of a larger volume, *500 Curries*

PUBLISHER'S NOTE
Although the advice and information in this book are believed to be accurate and true at the time
of going to press, neither the authors nor the publisher can accept any legal responsibility or liability for
any errors or omissions that may have been made nor for any inaccuracies nor for any loss, harm or injury
that comes about from following instructions or advice in this book.

Notes

Bracketed terms are intended for American readers.
For all recipes, quantities are given in both metric and imperial measures and, where appropriate, in standard
cups and spoons. Follow one set of measures, but not a mixture, because they are not interchangeable.
Standard spoon and cup measures are level. 1 tsp = 5ml, 1 tbsp = 15ml, 1 cup = 250ml/8fl oz. Australian standard tablespoons
are 20ml. Australian readers should use 3 tsp in place of 1 tbsp for measuring small quantities.
American pints are 16fl oz/2 cups. American readers should use 20fl oz/2.5 cups in place of 1 pint when measuring liquids.
Electric oven temperatures in this book are for conventional ovens. When using a fan oven, the temperature will probably need to
be reduced by about 10–20°C/20–40°F. Since ovens vary, you should check with your manufacturer's instruction book for guidance.

The nutritional analysis given for each recipe is calculated per portion (i.e. serving or item), unless otherwise stated.
If the recipe gives a range, such as Serves 4–6, then the nutritional analysis will be for the smaller portion size, i.e. 6 servings.
The analysis does not include optional ingredients, such as salt added to taste.
Medium (US large) eggs are used unless otherwise stated.
Vegetable ghee has been used in the recipes, but ghee made from butter can be used instead.

Main front cover image shows Aubergine Pilaff with Cinnamon – for recipe, see page 52

Contents

Introduction

Spice up your cooking with this fabulous collection of over 175 sizzling step-by-step recipes. Superb vegetarian dishes from around the world have been brought together in this

fabulous collection of dishes from as far afield as the Middle East, Morocco and the Caribbean. Since many ancient religions that promote vegetarianism originated in ancient India and South-east Asia, including Hinduism and Buddhism, these cuisines are especially rich in excellent, appetizing recipes that make the very best of vegetarian and vegan cooking. Here are perfect recipes for vegetable samosas, balti mushrooms in a garlic and chilli sauce and a spectacular spiced Indian rice with spinach, tomatoes and cashew nuts. Easy-to-follow vegetarian recipes with step-by-step instructions allow cooks of all abilities to create wonderful, memorable curry meals.

Exotic spiced sauces, or curries, have been used for thousands of years to liven up the daily staples of rice, noodles and bread. Turmeric, cumin, coriander, cardamom, chilli and many other pungent spices and scented flavourings contribute magical tastes and aromas to dishes. It is the careful blending of these various spices, herbs and other aromatics, often into a mixed powder or blended into a paste to which other ingredients are then added, that defines much of the art of creating mouthwatering curries. You will find that many of the spices, herbs and aromatics used in this book are readily available from stores and supermarkets. Some ingredients may be harder to buy – mango powder, asafoetida, galangal and fennel, as well as fresh leaves such as curry leaves, kaffir lime leaves and fenugreek – however, there are many Asian speciality stores where these ingredients can be bought or you can look for them online or through mail order.

With their fabulous flavours, fresh ingredients and speedy preparation time, vegetable curries are perfect for healthy modern living. Traditionally, curry in India is accompanied by rice or breads, and in South-east Asia by rice or noodles. Main courses are usually served in small quantities, surrounded by inviting little side dishes, such as pickles, chutneys, salads and sambals, flavoured with fresh herbs and chillies, yogurt or soy sauce, which are used to spice up the main meals.

Since earliest times, India has been known as the spice bowl of the world, and South-east Asia, too, has its own important place in the international history of the spice trade. The use of spices in curry was an established way of life in these sun-drenched, monsoon-fed lands long before traders and merchants, including Arabs, English, Dutch, Portuguese and Spanish, were lured by the value of these exotic ingredients.

Although the origins of the word curry are shrouded in antiquity, the word is generally believed to be an anglicized version of the south Indian word *kaari*. In India, the word refers to a sauce or gravy used as an accompaniment to moisten rice or to make bread more enjoyable. Other theories suggest the word *cury* has existed in English in the context of cooking since the 14th century, and that it was originally derived from the French verb *cuire* (to cook).

Spicy food is universally popular, and this collection brings together vegetarian dishes from countries all around the world, including red-hot recipes from India, the Caribbean, Korea, Malaysia, Burma, Thailand, Japan, North Africa and the Mediterranean. Travel into the exotic world of spice with Thai curry spiced potato samosas, Moroccan spiced aubergine tagine, hot Masala okra with coriander, and Madras sambal with chilli and spices.

Recipes are clearly organized by type, making the book instantly accessible for any lover of hot and spicy vegetable curries. Sections include appetizers and soups; vegetable curries; main course rice; rice side dishes and breads; side dishes; chutneys, relishes and pickles; and salads and slaws. With every recipe clearly explained and a photograph of the finished dish, you are sure to find a curry dish that is perfect for you.

Curry Crackers

Crisp curry-flavoured crackers are very good with creamy cheese or yogurt dips and make an unusual nibble with pre-dinner drinks. Add a pinch of cayenne pepper for an extra kick.

Makes about 30

175g/6oz/1½ cups self-raising (self-rising) flour, plus extra for dusting

pinch of salt
10ml/2 tsp garam masala
75g/3oz/6 tbsp butter, diced
5ml/1 tsp finely chopped fresh coriander (cilantro)
1 egg, beaten

For the topping
1 egg, beaten
black onion seeds
garam masala

1 Preheat the oven to 200°C/400°F/Gas 6. Put the flour, salt and garam masala into a bowl. Rub in the butter until the mixture resembles fine breadcrumbs. Stir in the coriander, add the egg and mix to a soft dough.

2 Turn out on to a lightly floured surface and knead gently until smooth. Roll out to a thickness of about 3mm/⅛in.

3 Cut the dough into neat rectangles measuring about 7.5 × 2.5cm/3 × 1in. Brush with a little beaten egg and sprinkle each cracker with a few black onion seeds. Place on non-stick baking sheets and bake in the oven for about 12 minutes, until the crackers are light golden brown all over.

4 Remove from the oven and, using a metal spatula, transfer to a wire rack. Put a little garam masala in a saucer and, using a dry pastry brush, dust each cracker with a little of the spice mixture. Leave to cool before serving.

> **Cook's Tip**
> Garam masala is a mixture of Indian spices that usually contains a blend of cinnamon, cloves, peppercorns, cardamom seeds and cumin seeds. You can buy it ready-made from supermarkets or Asian stores or make your own.

Low-fat Curry Thins

These spicy little crackers are low in fat and are ideal as a tasty pre-dinner snack.

Makes 12

50g/2oz/1½ cups plain (all-purpose) flour, plus extra for dusting

pinch of salt
5ml/1 tsp curry powder
1.5ml/¼ tsp chilli powder
15ml/1 tbsp chopped fresh coriander (cilantro)
30ml/2 tbsp water

1 Preheat the oven to 180°C/350°F/Gas 4.

2 Sift the flour and salt into a mixing bowl. Add the curry powder and the chilli powder. Make a well in the centre and add the coriander and water. Gradually incorporate the flour and mix to a firm dough.

3 Turn out the dough on to a lightly floured surface, knead with your hands until the dough is smooth and then set it aside to rest for 5 minutes.

4 Cut the dough into 12 equal pieces and knead each into a small ball. Roll out each ball very thinly to a 10cm/4in round, sprinkling more flour over the dough if necessary to prevent it from sticking to the rolling pin.

5 Arrange the rounds on two ungreased baking sheets, spaced apart, then bake in the preheated oven for 15 minutes. Use a metal spatula to turn the crackers over once during cooking. When very lightly browned, using a metal spatula, carefully transfer the crackers to a wire rack to cool.

> **Cook's Tip**
> Commercial curry powders vary enormously in flavour and their degree of heat, depending on the specific spices used and their proportions. The best-quality ones tend to be more expensive, but this is not invariably the case. Try different brands until you find one that you like.

Curry Crackers Energy 39kcal/164kJ; Protein 0.6g; Carbohydrate 4.6g, of which sugars 0.1g; Fat 2.2g, of which saturates 1.3g; Cholesterol 5mg; Calcium 11mg; Fibre 0.3g; Sodium 17mg.
Low-fat Curry Thins Energy 17kcal/73kJ; Protein 0.5g; Carbohydrate 3.6g, of which sugars 0.1g; Fat 0.2g, of which saturates 0g; Cholesterol 0mg; Calcium 14mg; Fibre 0.4g; Sodium 6mg.

Crisp Fried Spicy Aubergine

The spicy gram flour coating on these slices is deliciously crisp, revealing the succulent aubergine beneath. Choose a firm aubergine with a glossy skin.

Serves 4

50g/2oz/½ cup gram flour
15ml/1 tbsp semolina or ground rice
2.5ml/½ tsp onion seeds
5ml/1 tsp cumin seeds
2.5ml/½ tsp fennel seeds or aniseeds
2.5–5ml/½–1 tsp hot chilli powder
2.5ml/½ tsp salt, or to taste
1 large aubergine (eggplant)
vegetable oil, for deep-frying
chutney, to serve

1 Sift the gram flour into a large mixing bowl and add the semolina or ground rice with the onion and cumin seeds, fennel or aniseeds, and the hot chilli powder and salt.

2 Halve the aubergine lengthways and cut each half into 5mm/¼in thick slices. Rinse them and shake off the excess water, but do not pat dry. With some of the water still clinging to the slices, add them to the spiced gram flour mixture. Toss them around until they are evenly coated with the flour. Use a spoon if necessary to ensure that all the flour is used.

3 Heat the oil in a karahi, wok or deep-fryer to a temperature of 190°C/375°F, or until a cube of bread dropped in the oil browns in about 45 seconds. If it floats immediately, the oil has reached the right temperature.

4 Fry the spice-coated aubergine slices in a single layer. Avoid overcrowding the pan as this will lower the temperature, resulting in a soggy texture. Fry until crisp and well browned. Drain on kitchen paper and serve with a chutney.

> **Cook's Tip**
> *Fennel and aniseeds aid digestion, and many deep-fried Indian recipes use them for this reason. As with most seeds, they should be stored in a cool, dark place for no more than six months.*

Curried Sweet Potato Balls

These sweet potato balls, with roots in Chinese and South-east Asian cooking, are delicious dipped in a fiery red chilli sauce, fried black chilli sauce or hot peanut dipping sauce. They are ideal for serving as a pre-appetizer.

Serves 4

450g/1lb sweet potatoes or taro root, boiled or baked, and peeled
30ml/2 tbsp sugar
15ml/1 tbsp Indian curry powder or spice blend of your choice
25g/1oz fresh root ginger, peeled and grated
150g/5oz/1¼ cups glutinous rice flour or plain (all-purpose) flour
salt
sesame seeds or poppy seeds
vegetable oil, for deep-frying
dipping sauce, to serve

1 In a large bowl, mash the cooked sweet potatoes or taro root. Beat in the sugar, curry powder and ginger.

2 Add the rice or plain flour (sift it if you are using plain flour) and salt to the bowl, and mix well to work into a stiff dough, adding more flour if necessary.

3 Pull off lumps of the dough and mould them into small balls with your hands – you should be able to make roughly 24 balls. Roll the balls on a bed of sesame seeds or poppy seeds until they are completely coated.

4 Heat enough oil for deep-frying in a wok. Fry the sweet potato balls in batches, until golden. Drain on kitchen paper. Serve the balls with wooden skewers to make it easier to dip them into a dipping sauce of your choice.

> **Variation**
> *Also known as dasheen, taro root is a starchy tuber cultivated in many parts of Asia. If you opt to use it instead of the sweet potato in this recipe, you may need to add more sugar as it has a much more nutty taste when cooked.*

Spiced Sweet Potato Turnovers

The lightly spiced sweet potatoes make a great filling for this recipe.

Serves 4

1 sweet potato, about 225g/8oz
30ml/2 tbsp vegetable oil
2 shallots, finely chopped
10ml/2 tsp coriander
    seeds, crushed
5ml/1 tsp ground cumin
5ml/1 tsp garam masala
115g/4oz/1 cup frozen peas
15ml/1 tbsp chopped
    fresh mint

salt and ground black pepper
mint sprigs, to garnish

For the pastry

15ml/1 tbsp olive oil
1 small egg, plus extra to glaze
150ml/¼ pint/⅔ cup natural
    (plain) yogurt
115g/4oz/8 tbsp butter, melted
275g/10oz/2½ cups plain
    (all-purpose) flour
1.5ml/¼ tsp bicarbonate of soda
    (baking soda)
10ml/2 tsp paprika
5ml/1 tsp salt

1 Cook the sweet potato in boiling water for 15–20 minutes, until tender. Drain well and leave to cool. When cool enough to handle, peel the potato and cut into 1cm/½in cubes.

2 Heat the oil in a frying pan, add the shallots and cook until softened. Add the sweet potato and fry until it browns at the edges. Add the spices and fry for a few seconds. Remove from the heat and add the peas, mint and seasoning. Leave to cool.

3 Preheat the oven to 200°C/400°F/Gas 6. Grease a baking sheet. To make the pastry, whisk together the oil and egg, stir in the yogurt, then add the melted butter. Sift the flour, bicarbonate of soda, paprika and salt into a bowl, then stir into the yogurt mixture to form a soft dough. Turn out the dough, and knead gently. Roll it out, then stamp it out into rounds.

4 Spoon 10ml/2 tsp of the filling on to one side of each round, then fold over and seal the edges. Re-roll the trimmings and stamp out more rounds until the filling has all been used.

5 Arrange the turnovers on the baking sheet and brush the tops with beaten egg. Bake in the oven for about 20 minutes until crisp and golden brown. Serve hot, garnished with the mint.

Vegetable Samosas

Throughout the East, these spicy snacks are sold by street vendors, and eaten at any time of day.

Makes about 20

1 packet 25cm/10in square
    spring roll wrappers, thawed
    if frozen
30ml/2 tbsp plain (all-purpose)
    flour, mixed to a paste with
    a little water
vegetable oil, for deep-frying
coriander (cilantro) leaves,
    to garnish

For the filling

25g/1oz/2 tbsp ghee or
    unsalted butter

1 small onion, finely chopped
1cm/½in piece fresh root ginger,
    peeled and chopped
1 garlic clove, crushed
2.5ml/½ tsp chilli powder
1 large potato, about 225g/8oz,
    cooked until just tender and
    finely diced
50g/2oz/½ cup cauliflower
    florets, lightly cooked, chopped
    into small pieces
50g/2oz/½ cup frozen
    peas, thawed
5–10ml/1–2 tsp garam masala
15ml/1 tbsp chopped fresh
    coriander (cilantro) leaves
    and stems
squeeze of lemon juice
salt

1 To make the filling, heat the ghee or butter in a large frying pan and fry the onion, ginger and garlic for 5 minutes until the onion has softened but not browned.

2 Add the chilli powder and cook for 1 minute, then stir in the potato, cauliflower and peas. Sprinkle with garam masala and set aside to cool. Stir in the coriander, lemon juice and salt.

3 Cut the spring roll wrappers into three equal strips (or two for larger samosas). Brush the edges with a little of the flour paste. Place a small spoonful of filling about 2cm/¾in in from the edge of one strip. Fold one corner over the filling to make a triangle and continue this folding until the entire strip has been used and a triangular pastry has been formed. Seal any open edges with more flour and water paste.

4 Heat the oil for deep-frying to 190°C/375°F and fry the samosas, a few at a time, until golden and crisp. Drain well on kitchen paper and serve hot, garnished with coriander leaves.

Potato Turnovers Energy 660kcal/2760kJ; Protein 13.9g; Carbohydrate 75.8g, of which sugars 9.3g; Fat 35.9g, of which saturates 17g; Cholesterol 105mg; Calcium 216mg; Fibre 5.2g; Sodium 740mg.
Vegetable Samosas Energy 56kcal/235kJ; Protein 1.3g; Carbohydrate 10g, of which sugars 0.8g; Fat 1.4g, of which saturates 0.2g; Cholesterol 0mg; Calcium 16mg; Fibre 0.7g; Sodium 8mg.

Green Curry Puffs

Shrimp paste and green curry sauce, used judiciously, give these puffs their distinctive spicy, savoury flavour, and the addition of chilli steps up the heat.

Makes 24

24 small wonton wrappers, about
  8cm/3¼in square, thawed
  if frozen
15ml/1 tbsp cornflour
  (cornstarch), mixed to a paste
  with 30ml/2 tbsp water
vegetable oil, for deep-frying

For the filling

1 small potato, about 115g/4oz,
  boiled and mashed
25g/1oz/3 tbsp cooked petits pois
  (baby peas)
25g/1oz/3 tbsp cooked corn
few sprigs fresh coriander
  (cilantro), chopped
1 small fresh red chilli, seeded
  and finely chopped
½ lemon grass stalk,
  finely chopped
15ml/1 tbsp soy sauce
5ml/1 tsp shrimp paste or
  fish sauce
5ml/1 tsp Thai green curry paste

1 To make the filling combine the mashed potato, peas, corn, coriander, chilli and lemon grass in a bowl. Stir in the soy sauce, shrimp paste or fish sauce and Thai green curry paste.

2 Lay out one wonton wrapper on a chopping board or clean work surface and place a teaspoon of the filling in the centre of the wrapper. Brush a little of the cornflour paste along two sides of the square wrapper.

3 Fold the other two sides over to meet them, then press together to make a triangular pastry and seal in the filling. Make more pastries in the same way.

4 Heat the oil in a wok to 190°C/375°F or until a cube of bread, added to the oil, browns in about 45 seconds. Add the pastries to the oil, a few at a time, and fry them for about 5 minutes, until golden brown.

5 Remove from the wok and drain on kitchen paper. If you intend serving the puffs hot, place them in a single layer on a serving plate in a low oven while cooking successive batches. The puffs also taste good when served cold.

Thai Curry-spiced Potato Samosas

Most samosas are deep-fried, but these are baked, making them a healthier option. They are also perfect for parties as they are easier to cook.

Makes 25

1 large potato, about
  250g/9oz, diced
15ml/1 tbsp groundnut
  (peanut) oil
2 shallots, finely chopped
1 garlic clove, finely chopped
60ml/4 tbsp coconut milk
5ml/1 tsp Thai red or green
  curry paste
75g/3oz/¾ cup peas
juice of ½ lime
25 samosa wrappers or
  10 x 5cm/4 x 2in strips
  of filo pastry
salt and ground black pepper
vegetable oil, for brushing

1 Preheat the oven to 220°C/425°F/Gas 7. Bring a small pan of water to the boil, add the diced potato, cover and cook for 10–15 minutes, until tender. Drain and set aside.

2 Meanwhile, heat the groundnut oil in a large frying pan and cook the shallots and garlic over medium heat, stirring occasionally, for 4–5 minutes, until softened and golden.

3 Add the drained potato, coconut milk, red or green curry paste, peas and lime juice to the frying pan. Mash coarsely with a wooden spoon. Season to taste with salt and pepper and cook over a low heat for 2–3 minutes, then remove the pan from the heat and set aside until the mixture has cooled a little.

4 Lay a samosa wrapper or filo strip flat on the work surface. Brush with a little oil, then place a generous teaspoonful of the mixture in the middle of one end. Turn one corner diagonally over the filling to meet the long edge.

5 Continue folding over the filling, keeping the triangular shape as you work down the strip. Brush with a little more oil if necessary and place on a baking sheet. Prepare all the other samosas in the same way.

6 Bake for 15 minutes, or until the pastry is golden and crisp. Leave to cool slightly before serving.

Green Curry Puffs Energy 69kcal/291kJ; Protein 1.4g; Carbohydrate 9.9g, of which sugars 0.4g; Fat 3g, of which saturates 0.4g; Cholesterol 1mg; Calcium 22mg; Fibre 0.5g; Sodium 58mg.
Thai Potato Samosas Energy 42kcal/178kJ; Protein 1.2g; Carbohydrate 8.5g, of which sugars 0.6g; Fat 0.6g, of which saturates 0.1g; Cholesterol 0mg; Calcium 14mg; Fibre 0.5g; Sodium 4mg.

Spicy Potato Pancakes

Although called a pancake, these crispy spiced cakes are more like a traditional Indian bhaji. They make an ideal appetizer for a meal.

Makes 10
300g/11oz potatoes
25ml/1½ tsp garam masala or curry powder
4 spring onions (scallions), finely chopped
1 large (US extra large) egg white, lightly beaten
30ml/2 tbsp sunflower or olive oil
salt and ground black pepper
Indian chutney and relishes, to serve

1 Peel and grate the potatoes into a large bowl. Using your hands, squeeze the excess liquid from the grated potatoes and pat dry with kitchen paper.

2 Place the dry, grated potatoes in a separate bowl and add the spices, spring onions, egg white and seasoning. Stir to combine the ingredients.

3 Heat a large, non-stick frying pan over medium heat and add the vegetable oil.

4 Drop tablespoonfuls of the potato on to the pan and flatten out with the back of a spoon (you will need to cook the pancakes in two batches).

5 Cook the first batch for a few minutes and then flip over the pancakes. Cook for a further 3 minutes. Remove them from the pan and keep them warm in a preheated low oven while you cook the remaining batch.

6 Drain the pancakes well on kitchen paper and serve immediately with chutney and relishes.

Cook's Tip
Don't grate the potatoes too soon before you intend to use them as the flesh will quickly turn brown.

Curry-spiced Pakoras

These delicious batter balls make a wonderful snack with this fragrant chutney.

Makes 25
15ml/1 tbsp sunflower oil
20ml/4 tsp cumin seeds
5ml/1 tsp black mustard seeds
1 small onion, finely chopped
10ml/2 tsp grated fresh root ginger
2 green chillies, seeded and chopped
600g/1lb 5oz potatoes, cooked
200g/7oz fresh peas
juice of 1 lemon
90ml/6 tbsp chopped fresh coriander (cilantro) leaves
115g/4oz/1 cup gram flour
25g/1oz/¼ cup self-raising (self-rising) flour
40g/1½oz/⅓ cup rice flour
large pinch of turmeric
10ml/2 tsp crushed coriander seeds
350ml/12fl oz/1½ cups water
vegetable oil, for frying
salt and ground black pepper

For the chutney
105ml/7 tbsp coconut cream
200ml/7fl oz/scant 1 cup natural (plain) yogurt
50g/2oz mint leaves, finely chopped
5ml/1 tsp golden caster (superfine) sugar
juice of 1 lime

1 Heat a wok over medium heat and add the sunflower oil. When hot, fry the cumin and mustard seeds for 1–2 minutes. Add the onion, ginger and chillies to the wok and cook for 3–4 minutes. Add the cooked potatoes and peas and stir-fry for a further 5–6 minutes. Season, then stir in the lemon juice and coriander leaves. Leave the mixture to cool slightly, then divide into 25 portions. Shape each portion into a ball with your hands and chill in the refrigerator.

2 To make the chutney, place all the ingredients in a blender and process until smooth. Season, then chill. To make the batter, put the gram flour, self-raising flour and rice flour in a bowl. Season and add the turmeric and coriander seeds. Gradually whisk in the water to make a smooth batter.

3 Fill a wok one-third full of oil and heat to 180°C/350°F. Working in batches, dip the chilled balls in the batter, then drop into the oil and deep-fry for 1–2 minutes, or until golden. Drain on kitchen paper, and serve immediately with the chutney.

Potato Pancakes Energy 50kcal/210kJ; Protein 1.3g; Carbohydrate 5.8g, of which sugars 0.5g; Fat 2.6g, of which saturates 0.3g; Cholesterol 0mg; Calcium 8mg; Fibre 0.4g; Sodium 11mg.
Curry-spiced Pakoras Energy 126kcal/525kJ; Protein 4.1g; Carbohydrate 8.3g, of which sugars 2.6g; Fat 8.8g, of which saturates 5.2g; Cholesterol 0mg; Calcium 35mg; Fibre 1.3g; Sodium 16mg.

Onion Pakora

These delicious Indian onion fritters are made with chickpea flour, otherwise known as gram flour or besan. Serve with chutney or a yogurt dip.

Serves 4–5
675g/1½lb onions
5ml/1 tsp salt
5ml/1 tsp ground coriander
5ml/1 tsp ground cumin
2.5ml/½ tsp ground turmeric

1–2 green chillies, seeded and finely chopped
45ml/3 tbsp chopped fresh coriander (cilantro)
90g/3½oz/¾ cup gram flour
2.5ml/½ tsp baking powder
vegetable oil, for deep-frying

To serve
lemon wedges (optional)
fresh coriander (cilantro) sprigs
chutney or a yogurt and cucumber dip

1 Halve and thinly slice the onions in a colander, add the salt and toss. Place on a plate and leave to stand for 45 minutes, tossing once or twice. Rinse the onions, then squeeze out any excess moisture.

2 Place the onions in a bowl. Add the ground coriander, cumin, turmeric, chillies and fresh coriander. Mix well.

3 Add the gram flour and baking powder, then use your hands to mix the ingredients thoroughly. Shape the mixture by hand into 12–15 pakoras, about the size of golf balls.

4 Heat the oil for deep-frying to 180°C/350°F or until a cube of day-old bread browns in 30 seconds. Fry the pakoras, a few at a time, until they are deep golden brown all over. Drain each batch on kitchen paper and keep warm in a low oven until all the pakoras are cooked. Serve with lemon wedges, coriander sprigs and chutney or a yogurt and cucumber dip.

> **Cook's Tip**
> For a cucumber dip, stir half a diced cucumber and 1 seeded and chopped fresh green chilli into 250ml/8fl oz/1 cup natural (plain) yogurt. Season with salt and cumin.

Onion Bhajias

A favourite snack in India, bhajias consist of a savoury vegetable mixture in a crisp and spicy batter. They can be served as an appetizer or as a side dish with curries.

Makes 20–25
2 large onions
225g/8oz/2 cups gram flour
2.5ml/½ tsp chilli powder
5ml/1 tsp ground turmeric

5ml/1 tsp baking powder
1.5ml/¼ tsp asafoetida
2.5ml/½ tsp each nigella, fennel, cumin and onion seeds, coarsely crushed
2 fresh green chillies, finely chopped
50g/2oz/2 cups fresh coriander (cilantro), chopped
vegetable oil, for deep-frying
salt

1 Using a sharp knife, slice the onions into thin rounds. Separate the slices and set them aside on a plate.

2 In a bowl mix together the flour, chilli powder, ground turmeric, baking powder and asafoetida. Add salt to taste. Sift the mixture into a large mixing bowl.

3 Add the coarsely crushed seeds, onion slices, green chillies and fresh coriander to the bowl. Mix well until all the ingredients are combined.

4 Add enough cold water to make a paste, then stir in more water to make a thick batter that coats the onions and spices.

5 Heat enough oil in a wok for deep-frying to 180°C/350°F or until a cube of day-old bread browns in 30 seconds. Drop spoonfuls of the mixture into the hot oil, and fry the bhajias until they are golden brown. Turn the bhajias over during cooking. Drain well on kitchen paper and serve hot.

> **Variation**
> This versatile bhajia batter can be used with many other vegetables, including okra, cauliflower and broccoli. Cubes of potato also work well for a more filling snack.

Pakora Energy 207kcal/861kJ; Protein 5.4g; Carbohydrate 19.8g, of which sugars 8.2g; Fat 12.3g, of which saturates 1.4g; Cholesterol 0mg; Calcium 84mg; Fibre 4.3g; Sodium 14mg.
Onion Bhajias Energy 72kcal/301kJ; Protein 1.2g; Carbohydrate 8.8g, of which sugars 1.3g; Fat 3.8g, of which saturates 0.4g; Cholesterol 0mg; Calcium 23mg; Fibre 0.7g; Sodium 2mg.

Curried Parsnip Soup

The mild sweetness of parsnips and mango chutney is given an exciting lift with a blend of spices in this simple soup.

Serves 4

30ml/2 tbsp olive oil
1 onion, chopped
1 garlic clove, crushed
1 small green chilli, seeded and
   finely chopped
15ml/1 tbsp grated fresh
   root ginger
5 large parsnips, diced
5ml/1 tsp cumin seeds

5ml/1 tsp ground coriander
2.5ml/½ tsp ground turmeric
30ml/2 tbsp mango chutney
1.2 litres/2 pints/5 cups water
juice of 1 lime
salt and ground black pepper
60ml/4 tbsp natural (plain) yogurt
   and mango chutney, to serve
chopped fresh coriander (cilantro),
   to garnish (optional)

For the sesame naan croûtons

45ml/3 tbsp olive oil
1 large naan, cut into small dice
15ml/1 tbsp sesame seeds

1 Heat the oil in a large pan and add the onion, garlic, chilli and ginger. Cook for 4–5 minutes, until the onion has softened. Add the parsnips and cook for 2–3 minutes. Sprinkle in the cumin seeds, ground coriander and turmeric, and cook for 1 minute, stirring.

2 Add the chutney and the water. Season well with salt and pepper and bring to the boil. Reduce the heat, cover and simmer for 15 minutes, until the parsnips are soft.

3 Cool the soup slightly, then purée it in a food processor or blender and return it to the pan. Stir in the lime juice.

4 To make the naan croûtons, heat the oil in a large frying pan and cook the diced naan for 3–4 minutes, stirring, until golden all over. Remove from the heat and drain off any excess oil. Add the sesame seeds and return the pan to the heat for no more than 30 seconds, until the seeds are pale golden.

5 Ladle the soup into bowls. Spoon a little yogurt into each portion, then top with a little mango chutney and some of the sesame naan croûtons. Garnish with chopped fresh coriander, if you like.

Spiced Mango Soup

This delicious dish was invented at Chutney Mary's, the Anglo-Indian restaurant in London. It is best served lightly chilled. Gram flour, also known as besan or chickpea flour, is available from Asian stores.

Serves 4

2 ripe mangoes
15ml/1 tbsp gram flour
120ml/4fl oz/½ cup natural
   (plain) yogurt

900ml/1½ pints/3¾ cups cold
   or chilled water
2.5ml/½ tsp grated fresh
   root ginger
2 fresh red chillies, seeded and
   finely chopped
30ml/2 tbsp olive oil
2.5ml/½ tsp mustard seeds
2.5ml/½ tsp cumin seeds
8 curry leaves
salt and ground black pepper
fresh mint leaves, shredded,
   to garnish
natural (plain) yogurt, to serve

1 Peel the mangoes, remove the stones (pits) and cut the flesh into chunks. Purée in a food processor or blender until smooth. Pour the purée into a pan and stir in the gram flour, yogurt, measured water, ginger and chillies.

2 Bring all the ingredients slowly to the boil, stirring them occasionally. Simmer for about 4–5 minutes until thickened slightly, then set aside off the heat.

3 Heat the oil in a frying pan over medium to low heat. Add the mustard seeds, cover the pan, and cook for a few seconds until they begin to pop, then add the cumin seeds.

4 Add the curry leaves to the pan and then cook for about 5 minutes. Stir the spice mixture into the soup, return it to the heat and simmer for 10 minutes.

5 Press through a sieve (strainer), if you like, then season to taste with salt and black pepper. Leave the soup to cool completely, then chill for at least 1 hour.

6 Ladle the soup into chilled serving bowls, and top each with a dollop of natural yogurt. Garnish with the shredded fresh mint leaves and serve immediately.

Curried Parsnip Energy 150kcal/623kJ; Protein 4.7g; Carbohydrate 7.8g, of which sugars 6.8g; Fat 11.4g, of which saturates 7g; Cholesterol 32mg; Calcium 170mg; Fibre 0.8g; Sodium 112mg.
Spiced Mango Energy 83kcal/354kJ; Protein 3g; Carbohydrate 14.4g, of which sugars 12.7g; Fat 2g, of which saturates 0.5g; Cholesterol 0mg; Calcium 72mg; Fibre 2g; Sodium 28mg.

Forest Curry Soup

This is a thin, soupy curry with lots of fresh green vegetables and robust flavours. It originated in the forested regions of Thailand, where it would be made using wild leaves and roots.

Serves 2
600ml/1 pint/2½ cups water
5ml/1 tsp Thai vegetarian red
 curry paste
5cm/2in piece fresh galangal or
 fresh root ginger
90g/3½oz/scant 1 cup
 green beans
2 kaffir lime leaves, torn
8 baby corn cobs,
 halved widthways
2 heads Chinese
 broccoli, chopped
90g/3½oz/generous 3 cups
 beansprouts
15ml/1 tbsp drained bottled
 green peppercorns, crushed
10ml/2 tsp sugar
5ml/1 tsp salt

1 Heat the water in a large pan. Add the red curry paste and stir until it has dissolved completely. Bring to the boil.

2 Meanwhile, using a sharp knife, peel and finely chop the fresh galangal or root ginger.

3 Add the galangal or ginger, green beans, lime leaves, baby corn cobs, broccoli and beansprouts to the pan. Stir in the crushed peppercorns, sugar and salt. Bring back to the boil, then reduce the heat to low and simmer for 2 minutes. Serve immediately in warmed bowls.

Cook's Tip
You can serve this soup with plain rice or noodles for a simple lunch or a quick and easy supper.

Variation
Garnish the soup with some thinly sliced hard-boiled egg just before serving, or, if you prefer, provide a couple of whole hard-boiled eggs to serve on the side.

Potato Soup with Garlic Samosas

Soup and samosas are the ideal partners. Bought samosas are given an easy, but clever, flavour lift in this simple recipe.

Serves 4
60ml/4 tbsp sunflower oil
10ml/2 tsp black
 mustard seeds
1 large onion, chopped
1 fresh red chilli, seeded
 and chopped
2.5ml/½ tsp ground turmeric
1.5ml/¼ tsp cayenne pepper
900g/2lb potatoes, cut into cubes
4 fresh curry leaves
750ml/1¼ pint/3 cups
 vegetable stock
225g/8oz spinach leaves, torn
 if large
400ml/14fl oz/1⅔ cups
 coconut milk
handful of fresh coriander
 (cilantro) leaves
salt and black pepper

For the garlic samosas
1 large garlic clove, crushed
25g/1oz/2 tbsp butter
6 vegetable samosas

1 Heat the oil in a large pan. Add the mustard seeds, cover and cook until they begin to pop. Add the onion and chilli and cook for 5–6 minutes, until softened.

2 Stir the turmeric, cayenne, potatoes, curry leaves and stock into the pan. Bring to the boil, reduce the heat and cover the pan. Simmer for about 15 minutes, stirring occasionally, until the potatoes are just tender.

3 Meanwhile, prepare the samosas. Preheat the oven to 180°C/350°F/Gas 4. Melt the garlic with the butter in a small pan, stirring and crushing the garlic into the butter.

4 Place the samosas on an ovenproof dish – a gratin dish or quiche dish is ideal. Brush them lightly with the butter, turn them over and brush with the remaining butter. Heat through in the oven for about 5 minutes, until piping hot.

5 Add the spinach to the soup and cook for 5 minutes. Stir in the coconut milk and cook for a further 5 minutes. Season and add the coriander leaves before ladling the soup into bowls. Serve with the garlic samosas.

Forest Curry Energy 154kcal/643kJ; Protein 14.9g; Carbohydrate 14.1g, of which sugars 11.8g; Fat 4.5g, of which saturates 0.8g, Cholesterol 0mg; Calcium 173mg; Fibre 9.1g; Sodium 678mg.
Potato with Samosas Energy 658kcal/2744kJ; Protein 8.8g; Carbohydrate 63.4g, of which sugars 15.5g; Fat 42.8g, of which saturates 5.1g; Cholesterol 13mg; Calcium 184mg; Fibre 5.9g; Sodium 375mg.

Tofu, Green Bean and Mushroom Red Curry

This is one of those versatile recipes that should be in every curry lover's repertoire. This version uses green beans, but other types of vegetable work equally well.

Serves 4–6
600ml/1 pint/2½ cups
 coconut milk
10ml/2 tsp palm sugar (jaggery)
 or honey
15ml/1 tbsp Thai red
 curry paste
225g/8oz/3¼ cups button
 (white) mushrooms
115g/4oz green beans, trimmed
175g/6oz firm tofu, rinsed,
 drained and cut into
 2cm/¾in cubes
4 kaffir lime leaves, torn
2 fresh red chillies, seeded
 and sliced
fresh coriander (cilantro) leaves,
 to garnish

1 Pour about one-third of the coconut milk into a wok or pan. Cook until it starts to separate and an oily sheen appears on the surface of the hot liquid.

2 Add the palm sugar or honey and red curry paste to the coconut milk. Mix thoroughly, then add the mushrooms. Stir and cook for 1 minute over a medium heat.

3 Stir in the remaining coconut milk. Bring back to the boil, then add the green beans and tofu cubes. Simmer gently for 4–5 minutes more, stirring occasionally.

4 Stir in the kaffir lime leaves and sliced red chillies. Spoon the tofu and green bean curry into a serving dish, garnish with the coriander leaves and serve immediately.

> **Cook's Tip**
> Unless there are compelling health reasons, do not use low-fat coconut milk for this curry. The flavour of the full-cream product is superior. If you buy the canned product and have some left over, freeze it in ice cube trays – handy for future sauces.

Spicy Tofu with Basil and Peanuts

In Vietnam, aromatic pepper leaves are often used as the herb element in this dish but, because these are quite difficult to find outside South-east Asia, you can use basil leaves instead. Tofu can be very bland in flavour, but when marinated in lemon grass, chillies and spices, it becomes a memorable dish.

Serves 3–4
3 lemon grass stalks,
 finely chopped
45ml/3 tbsp soy sauce
2 red Serrano chillies, seeded
 and finely chopped
2 garlic cloves, crushed
5ml/1 tsp ground turmeric
10ml/2 tsp sugar
300g/11oz tofu, rinsed, drained,
 patted dry and cut into
 bitesize cubes
30ml/2 tbsp groundnut
 (peanut) oil
45ml/3 tbsp roasted
 peanuts, chopped
1 bunch fresh basil, stalks
 removed
salt

1 In a large mixing bowl, stir together the lemon grass, soy sauce, chopped chillies, garlic, turmeric and sugar, stirring briskly until the sugar has dissolved.

2 Add a little salt to the bowl to taste and add the tofu, making sure it is well coated in the marinade. Set aside to marinate for at least 1 hour.

3 Heat a wok or heavy pan. Pour in the oil, add the marinated tofu, and fry, stirring frequently, until it is golden brown on all sides. Add the peanuts and most of the basil leaves to the pan and mix well to combine the ingredients.

4 Divide the tofu among individual serving dishes, sprinkle the remaining basil leaves over the top and serve the curry either hot or at room temperature.

> **Variation**
> Lime, coriander (cilantro) or curry leaves would all work well in this simple and delicious stir-fry.

Tofu Curry Energy 59kcal/250kJ; Protein 3.8g; Carbohydrate 7.5g, of which sugars 7.1g; Fat 1.8g, of which saturates 0.4g; Cholesterol 0mg; Calcium 188mg; Fibre 0.8g; Sodium 291mg.
Spicy Tofu with Basil Energy 120kcal/500kJ; Protein 3g; Carbohydrate 5g, of which sugars 3g; Fat 10g, of which saturates 2g; Cholesterol 0mg; Calcium 36mg; Fibre 3.3g; Sodium 200mg.

Okra and Tomato Tagine with Garlic and Coriander

Although this spicy vegetable stew is a North African speciality, similar dishes exist throughout the Middle East.

Serves 4

350g/12oz okra
5–6 tomatoes
2 small onions
2 garlic cloves, crushed
1 fresh green chilli, seeded and roughly chopped
5ml/1 tsp paprika
small handful of fresh coriander (cilantro)
30ml/2 tbsp sunflower oil
juice of 1 lemon

1 Trim the okra and then cut it into 1cm/½in lengths. Skin and seed the tomatoes and roughly chop the flesh.

2 Roughly chop one of the onions and place it in a blender or food processor with the garlic, chilli, paprika, coriander and 60ml/4 tbsp water. Process to make a paste.

3 Thinly slice the second onion and fry it in the oil in a pan for 5–6 minutes, until golden brown. Transfer to a plate and set aside. Reduce the heat and pour the onion and coriander paste into the pan. Cook for 1–2 minutes, stirring frequently.

4 Add the okra, tomatoes, lemon juice and about 120ml/4fl oz/ ½ cup water. Stir well to mix, cover tightly and simmer over a low heat for about 15 minutes, until the okra is tender. Transfer to a serving dish, sprinkle with the fried onion rings and serve.

> **Variations**
> • Okra is a vegetable that is particularly popular in Egypt, where it is cultivated commercially on a grand scale.
> The vegetable is also known as 'ladies' fingers'. When cut before being cooked, the pods ooze a glue-like substance, which gives the dish a distinctive texture.
> • Use three or four shallots instead of onions, for a milder flavour, plus canned chopped tomatoes, if you prefer.

Israeli Vegetable Curry

This fiery tomato and aubergine stew is typical of Israeli cooking, for which aubergines and all things hot and spicy are staples.

Serves 4–6

about 60ml/4 tbsp olive oil
1 large aubergine (eggplant) cut into bitesize chunks
2 onions, thinly sliced
3–5 garlic cloves, chopped
1–2 green (bell) peppers, thinly sliced or chopped
1–2 fresh hot chillies, chopped
4 fresh or canned tomatoes, diced
30–45ml/2–3 tbsp tomato purée (paste), if using fresh tomatoes
5ml/1 tsp ground turmeric
pinch of curry powder or ras al hanout
cayenne pepper, to taste
400g/14oz can chickpeas, drained and rinsed
juice of ½–1 lemon
30–45ml/2–3 tbsp chopped fresh coriander (cilantro) leaves
salt

1 Heat half the oil in a frying pan, add the aubergine chunks and fry until brown, adding more oil if necessary. When cooked, transfer the aubergine to a strainer, standing over a large bowl, and leave to drain thoroughly on kitchen paper.

2 Heat the remaining oil in the pan, add the onions, garlic, peppers and chillies and fry until softened.

3 Add the diced tomatoes, tomato purée, if using, spices and salt, and cook, stirring, until the mixture thickens to a sauce consistency. Add a little water if necessary.

4 Add the chickpeas to the sauce and cook for about 5 minutes, then add the aubergine, stir to mix well and cook for 5–10 minutes until the flavours are well combined. Add lemon juice to taste, then add the coriander leaves. Chill before serving.

> **Variation**
> To make a Middle Eastern-style ratatouille, cut two courgettes (zucchini) and one red (bell) pepper into chunks. Add to the pan with the onions and garlic and continue as before.

Okra Tagine Energy 113kcal/471kJ; Protein 4.1g; Carbohydrate 9.2g, of which sugars 8g; Fat 7g, of which saturates 1.1g; Cholesterol 0mg; Calcium 181mg; Fibre 5.8g; Sodium 23mg.
Israeli Vegetable Curry Energy 362kcal/1536kJ; Protein 26g; Carbohydrate 60.9g, of which sugars 5.2g; Fat 3.6g, of which saturates 0.6g; Cholesterol 0mg; Calcium 117mg; Fibre 8g; Sodium 46mg.

Moroccan-spiced Aubergine Tagine

Cambodian Aubergine Curry

Spiced with coriander, cumin, cinnamon, turmeric and a dash of chilli sauce, this Moroccan-style stew makes a filling supper dish when served with couscous.

Serves 4

1 small aubergine (eggplant), cut into 1cm/½in dice
2 courgettes (zucchini), sliced
60ml/4 tbsp olive oil
1 large onion, sliced
2 garlic cloves, chopped
150g/5oz/2 cups brown cap (cremini) mushrooms, halved
15ml/1 tbsp ground coriander
10ml/2 tsp cumin seeds
15ml/1 tbsp ground cinnamon
10ml/2 tsp ground turmeric
225g/8oz new potatoes, quartered
600ml/1 pint/2½ cups passata (bottled strained tomatoes)
15ml/1 tbsp tomato purée (paste)
15ml/1 tbsp chilli sauce
75g/3oz/½ cup ready-to-eat unsulphured dried apricots
400g/14oz/3 cups canned chickpeas, drained and rinsed
salt and ground black pepper
15ml/1 tbsp chopped fresh coriander (cilantro), to garnish

1 Place the the aubergine and courgettes in a colander, sprinkle with salt and leave for 30 minutes. Rinse and pat dry with a dish towel. Heat the grill (broiler) to high. Arrange the courgettes and aubergine on a baking tray and toss in 30ml/2 tbsp of the olive oil. Cook for 20 minutes, turning occasionally, until tender and golden.

2 Meanwhile, heat the remaining oil in a large heavy pan and cook the onion and garlic for 5 minutes until softened, stirring occasionally. Add the mushrooms and sauté for 3 minutes until tender. Add the spices and cook for 1 minute more, stirring, to allow the flavours to mingle.

3 Add the potatoes and cook for about 3 minutes, stirring. Pour in the passata, tomato purée and 150ml/¼ pint/⅔ cup water. Cover and cook for 10 minutes to thicken the sauce.

4 Add the aubergine, courgettes, chilli sauce, apricots and chickpeas. Season and cook, partially covered, for about 15 minutes until the potatoes are tender. Add a little extra water if the tagine becomes too dry. Sprinkle with chopped fresh coriander and serve immediately.

Aubergine curries are popular throughout South-east Asia, the Thai version being the most famous. All are hot and aromatic, enriched with coconut milk. This spicy Cambodian recipe uses the herbal paste kroeung.

Serves 4–6

15ml/1 tbsp vegetable oil
4 garlic cloves, crushed
2 shallots, sliced
2 dried chillies
45ml/3 tbsp kroeung
15ml/1 tbsp vegetable paste or mam roi
15ml/1 tbsp palm sugar (jaggery)
600ml/1 pint/2½ cups coconut milk
250ml/8fl oz/1 cup vegetable stock
4 aubergines (eggplants), trimmed and cut into bitesize pieces
6 kaffir lime leaves
1 bunch fresh basil, stalks removed, leaves chopped
salt and ground black pepper
fragrant jasmine rice and 2 limes, cut into quarters, to serve

1 Heat the oil in a wok or heavy pan. Stir in the garlic, shallots and whole chillies and stir-fry until they begin to colour.

2 Stir in the kroeung, vegetable paste or mam roi and palm sugar and stir-fry until the mixture begins to darken.

3 Pour the coconut milk and stock into the pan, and add the aubergines and lime leaves. Stir well so that all the ingredients are well combined. Bring slowly to the boil.

4 Partially cover the pan and simmer over a low heat for about 25–30 minutes until the aubergines are tender. Stir in the chopped fresh basil and check the seasoning. Serve the curry immediately with jasmine rice and lime wedges.

> **Cook's Tip**
> *Kroeung is an aromatic, medium to hot red curry paste. A typical formulation of this popular ingredient contains dried red chillies, galangal root, coriander root, shallots, chopped kaffir lime rind and leaves, lemon grass, garlic and turmeric. Look for it in large supermarkets and Asian stores.*

Aubergine Tagine Energy 359kcal/1509kJ; Protein 13.9g; Carbohydrate 45g, of which sugars 19.3g; Fat 15g, of which saturates 2.1g; Cholesterol 0mg; Calcium 123mg; Fibre 9.7g; Sodium 597mg.
Aubergine Curry Energy 72kcal/305kJ; Protein 1.6g; Carbohydrate 11.2g, of which sugars 10.7g; Fat 3g, of which saturates 1g; Cholesterol 0mg; Calcium 46mg; Fibre 2.8g; Sodium 113mg.

Pumpkin and Peanut Yellow Curry

This is a hearty, soothing Thai curry that is perfect for autumn or winter evenings. Its cheerful colour alone will brighten you up – and it tastes terrific.

Serves 4

30ml/2 tbsp vegetable oil
4 garlic cloves, crushed
4 shallots, finely chopped
30ml/2 tbsp Thai yellow
   curry paste
600ml/1 pint/2½ cups
   vegetable stock
2 kaffir lime leaves, torn

15ml/1 tbsp chopped galangal
450g/1lb pumpkin, peeled, seeded
   and diced
225g/8oz sweet potatoes, diced
90g/3½oz/scant 1 cup peanuts,
   roasted and chopped
300ml/½ pint/1¼ cups
   coconut milk
90g/3½oz/1½ cups brown cap
   (cremini) mushrooms, sliced
15ml/1 tbsp soy sauce
30ml/2 tbsp Thai
   mushroom ketchup
50g/2oz/⅓ cup pumpkin seeds,
   toasted, and fresh green chilli
   flowers, to garnish

1 Heat the oil in a large pan. Add the garlic and shallots and cook over a medium heat, stirring occasionally, for 10 minutes, until softened and golden. Do not let them burn.

2 Add the yellow curry paste and stir-fry over a medium heat for 30 seconds, until the mixture is fragrant.

3 Add the stock, lime leaves, galangal, pumpkin and sweet potatoes. Bring to the boil, stirring frequently, then reduce the heat to low and simmer gently for 15 minutes.

4 Add the peanuts, coconut milk and mushrooms. Stir in the soy sauce and mushroom ketchup and simmer for 5 minutes more. Spoon into warmed individual serving bowls, garnish with the pumpkin seeds and chilli flowers and serve.

> **Cook's Tip**
> *The well-drained vegetables from a curry of this kind would make a very tasty filling for a pastry or pie. This may not be a Thai tradition, but it is a good example of fusion food.*

Corn and Cashew Nut Curry

This is a substantial curry, thanks largely to the potatoes and corn kernels, which makes it a great winter-warming dish. It is deliciously aromatic, but, as the spices are added in relatively small amounts, the resulting flavour and heat is fairly mild.

Serves 4

30ml/2 tbsp vegetable oil
4 shallots, chopped
90g/3½ oz/scant 1 cup
   cashew nuts
5ml/1 tsp red curry paste
400g/14oz potatoes, peeled
   and cut into chunks
1 lemon grass stalk, finely chopped

200g/7oz can chopped tomatoes
600ml/1 pint/2½ cups
   boiling water
200g/7oz/generous 1 cup
   drained canned whole
   kernel corn
4 celery sticks, sliced
2 kaffir lime leaves, central rib
   removed, rolled into cylinders
   and thinly sliced
15ml/1 tbsp tomato ketchup
15ml/1 tbsp light soy sauce
5ml/1 tsp palm sugar (jaggery)
   or light muscovado
   (brown) sugar
4 spring onions (scallions),
   thinly sliced
small bunch fresh basil,
   roughly chopped

1 Heat the oil in a wok or deep frying pan. Add the shallots and stir-fry over a medium heat for 2–3 minutes, until softened. Add the cashew nuts to the pan and stir-fry for a few minutes until they are golden but take care not to let them burn.

2 Stir the red curry paste into the pan. Cook for 1 minute, stirring constantly, then add the potatoes, lemon grass, tomatoes and boiling water and stir well.

3 Bring back to the boil, then reduce the heat to low, cover and simmer gently for 15–20 minutes, or until the potatoes are tender when tested with the tip of a knife.

4 Stir the corn, celery, lime leaves, ketchup, soy sauce and sugar into the pan. Simmer further for about 5 minutes, until heated through, then spoon the curry into warmed serving bowls. Sprinkle with the sliced spring onions and chopped fresh basil and serve immediately.

Pumpkin Curry Energy 306kcal/1279kJ; Protein 9.6g; Carbohydrate 24.5g, of which sugars 11.4g; Fat 19.6g, of which saturates 3.3g; Cholesterol 0mg; Calcium 160mg; Fibre 6.4g; Sodium 409mg.
Corn and Cashew Curry Energy 298kcal/1245kJ; Protein 8.8g; Carbohydrate 27.6g, of which sugars 8.9g; Fat 17.7g, of which saturates 3.1g; Cholesterol 0mg; Calcium 33mg; Fibre 3.5g; Sodium 981mg.

Middle Eastern Stuffed Onions, Potatoes and Courgettes

The vegetarian filling of these vegetables is tomato-red, Yemenite-spiced and accented with the tart taste of lemon. They are delicious cold and are good served as an appetizer as well as a main course.

Serves 4
4 potatoes, peeled
4 onions, skinned
4 courgettes (zucchini), cut in
   half widthways
2–4 garlic cloves, chopped
45–60ml/3–4 tbsp olive oil
45–60ml/3–4 tbsp tomato
   purée (paste)
1.5ml/¼ tsp ras al hanout
   or curry powder
large pinch of ground allspice
seeds of 2–3 cardamom pods
juice of ½ lemon
30–45ml/2–3 tbsp chopped
   fresh parsley
90–120ml/6–8 tbsp
   vegetable stock
salt and ground black pepper
salad, to serve (optional)

1 Bring a large pan of salted water to the boil. Starting with the potatoes, then the onions and finally the courgettes, add to the boiling water and cook until they become almost tender but not cooked right through. Allow about 10 minutes for the potatoes, 8 minutes for the onions and about 4–6 minutes for the courgettes. Remove the vegetables from the pan and set aside to cool slightly.

2 When the vegetables are cool enough to handle, hollow them out. Preheat the oven to 190°C/375°F/Gas 5.

3 Finely chop the cut-out vegetable flesh and put it in a bowl. Add the garlic, half the olive oil, the tomato purée, ras al hanout or curry powder, allspice, cardamom seeds, lemon juice, parsley, salt and pepper and mix well together. Use the stuffing mixture to fill the hollowed vegetables.

4 Arrange the stuffed vegetables in a baking tin (pan) and drizzle with the stock and the remaining oil. Roast for about 35–40 minutes, or until golden brown. Serve warm with a simple salad, if you like.

Red Curry Stuffed Sweet Peppers

This is an unusual recipe where the stuffed peppers are steamed rather than baked, but the result is beautifully light and tender. The filling incorporates typical Thai ingredients such as red curry paste and soy sauce. Kaffir lime leaves also add a delicate citrus flavour.

Serves 4
3 garlic cloves
2 coriander (cilantro) roots
400g/14oz/3 cups brown cap
   (cremini) or button (white)
   mushrooms, quartered
5ml/1 tsp Thai red curry paste
1 egg, lightly beaten
30ml/2 tbsp soy sauce or light
   soy sauce
2.5ml/½ tsp sugar
3 kaffir lime leaves,
   finely chopped
4 yellow (bell) peppers, halved
   lengthways and seeded

1 Finely chop the garlic cloves and coriander roots. Pound or blend the garlic with the coriander roots using a pestle and mortar or spice grinder. Scrape into a bowl.

2 Put the mushrooms in a food processor and pulse briefly until they are finely chopped.

3 Add to the garlic mixture, then stir in the Thai red curry paste, beaten egg and soy sauce. Add the sugar and kaffir lime leaves to the mixture.

4 Place the pepper halves in a single layer in a steamer basket. Spoon the mixture loosely into the pepper halves. Do not pack the mixture down tightly or the filling will dry out too much.

5 Bring the water in the steamer to the boil, then lower the heat to a simmer. Steam the peppers for 15 minutes, or until the flesh is tender. Serve hot.

> **Variations**
> Use red or orange (bell) peppers rather than yellow, if you prefer, or a combination of the two.

Spiced Peppers with Eggs and Lentils

These oven-baked filled peppers make a tasty side dish. They are delicious with fish or pork chops, but also make an excellent light meal for vegetarians.

Serves 4
75g/3oz/½ cup Puy lentils
2.5ml/½ tsp ground turmeric
2.5ml/½ tsp ground coriander
2.5ml/½ tsp paprika
450ml/¾ pint/1¾ cups vegetable stock
2 large (bell) peppers, halved lengthways and seeded
a little vegetable oil
15ml/1 tbsp chopped fresh mint
4 eggs
salt and ground black pepper
sprigs of coriander (cilantro), to garnish

1 Put the lentils in a pan with the spices and stock. Bring to the boil, stirring occasionally, and simmer for 30–40 minutes. If necessary, add more water during cooking.

2 Brush the peppers with oil and place them close together on a baking tray.

3 Stir the mint into the lentils, then fill the peppers with the mixture. Preheat the oven to 190°C/375°F/Gas 5.

4 Crack the eggs, one at a time, into a small saucer and carefully pour into the middle of a pepper. Stir into the lentils and sprinkle with seasoning. Bake the dish for 10 minutes until the egg white is just set. Garnish the peppers with the sprigs of coriander and serve.

> **Variations**
> • Use large beefsteak tomatoes instead of the peppers. Cut a lid off the tomatoes and scoop out their middles using a spoon. Fill with lentils and eggs and bake as before.
> • You can add a little extra flavour to the lentil mixture by adding chopped onion and tomatoes that have been sautéed in olive oil.

Fiery Jungle Curry

This fiery, flavoursome vegetarian curry is almost dominated by the chilli. Its many variations make it a favourite with Buddhist monks who value the way it adds variety to their vegetarian diet. Jungle curry can be served with plain rice or noodles, or chunks of crusty bread. It can be eaten for breakfast or enjoyed as a pick-me-up at any time of day.

Serves 4
30ml/2 tbsp vegetable oil or extra virgin olive oil
2 onions, roughly chopped
2 lemon grass stalks, roughly chopped and bruised
4 fresh green chillies, seeded and finely sliced
4cm/1½in galangal or fresh root ginger, peeled and chopped
3 carrots, peeled, halved lengthways and sliced
115g/4oz yard-long beans
grated rind of 1 lime
15ml/3 tsp soy sauce
15ml/1 tbsp rice vinegar
5ml/1 tsp black peppercorns, crushed
15ml/1 tbsp sugar
10ml/2 tsp ground turmeric
115g/4oz canned bamboo shoots
75g/3oz spinach, steamed and roughly chopped
150ml/¼ pint/⅔ cup coconut milk
chopped fresh coriander (cilantro) and mint leaves, to garnish

1 Heat a wok or heavy frying pan and add the oil. Once hot, stir in the onions, lemon grass, chillies and galangal or ginger and stir-fry for 2–3 minutes.

2 Add the carrots and beans to the pan along with the lime rind and stir-fry for 1–2 minutes.

3 Stir in the soy sauce and rice vinegar and mix well.

4 Add the crushed peppercorns, sugar and turmeric to the pan, then stir in the bamboo shoots and the chopped spinach.

5 Stir the coconut milk into the pan and simmer over a low heat for about 10 minutes, until all the vegetables are tender.

6 Garnish with chopped fresh coriander and mint leaves and serve the curry immediately with rice, noodles or crusty bread.

Spiced Peppers Energy 188kcal/788kJ; Protein 11.8g; Carbohydrate 16.3g, of which sugars 5.9g; Fat 9g, of which saturates 2.1g; Cholesterol 190mg; Calcium 58mg; Fibre 2.6g; Sodium 82mg.
Fiery Jungle Curry Energy 119kcal/496kJ; Protein 3.8g; Carbohydrate 18.6g, of which sugars 15.3g; Fat 3.8g, of which saturates 0.5g; Cholesterol 0mg; Calcium 125mg; Fibre 4.3g; Sodium 60mg.

Cauliflower and Coconut Milk Curry

This delicious vegetable
curry combines rich
coconut milk with spices,
and is perfect as a
vegetarian main course
or as part of a buffet.

Serves 4

1 cauliflower
2 medium tomatoes
1 onion, chopped
2 garlic cloves, crushed

1 fresh green chilli, seeded and
   roughly chopped
2.5ml/½ tsp ground turmeric
30ml/2 tbsp sunflower oil
400ml/14fl oz/1⅔ cups
   coconut milk
250ml/8fl oz/1 cup water
5ml/1 tsp sugar
5ml/1 tsp tamarind pulp,
   soaked in 45ml/3 tbsp
   warm water
salt

1 Trim the stalk from the cauliflower and divide into small
florets. Peel the tomatoes if you like, then chop them into even
pieces, roughly 1–2.5cm/½–1in long.

2 Grind the chopped onion, garlic, green chilli and ground
turmeric to a paste in a food processor.

3 Heat the oil in a karahi, wok or large frying pan and stir-fry
the spice paste until the aromatic flavours are released, without
allowing it to brown or burn.

4 Add the cauliflower florets to the pan and toss well to coat in
the spice mixture. Stir in the coconut milk, water and sugar, and
add salt to taste. Simmer for about 5 minutes. Strain the
tamarind, discard the pulp and reserve the juice.

5 Add the tamarind juice and chopped tomatoes to the pan
then cook for 2–3 minutes only. Taste and adjust the seasoning
if necessary, then serve immediately.

> **Cook's Tip**
> *Always be careful when preparing fresh or dried chillies as they
> can irritate sensitive skin. Wear plastic gloves or ensure you
> wash your hands thoroughly after preparation.*

Okra in Chilli Yogurt

This tangy vegetable curry
can be served as an
accompaniment, but also
makes an excellent
vegetarian meal served with
tarka dhal and chapatis or
other Indian breads. The
secret of cooking okra is
not to overcook it, as the
resulting sticky juices can be
somewhat unpleasant.

Serves 4

450g/1lb okra
30ml/2 tbsp vegetable oil

2.5ml/½ tsp onion seeds
3 fresh red or green chillies,
   seeded and chopped
1 onion, sliced
1.5ml/¼ tsp ground turmeric
10ml/2 tsp desiccated
   (dry unsweetened
   shredded) coconut
2.5ml/½ tsp salt
15ml/1 tbsp natural
   (plain) yogurt
2 tomatoes, quartered
15ml/1 tbsp chopped fresh
   coriander (cilantro)

1 Wash and trim the okra. Cut each one into pieces roughly
1cm/½in long and set aside.

2 Heat the vegetable oil in a wok, karahi or large frying pan.
Add the onion seeds, red or green chillies and onion, and cook
for about 5 minutes, stirring frequently.

3 When the onion is golden brown, lower the heat and
add the turmeric, desiccated coconut and salt. Fry for about
1 minute, stirring all the time.

4 Add the okra to the pan. Increase the heat to medium-high
and cook briskly for a few minutes, stirring all the time until
the okra has turned lightly golden. Take care not to overcook the
okra as it will begin to release its glutinous juices.

5 Add the yogurt, tomatoes and fresh coriander to the pan.
Stir well to ensure all the ingredients are well combined.

6 Cook the curry for a further 4–5 minutes until everything is
warmed through. Transfer to a warmed serving dish and serve
immediately as a side dish or as a main course accompanied
by dhal and Indian bread.

Cauliflower Curry Energy 122kcal/504kJ; Protein 3.7g; Carbohydrate 7.4g, of which sugars 3.3g; Fat 8.8g, of which saturates 1.2g; Cholesterol 0mg; Calcium 34mg; Fibre 1.4g; Sodium 41mg.
Okra in Chilli Yogurt Energy 211kcal/873kJ; Protein 5g; Carbohydrate 6.3g, of which sugars 5.2g; Fat 18.7g, of which saturates 7.1g; Cholesterol 0mg; Calcium 246mg; Fibre 7.6g; Sodium 15mg.

Hot Masala Okra with Coriander

Okra, or 'ladies' fingers', are a popular Indian vegetable. In this recipe they are stir-fried with a dry masala spice mixture to make a delicious side dish.

Serves 4
450g/1lb okra
2.5ml/½ tsp ground turmeric
5ml/1 tsp chilli powder
15ml/1 tbsp ground cumin
15ml/1 tbsp ground coriander
1.5ml/¼ tsp salt
1.5ml/¼ tsp sugar
15ml/1 tbsp lemon juice
15ml/1 tbsp desiccated (dry unsweetened shredded) coconut
30ml/2 tbsp chopped fresh coriander (cilantro)
45ml/3 tbsp vegetable oil
2.5ml/½ tsp cumin seeds
2.5ml/½ tsp black mustard seeds
chopped fresh tomatoes, to garnish
poppadums, to serve

1 Wash, pat dry and trim the the ends of the okra. In a mixing bowl, mix together the turmeric, chilli powder, cumin, ground coriander, salt, sugar, lemon juice, desiccated coconut and the chopped fresh coriander. Mix well to combine.

2 Heat the vegetable oil in a wok or large, heavy frying pan that has a tight-fitting lid. Add the cumin seeds and mustard seeds to the pan and fry, stirring constantly, for about 2–3 minutes, or until the seeds begin to splutter and release their aromatic fragrances.

3 Add the spice mixture to the pan and continue to cook, stirring constantly, for 2 minutes.

4 Add the okra to the pan, cover, and cook over a low heat for about 10 minutes, or until the okra is tender.

5 Transfer to a serving dish and garnish with the chopped fresh tomatoes. Serve immediately with poppadums.

Cook's Tip
Poppadums are wafer-thin crisp breads from India. Buy them in Asian stores and look out for the versions with added spices.

Corn and Pea Chilli Curry

Tender corn on the cob is cooked in a spicy tomato sauce. Indian breads, such as chapatis, make the perfect accompaniment to this curry.

Serves 4
6 pieces of fresh corn on the cob
45ml/3 tbsp vegetable oil
2.5ml/½ tsp cumin seeds
1 onion, finely chopped
2 garlic cloves, crushed
1 green chilli, finely chopped
15ml/1 tbsp curry paste
5ml/1 tsp ground coriander
5ml/1 tsp ground cumin
1.5ml/¼ tsp ground turmeric
2.5ml/½ tsp salt
2.5ml/½ tsp sugar
400g/14oz can chopped tomatoes
15ml/1 tbsp tomato purée (paste)
150ml/¼ pint/⅔ cup water
115g/4oz frozen peas, thawed
30ml/2 tbsp chopped fresh coriander (cilantro)
chapatis, to serve (optional)

1 With a sharp knife, cut each piece of corn in half crossways to make 12 equal pieces in total. Bring a large pan of water to the boil and cook the corn cob pieces for about 10–12 minutes. Drain well.

2 Heat the oil in a pan and fry the cumin seeds for 2 minutes, or until they begin to splutter. Add the chopped onion, garlic and chilli and fry for 5–6 minutes until the onion is golden.

3 Add the curry paste and fry for 2 minutes. Stir in the remaining spices, salt and sugar and fry for 2–3 minutes.

4 Add the tomatoes and tomato purée with the water and simmer for 5 minutes. Add the peas and cook for 5 minutes.

5 Add the pieces of corn and fresh coriander and cook for a further 6–8 minutes, or until the corn and peas are tender. Serve with chapatis, for mopping up the rich sauce, if you like.

Cook's Tip
If corn on the cob is out of season, this curry can also be made with the frozen variety of sliced corn cobs.

Masala Okra Energy 211kcal/873kJ; Protein 5g; Carbohydrate 6.3g, of which sugars 5.2g; Fat 18.7g, of which saturates 7.1g; Cholesterol 0mg; Calcium 246mg; Fibre 7.6g; Sodium 15mg.
Corn Curry Energy 260kcal/1089kJ; Protein 8.6g; Carbohydrate 29.7g, of which sugars 7.1g; Fat 12.9g, of which saturates 1.7g; Cholesterol 0mg; Calcium 68mg; Fibre 5.6g; Sodium 46mg.

Potato with Spicy Cottage Cheese

Always choose a variety of potato recommended for baking for this recipe, as the texture of the potato should not be too dry. This dish makes an excellent low-fat snack at any time of the day.

2.5ml/½ tsp ground coriander
2.5ml/½ tsp chilli powder
2.5ml/½ tsp salt
15ml/1 tbsp corn or
   sunflower oil
2.5ml/½ tsp mixed onion and
   mustard seeds
3 curry leaves
30ml/2 tbsp water

Serves 4

4 medium baking potatoes
225g/8oz/1 cup low-fat
   cottage cheese
10ml/2 tsp tomato
   purée (paste)
2.5ml/½ tsp ground cumin

For the garnish
mixed salad leaves
fresh coriander (cilantro) sprigs
lemon wedges
2 tomatoes, quartered

1 Preheat the oven to 180°C/350°F/Gas 4. Wash, pat dry and make a slit in the middle of each potato. Prick the potatoes a few times, then wrap in foil. Bake for about 1 hour until soft. Put the cottage cheese into a heatproof dish and set aside.

2 In a separate bowl, mix together the tomato purée, ground cumin, ground coriander, chilli powder and salt.

3 Heat the oil in a small pan for about 1 minute. Add the mixed onion and mustard seeds and the curry leaves. When the leaves turn a shade darker and release their aroma, pour the spice mixture into the pan and lower the heat.

4 Add the water and mix well. Cook for a further 1 minute, then pour the spicy tomato mixture on to the cottage cheese and blend everything together well.

5 Check that the potatoes are cooked right through by inserting a metal skewer. Unwrap the potatoes and divide the cottage cheese mixture equally between the four potatoes. Garnish the potatoes with the mixed salad leaves, fresh coriander sprigs, lemon wedges and tomato quarters.

Curry Fried Noodles

On its own, tofu has a fairly bland flavour, but it is very good at taking on the flavours of the other ingredients it is cooked with. This delicious curry takes advantage of that by cooking the tofu with traditional spice paste.

Serves 4

60ml/4 tbsp vegetable oil
30–45ml/2–3 tbsp curry paste
225g/8oz smoked tofu, cut into
   2.5cm/1in cubes

225g/8oz green beans, cut into
   2.5cm/1in lengths
1 red (bell) pepper, seeded and
   cut into fine strips
350g/12oz rice vermicelli, soaked
   in warm water until soft
15ml/1 tbsp soy sauce
salt and ground black pepper
2 spring onions (scallions),
   finely sliced, 2 red chillies,
   seeded and cut into thin slices,
   and 1 lime, cut into wedges,
   to garnish

1 Heat half the oil in a wok or large frying pan. Add the curry paste to the pan and stir-fry for a few minutes until it releases all the fragrant aromas.

2 Add the tofu to the pan and fry until golden brown all over. Using a slotted spoon remove the tofu cubes from the pan and set aside until required.

3 Add the remaining oil to the wok or pan. When the oil is hot, add the green beans and red pepper strips. Stir-fry for about 4–5 minutes until the vegetables are cooked. You may need to moisten them with a little water.

4 Drain the soaked noodles thoroughly and then add them to the wok or frying pan.

5 Continue to stir-fry until the noodles are heated through, then return the curried tofu to the wok or pan. Season with soy sauce, salt and black pepper.

6 Transfer the mixture to a warmed serving dish. Sprinkle with the sliced spring onions and chillies and serve immediately with the lime wedges on the side.

Potato with Cheese Energy 256kcal/1086kJ; Protein 12.4g; Carbohydrate 43.8g, of which sugars 5.4g; Fat 4.8g, of which saturates 1.1g; Cholesterol 3mg; Calcium 64mg; Fibre 2.6g; Sodium 249mg.
Curry Noodles Energy 479kcal/1996kJ; Protein 13.8g; Carbohydrate 73.7g, of which sugars 4.3g; Fat 14.2g, of which saturates 1.7g; Cholesterol 0mg; Calcium 332mg; Fibre 2g; Sodium 11mg.

Cheese with Mushrooms and Peas

An Indian cheese, known as paneer, is used in both sweet and savoury dishes. In India this cheese is often made at home, although in recent years it has become available commercially. It is a useful source of protein for the many vegetarians living in India.

Serves 4–6
90ml/6 tbsp ghee or vegetable oil
225g/8oz paneer, cubed
1 onion, finely chopped
a few fresh mint leaves, chopped,
    plus extra sprigs to garnish
50g/2oz chopped fresh
    coriander (cilantro)
3 fresh green chillies, chopped
3 garlic cloves
2.5cm/1in piece fresh root
    ginger, sliced
5ml/1 tsp ground turmeric
5ml/1 tsp chilli powder (optional)
5ml/1 tsp garam masala
225g/8oz/3 cups tiny button
    (white) mushrooms, washed
225g/8oz/2 cups frozen
    peas, thawed
175ml/6fl oz/³⁄₄ cup natural (plain)
    yogurt, mixed with 5ml/1 tsp
    cornflour (cornstarch)
salt

1 Heat the ghee or oil in a wok, karahi or large pan, and fry the paneer cubes until they are golden brown on all sides. Remove, drain on kitchen paper, and keep to one side.

2 Grind the onion, mint, coriander, chillies, garlic and ginger with a mortar and pestle or in a food processor or blender to a fairly smooth paste.

3 Remove to a bowl and mix in the turmeric, chilli powder, if using, and garam masala, and season with salt to taste.

4 Remove excess ghee or oil from the pan, leaving about 15ml/1 tbsp. Heat and fry the paste over a medium heat for 8–10 minutes, or until the oil separates.

5 Add the mushrooms, thawed peas and paneer, and mix well. Cool the mixture slightly and gradually fold in the yogurt.

6 Simmer for about 10 minutes, until the vegetables are tender and the flavours well mixed. Remove to a serving dish, garnish with sprigs of fresh mint and serve immediately.

Potato Curry with Yogurt

Variations of this simple Indian curry are popular in Singapore, where fusion dishes like this one cater for a community that includes people from all over Asia, as well as from Europe and the Americas.

Serves 4
6 garlic cloves, chopped
25g/1oz fresh root ginger, peeled
    and chopped
30ml/2 tbsp ghee, or 15ml/1 tbsp
    oil and 15g/¹⁄₂oz/1 tbsp butter
6 shallots, halved lengthways and
    sliced along the grain
2 fresh green chillies, seeded
    and finely sliced
10ml/2 tsp sugar
a handful of fresh or dried
    curry leaves
2 cinnamon sticks
5–10ml/1–2 tsp ground turmeric
15ml/1 tbsp garam masala
500g/1¹⁄₄lb waxy potatoes, cut
    into bitesize pieces
2 tomatoes, peeled, seeded
    and quartered
250ml/8fl oz/1 cup Greek
    (US strained plain) yogurt
salt and ground black pepper
5ml/1 tsp red chilli powder, and
    fresh coriander (cilantro)
    and mint leaves, finely chopped,
    to garnish
1 lemon, cut into quarters,
    to serve

1 Using a mortar and pestle or a food processor, grind the garlic and ginger to a coarse paste.

2 Heat the ghee or oil and butter in a heavy pan and stir in the shallots and chillies, until fragrant. Add the garlic and ginger paste with the sugar, and stir until the mixture begins to colour. Stir in the curry leaves, cinnamon sticks, turmeric and garam masala, and toss in the potatoes, making sure they are well coated in the spice mixture.

3 Pour just enough cold water into the pan to cover the potatoes. Bring to the boil, then reduce the heat and simmer until the potatoes are just cooked – they should still have a bite to them rather than being mushy.

4 Season with salt and pepper to taste. Gently toss in the tomatoes to heat them through. Fold in the yogurt so that it is streaky. Sprinkle with the chilli powder, coriander and mint. Serve immediately from the pan, with lemon to squeeze over.

Cheese with Mushrooms Energy 294kcal/1217kJ; Protein 14.4g; Carbohydrate 14g, of which sugars 7.3g; Fat 20.3g, of which saturates 3.7g; Cholesterol 10mg; Calcium 174mg; Fibre 3.5g; Sodium 210mg.
Potato Curry Energy 231kcal/967kJ; Protein 6.7g; Carbohydrate 26.2g, of which sugars 7.4g; Fat 12.4g, of which saturates 4.1g; Cholesterol 0mg; Calcium 110mg; Fibre 2g; Sodium 63mg.

Cabbage with Chilli and Cumin

This cabbage dish is only lightly spiced. It makes a good accompaniment to many other dishes, or a great main dish for a vegetarian lunch or a mid-week dinner.

Serves 4

15ml/1 tbsp corn oil
50g/2oz/4 tbsp butter
2.5ml/½ tsp coriander
 seeds, crushed
2.5ml/½ tsp white cumin seeds
6 dried red chillies
1 small Savoy cabbage,
 finely shredded
12 mangetouts (snow peas)
3 fresh red chillies, seeded
 and sliced
12 baby corn cobs
salt
25g/1oz/¼ cup flaked (sliced)
 almonds, toasted, and
5ml/1 tbsp chopped fresh
 coriander (cilantro), to garnish

1 Heat the oil and butter in a wok or a large, heavy frying pan and add the crushed coriander seeds, white cumin seeds and dried red chillies. Fry for about 1–2 minutes, stirring constantly, until the spices release their fragrances.

2 Add the shredded cabbage and the mangetouts to the pan and fry, stirring constantly, for about 5 minutes, until the vegetables are just tender.

3 Finally add the fresh red chillies, baby corn cobs and salt to the pan, and fry for a further 3 minutes.

4 Remove the pan from the heat and toss the ingredients together. Garnish with the toasted almonds and chopped fresh coriander, and serve immediately.

Variations
• Many other vegetables will work equally well in this dish. If mangetouts are out of season, you could replace them with any other green beans. You can also try adding some (bell) peppers in place of the baby corn cobs.
• If you prefer a little more heat, you can keep the seeds in the chillies or increase the amount of chillies used.

Mushroom and Okra Curry

The sliced okra not only flavours this unusual curry, but thickens it, too.

Serves 4

4 garlic cloves, roughly chopped
2.5cm/1in piece fresh root ginger,
 roughly chopped
1 or 2 fresh red chillies, seeded
 and chopped
175ml/6fl oz/¾ cup cold water
15ml/1 tbsp sunflower oil
5ml/1 tsp coriander seeds
5ml/1 tsp cumin seeds
5ml/1 tsp ground cumin
seeds from 2 green cardamom
 pods, ground
pinch of ground turmeric
400g/14oz can chopped
 tomatoes

450g/1lb/6 cups mushrooms,
 quartered if large
225g/8oz okra, trimmed
 and sliced
30ml/2 tbsp chopped fresh
 coriander (cilantro)
plain boiled basmati rice,
 to serve

For the mango relish

1 large ripe mango, about
 500g/1¼lb
1 small garlic clove, crushed
1 small onion, finely chopped
10ml/2 tsp grated fresh
 root ginger
1 fresh red chilli, seeded and
 finely chopped
a pinch each of salt and sugar

1 To make the mango relish, peel the mango, cut the flesh off the stone (pit) and chop it finely. Place the mango pieces in a bowl and mash with a fork. Add the garlic, onion, ginger, chilli, salt and sugar and mix well. Set aside.

2 Put the garlic, ginger, chillies and 45ml/3 tbsp of the water in a blender or food processor and blend to a smooth paste.

3 Heat the oil in a large pan. Add the coriander and cumin seeds, and the ground cumin, ground cardamom and turmeric, and cook for 1 minute, until aromatic. Scrape in the garlic paste, then add the tomatoes, mushrooms and okra. Pour in the remaining water. Stir to mix well, and bring to the boil. Reduce the heat, cover and simmer the curry for 5 minutes.

4 Remove the lid, increase the heat slightly and cook for 5–10 minutes more, until the okra is tender. Stir in the fresh coriander and serve with the rice and the mango relish.

Spicy Bitter Gourds

Bitter gourds are widely used in Indian cooking, both on their own as a side dish and combined with other vegetables in a curry.

Serves 4

675g/1½lb bitter gourds
60ml/4 tbsp vegetable oil
2.5ml/½ tsp cumin seeds
6 spring onions (scallions), chopped
5 tomatoes, finely chopped
2.5cm/1in piece root ginger, finely chopped
2 garlic cloves, crushed
2 fresh green chillies, seeded and finely chopped
2.5ml/½ tsp salt, plus extra to taste
2.5ml/½ tsp chilli powder
5ml/1 tsp ground coriander
5ml/1 tsp ground cumin
45ml/3 tbsp peanuts, crushed
45ml/3 tbsp soft dark brown sugar
15ml/1 tbsp gram flour
fresh coriander (cilantro) sprigs, to garnish

1 Bring a large pan of lightly salted water to the boil. Peel the bitter gourds using a small sharp knife and halve them. Discard the seeds. Cut into 2cm/¾in pieces, then cook in the water for about 10–15 minutes, or until they are tender. Drain well and set aside while you prepare the other ingredients.

2 Heat the oil in a large pan and fry the cumin seeds for about 2 minutes until they begin to splutter. Add the spring onions and fry for 3–4 minutes. Add the tomatoes, ginger, garlic and chillies and cook for 5 minutes.

3 Add the salt, remaining spices, the peanuts and sugar and cook for about 2–3 minutes, stirring constantly.

4 Add the bitter gourds and mix well. Sprinkle over the gram flour. Cover and simmer over a low heat for 5–8 minutes, or until all of the gram flour has been absorbed into the sauce. Serve garnished with fresh coriander sprigs.

> **Cook's Tip**
> *For a quick and easy way to crush peanuts, put into a food processor or blender and process for about 20–30 seconds.*

Spicy Courgette Curry

This is an excellent way to spice up an everyday vegetable. The courgettes are thickly sliced and then combined with authentic Indian spices for a delicious, colourful vegetable curry.

Serves 4

675g/1½lb courgettes (zucchini)
45ml/3 tbsp vegetable oil
2.5ml/½ tsp cumin seeds
2.5ml/½ tsp mustard seeds
1 onion, thinly sliced
2 garlic cloves, crushed
1.5ml/¼ tsp ground turmeric
1.5ml/¼ tsp chilli powder
5ml/1 tsp ground coriander
5ml/1 tsp ground cumin
2.5ml/½ tsp salt
15ml/1 tbsp tomato purée (paste)
400g/14oz can chopped tomatoes
150ml/¼ pint/⅔ cup water
15ml/1 tbsp chopped fresh coriander (cilantro)
5ml/1 tsp garam masala

1 Trim the ends from the courgettes and discard, then cut them into slices, about 1cm/½in thick.

2 Heat the oil in a wok or large frying pan and fry the cumin with the mustard seeds for about 2 minutes until they begin to splutter and release their aromatic fragrances.

3 Add the onion and garlic to the pan and fry for about 5–6 minutes until the onion begins to soften.

4 Add the ground turmeric, chilli powder, coriander, cumin and salt and fry for about 2–3 minutes, stirring constantly.

5 Add the sliced courgettes to the pan all at once, and cook for about 5–7 minutes until just tender.

6 Mix together the tomato purée and chopped tomatoes in a bowl and add to the pan with the water. Mix well until all the ingredients are well combined. Cover the pan and simmer for 10 minutes until the sauce thickens.

7 Stir in the fresh coriander and the garam masala, then cook for 5 minutes or until heated through. Transfer to a serving dish and serve immediately.

Spicy Bitter Gourds Energy 304kcal/1268kJ; Protein 8.9g; Carbohydrate 27g, of which sugars 19.6g; Fat 18.6g, of which saturates 2.8g; Cholesterol 0mg; Calcium 89mg; Fibre 3.8g; Sodium 19mg.
Courgette Curry Energy 161kcal/666kJ; Protein 5.8g; Carbohydrate 11g, of which sugars 6.5g; Fat 10.9g, of which saturates 1.5g; Cholesterol 0mg; Calcium 73mg; Fibre 2.6g; Sodium 24mg.

Mushroom Curry with Garam Masala

This is a delicious way of cooking mushrooms. It goes well with meat dishes, but is also great served on its own as a vegetarian main course.

Serves 4

30ml/2 tbsp vegetable oil
2.5ml/½ tsp cumin seeds
1.5ml/¼ tsp black peppercorns
4 green cardamom pods
1.5ml/¼ tsp ground turmeric
1 onion, finely chopped
5ml/1 tsp ground cumin
5ml/1 tsp ground coriander
2.5ml/½ tsp garam masala
1 fresh green chilli,
   finely chopped
2 garlic cloves, crushed
2.5cm/1in piece fresh root
   ginger, grated
400g/14oz can
   chopped tomatoes
1.5ml/¼ tsp salt
450g/1lb/6 cups button (white)
   mushrooms, halved
chopped fresh coriander
   (cilantro), to garnish

1 Heat the oil in a large, heavy pan and fry the cumin seeds, peppercorns, cardamom pods and turmeric for 2–3 minutes.

2 Add the onion and fry for about 5 minutes until golden. Stir in the cumin, ground coriander and garam masala and fry for a further 2 minutes.

3 Add the chilli, garlic and ginger and fry for 2–3 minutes, stirring all the time. Add the tomatoes and salt. Bring to the boil and simmer for 5 minutes.

4 Add the mushrooms. Cover and simmer over a low heat for 10 minutes. Garnish with chopped coriander before serving.

Cook's Tip
The distinctive flavour of mushrooms goes well with this mixture of spices. If you don't want to use button (white) mushrooms, you can substitute any other mushrooms. Dried mushrooms can be added, if you like. Soak dried mushrooms before using, and add them to the recipe with the tomatoes.

Aromatic Vegetable Curry with Mushrooms and Beans

Here the aim is to produce a subtle curry rather than an assault on the senses.

Serves 4

50g/2oz/¼ cup butter
2 onions, sliced
2 garlic cloves, crushed
2.5cm/1in piece fresh root
   ginger, grated
5ml/1 tsp ground cumin
15ml/1 tbsp ground coriander
6 cardamom pods
5cm/2in piece of cinnamon stick
5ml/1 tsp ground turmeric
1 fresh red chilli, seeded and
   finely chopped
1 potato, peeled and cut into
   2.5cm/1in cubes
1 small aubergine
   (eggplant), chopped
115g/4oz/1½ cups mushrooms,
   thickly sliced
175ml/6fl oz/¾ cup water
115g/4oz green beans, cut into
   2.5cm/1in lengths
60ml/4 tbsp natural (plain) yogurt
150ml/¼ pint/⅔ cup double
   (heavy) cream
5ml/1 tsp garam masala
salt and ground black pepper
fresh coriander (cilantro) sprigs,
   to garnish
plain boiled rice, to serve

1 Melt the butter in a heavy pan. Add the onions and cook for 5 minutes until soft. Add the garlic and ginger and cook for 2 minutes, then stir in the cumin, coriander, cardamom pods, cinnamon stick, turmeric and finely chopped chilli. Cook, stirring constantly, for 30 seconds.

2 Add the potato cubes, aubergine and mushrooms and the water. Cover the pan, bring to the boil, then lower the heat and simmer for 15 minutes.

3 Add the beans to the pan and cook, uncovered, for about 5 minutes. With a slotted spoon, remove the vegetables to a warmed serving dish and keep hot.

4 Allow the cooking liquid to bubble up until it has reduced a little. Season with salt and pepper to taste, then stir in the yogurt, double cream and garam masala. Pour the sauce over the vegetables and garnish with fresh coriander. Serve the curry immediately with plain boiled rice.

Mushroom Curry Energy 110kcal/459kJ; Protein 4.2g; Carbohydrate 7.1g, of which sugars 3.3g; Fat 7.7g, of which saturates 1.1g; Cholesterol 0mg; Calcium 32mg; Fibre 2.2g; Sodium 18mg.
Aromatic Curry Energy 183kcal/766kJ; Protein 7g; Carbohydrate 22.7g, of which sugars 10.5g; Fat 7.9g, of which saturates 1.1g; Cholesterol 0mg; Calcium 82mg; Fibre 6.6g; Sodium 253mg.

Punjab Roasted Aubergines with Spring Onions

This classic dish, made of roasted and mashed aubergines cooked with spring onions, is known as bharta in the Punjab region. Traditionally, the aubergine is roasted over charcoal, but a hot electric or gas oven will produce similar results, although the smoky flavour will be missing.

Serves 4
2 large aubergines (eggplants)
45ml/3 tbsp vegetable oil
2.5ml/¹/₂ tsp black mustard seeds
1 bunch spring onions (scallions), finely chopped
115g/4oz/1¹/₂ cups button (white) mushrooms, halved
2 garlic cloves, crushed
1 fresh red chilli, finely chopped
2.5ml/¹/₂ tsp chilli powder
5ml/1 tsp ground cumin
5ml/1 tsp ground coriander
1.5ml/¹/₄ tsp ground turmeric
5ml/1 tsp salt
400g/14oz can chopped tomatoes
15ml/1 tbsp chopped fresh coriander (cilantro), plus a few extra sprigs to garnish

1 Preheat the oven to 200°C/400°F/Gas 6. Place the aubergines in a baking dish, brush with 15ml/1 tbsp of the oil and prick with a fork. Bake for 30–35 minutes until soft.

2 Meanwhile, heat the remaining oil in a large pan and fry the black mustard seeds for about 2 minutes until they splutter.

3 Add the spring onions, mushrooms, garlic and chilli to the pan, and fry for about 5 minutes more.

4 Stir in the chilli powder, cumin, coriander, turmeric and salt and fry for 4 minutes. Add the tomatoes and cook for 5 minutes.

5 Cut the aubergines in half lengthwise and scoop out the soft flesh into a large mixing bowl. Mash the flesh to a coarse texture, using a fork or potato masher.

6 Add the aubergines to the pan with the coriander. Bring to the boil and simmer for 5 minutes until the sauce thickens. Serve garnished with the fresh coriander.

Spiced Potato Curry with Chilli and Paprika

This spicy potato curry is an Andean stew called ajiaco. It gets its name from aji, a generic word for hot pepper. The dish combines potatoes, fresh cheese and chilli: there are many variations but these three main ingredients are always included. It can be served with rice and vegetables, or with roasted or grilled meats. It is substantial and flexible – choose your own assortment of vegetables, such as pumpkin, butternut squash, winter melon, yams, aubergines or beans.

Serves 6
1kg/2¹/₄lb floury potatoes, such as King Edward
60ml/4 tbsp vegetable oil
6 spring onions (scallions), chopped
5ml/1 tsp grated garlic
30ml/2 tbsp chilli sauce
5ml/1 tsp paprika
250ml/8fl oz/1 cup evaporated milk
120ml/4fl oz/¹/₂ cup water
150g/5oz feta cheese
4 hard-boiled eggs, roughly chopped
salt and ground black pepper

1 Boil the potatoes in their skins in lightly salted water for 20 minutes, until tender.

2 Peel the potatoes and crush them lightly (they do not need to be mashed to a purée). Set aside.

3 Heat the oil in a heavy frying pan over a medium heat and fry the spring onions and garlic for about 8 minutes, stirring frequently, until browned.

4 Add the chilli sauce and paprika, season with salt and pepper, then stir in the potatoes, milk and water.

5 Mash the cheese with a fork and add to the potato mixture with the chopped eggs.

6 Stir with a wooden spoon and leave the mixture to simmer for 5 minutes before serving.

Punjab Aubergines Energy 136kcal/363kJ; Protein 3.6g; Carbohydrate 8.4g, of which sugars 5.5g; Fat 10.2g, of which saturates 0.7g; Cholesterol 0mg; Calcium 57mg; Fibre 4g; Sodium 19mg.
Spiced Potato Curry Energy 306kcal/1281kJ; Protein 11.6g; Carbohydrate 28.7g, of which sugars 2.8g; Fat 17.1g, of which saturates 5.5g; Cholesterol 144mg; Calcium 129mg; Fibre 1.8g; Sodium 427mg.

Stuffed Aubergines with Tamarind

The traditional way of cooking with tamarind is in a terracotta dish, which brings out the full fruity tartness of the tamarind. This spicy aubergine dish will add a refreshing tang to any meal.

Serves 4
12 baby aubergines (eggplants)
30ml/2 tbsp vegetable oil
1 small onion, chopped
10ml/2 tsp grated fresh
   root ginger
10ml/2 tsp crushed garlic

5ml/1 tsp coriander seeds
5ml/1 tsp cumin seeds
10ml/2 tsp white poppy seeds
10ml/2 tsp sesame seeds
10ml/2 tsp desiccated
   (dry unsweetened
   shredded) coconut
15ml/1 tbsp dry-roasted
   skinned peanuts
2.5–5ml/½–1 tsp chilli powder
5ml/1 tsp salt
6–8 curry leaves
1–2 dried red chillies, seeded
   and chopped
2.5ml/½ tsp concentrated
   tamarind paste

1 Make three deep slits lengthwise on each aubergine, without cutting through, then soak in salted water for 20 minutes.

2 Heat half the oil in a pan and fry the onion for 3–4 minutes. Add the ginger and garlic and cook for 30 seconds.

3 Add the coriander and cumin seeds and fry for 30 seconds, then add the poppy seeds, sesame seeds and coconut. Fry for 1 minute, stirring constantly. Allow to cool slightly, then grind the spices in a food processor, adding 105ml/7 tbsp warm water.

4 Mix the peanuts, chilli powder and salt into the spice paste. Drain the aubergines and dry on kitchen paper. Stuff each of the slits with the spice paste and reserve any remaining paste.

5 Heat the remaining oil in a large pan over a medium heat and add the curry leaves and chillies. Let the chillies blacken, then add the aubergines and the tamarind blended with 105ml/7 tbsp hot water. Stir in any remaining paste.

6 Cover the pan and simmer gently for 15–20 minutes or until the aubergines are tender. Serve immediately.

Vegetable Korma

Korma-style cooking was originally used for meat and poultry dishes, but it proved so popular that vegetarian recipes were created. This colourful curry is a combination of vegetables coated in a luxurious almond sauce, exotically spiced with cardamom and coriander.

Serves 4
115g/4oz fine green beans, cut
   into 5cm/2in pieces
375g/13oz cauliflower, divided
   into 1cm/½in florets
115g/4oz carrots, cut into batons

375g/13oz potatoes, boiled in
   their skins and cooled
50g/2oz blanched almonds,
   soaked in 150ml/5fl oz/⅔ cup
   boiling water for 20 minutes
60ml/4 tbsp sunflower oil or
   olive oil
2 medium onions, finely chopped
2 green chillies, seeded and
   finely chopped
10ml/2 tsp ginger purée
15ml/1 tbsp ground coriander
1.5ml/¼ tsp ground turmeric
2.5ml/½ tsp chilli powder
5ml/1 tsp salt, or to taste
2.5ml/½ tsp sugar
120ml/4fl oz/½ cup double
   (heavy) cream

1 Blanch all the vegetables separately – the beans for about 3 minutes, the cauliflower for 3 minutes and the carrots for 5 minutes – then plunge them immediately into cold water. Cut the cooked potatoes into 2.5cm/1in cubes.

2 Purée the blanched almonds in a blender or food processor with the water in which they were soaked, and set aside.

3 In a heavy frying pan, heat the oil over a medium heat and add the onions, green chillies and ginger purée. Fry them for 10–12 minutes, stirring regularly, until they turn a light brown colour and the onions have softened.

4 Add the coriander, turmeric and chilli powder. Reduce the heat to a low temperature and fry for 1 minute.

5 Add the vegetables, salt and sugar. Add 150ml/5fl oz/⅔ cup warm water, stir once and then bring to the boil. Reduce the heat to low, add the cream and cook for 2–3 minutes to heat through, then serve immediately.

Stuffed Aubergines Energy 132kcal/549kJ; Protein 2.9g; Carbohydrate 4.7g, of which sugars 3.8g; Fat 11.5g, of which saturates 3.3g; Cholesterol 0mg; Calcium 36mg; Fibre 3.7g; Sodium 5mg.
Vegetable Korma Energy 381kcal/1577kJ; Protein 5.1g; Carbohydrate 20.9g, of which sugars 9.9g; Fat 31.4g, of which saturates 19.3g; Cholesterol 78mg; Calcium 95mg; Fibre 3.9g; Sodium 108mg.

Creamy Black Lentils

Black lentils, or urad dhal, are available whole, split, and skinned and split. Generally, both split and skinned versions are used in west and south Indian cooking, whereas whole black lentils are a typical ingredient in the north.

Serves 4–6

175g/6oz/³⁄₄ cup black
　lentils, soaked overnight
50g/2oz/¹⁄₄ cup red split lentils
120ml/4fl oz/¹⁄₂ cup double (heavy)
　cream, plus extra to serve
120ml/4fl oz/¹⁄₂ cup natural
　(plain) yogurt
5ml/1 tsp cornflour (cornstarch)
45ml/3 tbsp ghee or vegetable oil
1 onion, finely chopped
5cm/2in piece fresh root
　ginger, crushed
4 fresh green chillies, chopped
1 tomato, chopped
2.5ml/¹⁄₂ tsp chilli powder
2.5ml/¹⁄₂ tsp ground turmeric
2.5ml/¹⁄₂ tsp ground cumin
2 garlic cloves, sliced
salt
coriander (cilantro) sprigs and
　sliced red chilli, to garnish

1 Drain the black lentils and place in a large pan with the red lentils. Cover with water and bring to the boil. Reduce the heat, cover the pan and simmer until tender. Mash the lentils with a spoon or fork, and set aside to cool.

2 In a large bowl, mix together the cream, yogurt and cornflour, and stir into the lentils in the pan.

3 Heat 15ml/1 tbsp of the ghee or oil in a wok, karahi or large pan, and fry the onion, ginger, two green chillies and the tomato until the onion is soft. Add the ground spices and salt and fry for a further 2 minutes. Stir into the lentil mixture and mix well to combine. Reheat, then transfer to a heatproof serving dish and keep warm.

4 Heat the remaining ghee or oil in a frying pan over a low heat and fry the garlic slices and remaining chillies until the garlic slices are golden brown.

5 Pour the garlic and chillies over the lentils and fold in just before serving. Place extra cream on the table for the diners to add more to their helping if they wish.

Purée of Spiced Lentils with Eggs

This unusual dish of brown lentils spiced with fresh coriander and mint makes an excellent supper or light lunch or an unusual breakfast dish. For a nuttier flavour you could add a 400g/14oz can of unsweetened chestnut purée to the lentil mixture.

Serves 4

450g/1lb/2 cups washed
　brown lentils
3 leeks, thinly sliced
10ml/2 tsp coriander seeds,
　crushed
15ml/1 tbsp chopped fresh
　coriander (cilantro)
30ml/2 tbsp chopped fresh
　mint leaves
15ml/1 tbsp red wine vinegar
1 litre/1³⁄₄ pints/4 cups
　vegetable stock
4 eggs
salt and ground black pepper
generous handful of fresh
　parsley, stalks removed,
　roughly chopped, to garnish

1 Put the lentils in a deep pan. Add the leeks, coriander seeds, fresh coriander, mint, vinegar and vegetable stock and stir until the ingredients are well combined.

2 Bring the mixture to the boil, then lower the heat and simmer for 30–40 minutes, until the lentils are cooked and have absorbed the liquid. Preheat the oven to 180°C/350°F/Gas 4.

3 Season the lentils with salt and pepper, and mix well. Spread them out in four lightly greased baking dishes.

4 Using the back of a spoon, make a hollow in the lentil mixture in each dish. Break an egg into each hollow.

5 Cover the dishes with foil and bake for 15–20 minutes, or until the egg whites are set and the yolks are still soft. Sprinkle with plenty of parsley and serve immediately.

> **Cook's Tip**
> If you prefer, the lentil mixture can be put into a large dish.
> Make four indentations in the mixture to hold the eggs.

Creamy Black Lentils Energy 309kcal/1289kJ; Protein 11g; Carbohydrate 26.2g, of which sugars 3.8g; Fat 18.6g, of which saturates 10.1g; Cholesterol 28mg; Calcium 77mg; Fibre 2.2g; Sodium 38mg.
Purée of Lentils Energy 470kcal/1990kJ; Protein 35.9g; Carbohydrate 68.4g, of which sugars 6g; Fat 7.9g, of which saturates 1.9g; Cholesterol 190mg; Calcium 148mg; Fibre 8.8g; Sodium 116mg.

Fried Hard-boiled Eggs in Red Sauce

A popular snack at street stalls in Malaysia and Singapore, this spicy egg dish originally comes from Indonesia. It is usually served wrapped in a banana leaf and eaten with plain steamed rice, sliced chillies, onion and fresh coriander, and it is ideal for a quick, tasty meal.

Serves 4

vegetable oil, for deep-frying
8 eggs, hard-boiled and shelled
1 lemon grass stalk, trimmed,
    quartered and crushed
2 large tomatoes, skinned,
    seeded and chopped to a pulp
5–10ml/1–2 tsp sugar
30ml/2 tbsp dark soy sauce
juice of 1 lime
fresh coriander (cilantro) and mint
    leaves, coarsely chopped,
    to garnish

For the spice paste
4–6 fresh red chillies, seeded
    and chopped
4 shallots, chopped
2 garlic cloves, peeled
    and chopped
2.5ml/½ tsp vegetable paste
    or mam roi

1 Using a mortar and pestle or a food processor, grind together the ingredients for the spice paste until smooth. Set aside while you prepare the other ingredients.

2 Heat enough oil for deep-frying in a wok or heavy pan and deep-fry the whole boiled eggs until they are golden brown. Lift them out and drain.

3 Reserve about 15ml/1 tbsp of the oil in the wok or pan and discard the rest. Heat the oil in the wok or heavy pan and stir in the spice paste. Cook, stirring frequently, for 2–3 minutes or until it becomes fragrant but not browned.

4 Add the lemon grass to the pan, followed by the chopped tomatoes and sugar. Cook over a medium heat for 2–3 minutes, until it forms a thick paste.

5 Reduce the heat and stir in the soy sauce and lime juice. Add 30ml/2 tbsp water to thin the sauce. Toss in the eggs, making sure they are thoroughly coated, and serve hot, garnished with chopped coriander and mint leaves.

Egg and Lentil Curry

Eggs are an excellent addition to vegetarian curries and, combined with lentils, make a substantial and extremely tasty curry.

Serves 4

75g/3oz/½ cup green lentils
750ml/1¼ pints/3 cups stock
6 eggs
30ml/2 tbsp vegetable oil
3 cloves
1.5ml/¼ tsp black peppercorns
1 onion, finely chopped
2 green chillies, finely chopped
2 garlic cloves, crushed
2.5cm/1in piece of fresh root
    ginger, peeled and
    finely chopped
30ml/2 tbsp curry paste
400g/14oz can chopped
    tomatoes
2.5ml/½ tsp sugar
2.5ml/½ tsp garam masala

1 Wash the lentils under cold running water, checking for small stones. Put the lentils in a large pan with the stock. Cover and simmer for 15 minutes or until soft. Drain and set aside.

2 Cook the eggs in boiling water for 10 minutes. Remove from the boiling water and set aside to cool slightly. When cool enough to handle, peel and cut in half lengthways.

3 Heat the oil in a large pan and fry the cloves and peppercorns for about 2 minutes. Add the onion, chillies, garlic and ginger to the pan and fry the mixture for a further 5–6 minutes, stirring frequently.

4 Stir the curry paste into the pan and fry for about 2 minutes, stirring constantly, until the aromatic fragrances are released.

5 Add the tomatoes and sugar and stir in 175ml/6fl oz/¾ cup water. Simmer for about 5 minutes until the sauce thickens, stirring occasionally. Add the eggs, drained lentils and garam masala. Cover and simmer for 10 minutes, then serve.

> **Variation**
> You can substitute red lentils for the green. Red lentils tend to disintegrate more when cooking, resulting in a smoother curry.

Fried Eggs Energy 271kcal/1125kJ; Protein 13.3g; Carbohydrate 5.5g, of which sugars 5g; Fat 22.3g, of which saturates 4.4g; Cholesterol 381mg; Calcium 67mg; Fibre 0.7g; Sodium 679mg.
Egg and Lentil Curry Energy 238kcal/997kJ; Protein 14.6g; Carbohydrate 14.2g, of which sugars 4.1g; Fat 14.4g, of which saturates 3.1g; Cholesterol 285mg; Calcium 60mg; Fibre 1.9g; Sodium 121mg.

Eggs Baked on Chipsticks

This is an unusual and delicious way of combining eggs with potato sticks. The potato sticks are cooked with spices to form a pancake. Eggs are then placed on top of the potato pancake and gently cooked.

Serves 4–6
225g/8oz salted chipsticks
2 fresh green chillies, seeded and
　finely chopped
a few coriander (cilantro)
　sprigs, chopped
1.5ml/¼ tsp ground turmeric
60ml/4 tbsp vegetable oil or
　sunflower oil
75ml/5 tbsp water
6 eggs
3 spring onions (scallions),
　finely chopped
salt and ground black pepper
warm chapatis and a simple
　mixed green salad,
　to serve (optional)

1 In a large mixing bowl, mix together the salted chipsticks, chopped chillies, coriander and turmeric.

2 Heat 30ml/2 tbsp of the oil in a heavy frying pan. Add the chipstick mixture and water. Cook until the chipsticks turn soft, and then crisp up again.

3 Place a dinner plate or chopping board over the frying pan, and hold it firmly in place as you turn the pan over and carefully transfer the chipstick pancake on to the plate or board.

4 Heat the remaining oil in the pan and slide the pancake back into the frying pan to brown the other side.

5 Gently break the eggs over the pancake, cover the frying pan and allow the eggs to set over a low heat. Season well and sprinkle with spring onions. Cook until the base is crisp. Serve immediately for breakfast, or with warm chapatis and a simple salad for a light lunch or supper.

> **Cook's Tip**
> There are a number of crisp (US potato chip) producers who make chipsticks. Look for them in supermarkets.

Spicy Omelette

This irresistible omelette is classic Parsi food, which originated along the shores of the Caspian Sea, and the cuisine offers some unique flavours, which appeal to both Eastern and Western palates. Serve at any time of day, whether for breakfast, a light lunch or a quick supper.

Serves 4–6
30ml/2 tbsp vegetable oil
1 onion, finely chopped
2.5ml/½ tsp ground cumin
1 garlic clove, crushed
1 or 2 fresh green chillies, seeded
　and finely chopped
a few coriander (cilantro) sprigs,
　chopped, plus a little extra,
　to garnish
1 firm tomato, chopped
1 small potato, cubed and boiled
　until just tender
25g/1oz/¼ cup cooked peas
25g/1oz/¼ cup cooked corn, or
　canned corn, drained
2 eggs, beaten
25g/1oz/¼ cup grated cheese
salt and ground black pepper

1 Heat the vegetable oil in a wok, karahi or large pan, and fry the onion for 5 minutes until beginning to soften.

2 Add the next eight ingredients to the pan and cook until they are well blended but the potato and tomato are still firm. Season to taste with salt and ground black pepper.

3 Increase the heat and pour in the beaten eggs. Reduce the heat, cover and cook until the bottom layer has browned.

4 Turn the omelette over and sprinkle with the grated cheese. Place under a hot grill (broiler) and cook until the egg sets and the cheese has melted and browned slightly.

5 Garnish the omelette with sprigs of coriander and serve with salad for a light lunch. If you prefer, serve it for a tasty breakfast.

> **Variation**
> You can use any vegetable with the potatoes. Try thickly sliced button (white) mushrooms, added in step 1.

Eggs on Chipsticks Energy 276kcal/1153kJ; Protein 8.7g; Carbohydrate 20.4g, of which sugars 0.6g; Fat 18.5g, of which saturates 6.8g; Cholesterol 190mg; Calcium 58mg; Fibre 2.5g; Sodium 373mg.
Spicy Omelette Energy 93kcal/388kJ; Protein 4g; Carbohydrate 3.7g, of which sugars 1.2g; Fat 7.1g, of which saturates 1.9g; Cholesterol 67mg; Calcium 46mg; Fibre 0.6g; Sodium 104mg.

Boiled Egg Curry

This spicy Indian dish is usually served with a biryani or pilau rice, but it is equally good served with some Indian bread such as naan or chapati.

Serves 4–6
10ml/2 tsp white poppy seeds
10ml/2 tsp white sesame seeds
10ml/2 tsp whole coriander seeds
10ml/2 tbsp desiccated
  (dry unsweetened
  shredded) coconut

350ml/12fl oz/1½ cups
  tomato juice
10ml/2 tsp gram flour
5ml/1 tsp grated fresh root ginger
5ml/1 tsp chilli powder
1.5ml/¼ tsp asafoetida
5ml/1 tsp sugar
6 hard-boiled eggs, halved
10ml/2 tbsp sesame oil
5ml/1 tsp cumin seeds
4 whole dried red chillies
6–8 curry leaves
4 garlic cloves, finely sliced
salt

1 Heat a frying pan and dry-fry the poppy, sesame and coriander seeds for 3–4 minutes until they release their aromatic fragrances and begin to splutter.

2 Add the coconut and dry-fry until it browns. Cool and grind the ingredients together using a mortar and pestle or a food processor or blender.

3 Pour a little of the tomato juice into a small bowl and mix with the gram flour to form a smooth paste.

4 Add the ginger, chilli powder, asafoetida, salt and sugar and the ground spices to the paste. Mix well until combined.

5 Add the remaining tomato juice to the bowl and mix well. Transfer the contents of the bowl into a heavy pan and simmer gently for 10 minutes.

6 Add the hard-boiled eggs to the pan and cover with the sauce. Heat the oil in a separate frying pan and fry the remaining ingredients until the chillies turn dark brown.

7 Pour the spices and oil over the egg curry, mix gently together and reheat for a minute. Serve immediately.

Indian-spiced Vegetable Curry

This is a very delicately spiced vegetable dish that makes a light meal when served with rice and bread. It is also a good partner to a heavily spiced meat curry.

Serves 4
350g/12oz mixed vegetables:
  beans, peas, potatoes,
  cauliflower, carrots, cabbage,
  mangetouts (snow peas) and
  button (white) mushrooms
30ml/2 tbsp vegetable oil
5ml/1 tsp cumin seeds, roasted

2.5ml/½ tsp mustard seeds
2.5ml/½ tsp onion seeds
5ml/1 tsp ground turmeric
2 garlic cloves, crushed
6–8 curry leaves
1 whole dried red chilli
5ml/1 tsp sugar
150ml/¼ pint/⅔ cup natural
  (plain) yogurt, mixed with
    5ml/1 tsp cornflour (cornstarch)
salt
boiled plain basmati rice and
  warm Indian breads,
  to serve

1 Prepare all the vegetables you have chosen: string the beans; thaw the peas, if frozen; cube the potatoes; cut the cauliflower into florets; dice the carrots; shred the cabbage; top and tail the mangetouts; wash the mushrooms and leave whole.

2 Heat a wok or large pan with enough water to cook all the vegetables and bring to the boil. First add the potatoes and carrots and cook until nearly tender, then add all the other vegetables and cook until still firm. All the vegetables should be crunchy except the potatoes. Drain well.

3 Heat the oil in a frying pan and add the cumin, mustard and onion seeds. Fry gently for 1–2 minutes, stirring constantly until the seeds begin to splutter.

4 Add the turmeric, garlic, curry leaves and dried red chilli to the pan. Fry gently until the garlic is golden brown and the chilli nearly burnt. Reduce the heat.

5 Fold in the drained vegetables, add the sugar and season with salt. Gradually add the yogurt mixed with the cornflour and stir well. Heat the curry until bubbling and serve immediately with rice and Indian breads.

Boiled Egg Curry Energy 229kcal/953kJ; Protein 10.7g; Carbohydrate 4.6g, of which sugars 3.7g; Fat 19g, of which saturates 6.7g; Cholesterol 254mg; Calcium 81mg; Fibre 1.7g; Sodium 276mg.
Indian-spiced Curry Energy 92kcal/384kJ; Protein 3.1g; Carbohydrate 10.2g, of which sugars 3.4g; Fat 4.7g, of which saturates 0.7g; Cholesterol 0mg; Calcium 99mg; Fibre 0.9g; Sodium 61mg.

Hot and Spicy Thai Vegetable Curry

This spicy curry made with coconut milk has a creamy richness that contrasts wonderfully with the heat of the chilli. Thai yellow curry paste is available in supermarkets, but you will really taste the difference when you make it yourself.

Serves 4
30ml/2 tbsp sunflower oil
200ml/7fl oz/scant 1 cup
   coconut cream
300ml/½ pint/1¼ cups
   coconut milk
150ml/¼ pint/⅔ cup vegetable
   stock
200g/7oz green beans, cut into
   2cm/¾in lengths
200g/7oz baby corn
4 baby courgettes (zucchini),
   thickly sliced

1 small aubergine (eggplant),
   cubed or sliced
30ml/2 tbsp Thai
   mushroom ketchup
10ml/2 tsp palm sugar (jaggery)
fresh coriander (cilantro) leaves,
   to garnish
noodles or rice, to serve

For the yellow curry paste
10ml/2 tsp hot chilli powder
10ml/2 tsp ground coriander
10ml/2 tsp ground cumin
5ml/1 tsp turmeric
15ml/1 tbsp chopped fresh
   galangal
10ml/2 tsp finely grated garlic
30ml/2 tbsp finely chopped
   lemon grass
4 red Asian or brown shallots,
   finely chopped
5ml/1 tsp finely chopped
   lime rind

1 To make the curry paste, place all the ingredients in a food processor and blend with 30–45ml/2–3 tbsp of cold water to make a smooth paste. Add a little more water to the paste if the mixture seems too dry.

2 Heat a large wok over a medium heat and add the sunflower oil. When hot add 30–45ml/2–3 tbsp of the curry paste and stir-fry for 1–2 minutes. Add the coconut cream and cook gently for 8–10 minutes, or until the mixture starts to separate.

3 Add the coconut milk, stock and vegetables and cook gently for 8–10 minutes, until the vegetables are just tender.

4 Stir in the mushroom ketchup and palm sugar, garnish with coriander leaves and serve with noodles or rice.

Tofu and Vegetable Thai Curry

Coconut milk, chillies, galangal, lemon grass and kaffir lime leaves give this curry a wonderful flavour.

Serves 4
175g/6oz firm tofu, drained
45ml/3 tbsp dark soy sauce
15ml/1 tbsp sesame oil
5ml/1 tsp chilli sauce
2.5cm/1in piece fresh root ginger,
   finely grated
30ml/2 tbsp vegetable oil
1 onion, sliced
400ml/14fl oz/1⅔ cups coconut milk
150ml/¼ pint/⅔ cup water
1 red (bell) pepper, seeded
   and chopped
175g/6oz green beans, halved

225g/8oz cauliflower florets
225g/8oz broccoli florets
115g/4oz/1½ cups shiitake
   or button (white)
   mushrooms, halved
shredded spring onions (scallions),
   to garnish
boiled rice or noodles, to serve

For the curry paste
2 fresh green chillies, seeded
   and chopped
1 lemon grass stalk, chopped
2.5cm/1in piece fresh
   galangal, chopped
2 kaffir lime leaves
10ml/2 tsp ground coriander
a few sprigs fresh coriander
   (cilantro), including the stalks

1 Cut the drained tofu into 2.5cm/1in cubes and place in an ovenproof dish. Mix together the soy sauce, sesame oil, chilli sauce and ginger and pour over the tofu. Toss gently, then leave to marinate for 4 hours or overnight, turning occasionally.

2 For the curry paste, place the ingredients and 45ml/3 tbsp water in a food processor and blend for a few seconds.

3 Preheat the oven to 190°C/375°F/Gas 5. Heat the oil in a flameproof casserole. Fry the onion for 7–8 minutes. Add the paste and the coconut milk. Add the water and bring to the boil.

4 Stir in the red pepper, beans, cauliflower and broccoli, then cover and place in the oven.

5 Place the tofu and marinade in the oven for 30 minutes. Stir them into the curry with the mushrooms. Reduce the oven to 180°C/350°F/Gas 4 and cook for a further 15 minutes. Garnish with spring onions and serve with rice or noodles.

Hot Thai Curry Energy 279kcal/1161kJ; Protein 9.8g; Carbohydrate 17.4g, of which sugars 13.3g; Fat 19.4g, of which saturates 3.6g; Cholesterol 5mg; Calcium 99mg; Fibre 3.3g; Sodium 824mg.
Tofu Thai Curry Energy 210kcal/873kJ; Protein 11g; Carbohydrate 15.1g, of which sugars 13.3g; Fat 12g, of which saturates 1.8g; Cholesterol 0mg; Calcium 328mg; Fibre 5g; Sodium 927mg.

Spicy Spinach Dhal

There are many different types of dhals eaten in India, with each region having its own speciality. This is a delicious, lightly spiced dish with a mild nutty flavour from the lentils, which combine beautifully with the spinach. Serve as a main meal with rice and breads or with a meat dish.

Serves 4

175g/6oz/1 cup chana dhal (yellow lentils) or yellow split peas

175ml/6fl oz/¾ cup water
30ml/2 tbsp vegetable oil
1.5ml/¼ tsp black mustard seeds
1 onion, thinly sliced
2 garlic cloves, crushed
2.5cm/1in piece fresh root ginger, grated
1 red chilli, seeded and finely chopped
275g/10oz frozen spinach, thawed
1.5ml/¼ tsp chilli powder
2.5ml/½ tsp ground coriander
2.5ml/½ tsp garam masala
2.5ml/½ tsp salt

1 Wash the chana dhal or split peas in several changes of cold water, carefully picking through it to remove any stones or bits of grit. Place in a large bowl and cover with plenty of cold water. Leave to soak for 30 minutes.

2 Drain the chana dhal or split peas and place in a large pan with the measured water. Bring to the boil, cover the pan, reduce the heat and simmer for about 20–25 minutes, or until the dhal or peas are soft and tender.

3 Meanwhile, heat the oil in a wok or large frying pan and fry the mustard seeds for 2 minutes until they begin to splutter.

4 Add the onion, garlic, ginger and chilli to the pan and fry for 5–6 minutes, stirring constantly. Add the spinach to the pan and cook for about 10–12 minutes, or until the spinach is dry and the liquid has evaporated.

5 Stir in the chilli powder, coriander, garam masala and salt and cook for a further 2–3 minutes.

6 Drain the chana dhal or split peas, add to the spinach mixture and cook for about 5 minutes. Serve immediately.

Balti Vegetables with Cashew Nuts

This quick and versatile stir-fry will accommodate most other combinations of vegetables – you do not have to use the selection suggested here.

Serves 4

2 medium carrots
1 medium red (bell) pepper, seeded
1 medium green (bell) pepper, seeded
2 courgettes (zucchini)
115g/4oz green beans
1 medium bunch spring onions (scallions)
15ml/1 tbsp vegetable oil
4–6 curry leaves
2.5ml/½ tsp cumin seeds
4 dried red chillies
10–12 cashew nuts
5ml/1 tsp salt
30ml/2 tbsp lemon juice
fresh mint leaves, to garnish

1 Prepare the vegetables: cut the carrots, peppers and courgettes into matchsticks, halve the beans and finely chop the spring onions. Set aside while you prepare the other ingredients.

2 Heat the vegetable oil in a karahi, wok or large heavy frying pan and fry the curry leaves, cumin seeds and dried red chillies for about 1 minute, stirring constantly.

3 Add the vegetables and nuts to the pan, and stir them in gently. Add the salt and lemon juice. Continue to stir and cook for about 3–5 minutes.

4 When all the ingredients are warmed through, transfer the vegetables to a warmed serving dish, garnish with the fresh mint leaves and serve immediately.

> **Variation**
> Small florets of broccoli or cauliflower are delicious cooked in a stir-fry like this. The florets should be cooked until they are only just tender so that they retain their crunch. You could use them instead of the courgettes (zucchini) in the recipe. Alternatively, use button (white) mushrooms, mangetouts (snow peas) and a handful of beansprouts.

Balti Vegetables Energy 105kcal/436kJ; Protein 4.2g; Carbohydrate 11.2g, of which sugars 10.1g; Fat 5.1g, of which saturates 0.9g; Cholesterol 0mg; Calcium 56mg; Fibre 3.9g; Sodium 510mg.
Spicy Dhal Energy 226kcal/949kJ; Protein 13.3g; Carbohydrate 28.7g, of which sugars 2.9g; Fat 7.3g, of which saturates 0.9g; Cholesterol 0mg; Calcium 152mg; Fibre 3.8g; Sodium 114mg.

Tarka Dhal

Tarka is a hot oil seasoning that is folded into a dish before serving. Dhal is cooked every day in an Indian household, and a much simpler version is made for most family meals. Tarka dhal is commonly found in Bengal, Assam and Bangladesh and it is the combination of spices that gives away its origin.

Serves 4–6
115g/4oz/½ cup red split lentils, washed
50g/2oz/¼ cup chana dhal (yellow lentils) or yellow split peas, washed
600ml/1 pint/2½ cups water
5ml/1 tsp grated fresh root ginger
5ml/1 tsp crushed garlic
2.5ml/½ tsp ground turmeric
2 fresh green chillies, seeded and chopped
7.5ml/1½ tsp salt

For the tarka
30ml/2 tbsp vegetable oil
1 onion, sliced
2.5ml/½ tsp mixed mustard and onion seeds
4 dried red chillies
1 tomato, sliced

To garnish
15ml/1 tbsp chopped fresh coriander (cilantro), 1–2 fresh green chillies, seeded and sliced, and 15ml/1 tbsp chopped mint

1 Pick over the washed lentils and chana dhal or yellow split peas and remove any stones, then place in a large pan.

2 Add the measured water with the ginger, garlic, turmeric and chopped green chillies, bring to the boil, lower the heat and simmer for about 15–20 minutes or until the lentils are soft.

3 Mash the lentils with the back of a spoon until they are of the same consistency as a thick soup. Add the salt. If the mixture looks too dry, add a little more water.

4 To prepare the tarka, heat the oil in another pan and fry the onion with the mustard and onion seeds, dried red chillies and sliced tomato for about 2 minutes.

5 Pour the tarka over the dhal in the pan and garnish with the chopped fresh coriander, fresh green chillies and chopped mint. Serve immediately.

Chilli Lentils and Spiced Vegetables

This deliciously spicy curry is often served for breakfast with Indian pancakes or rice dumplings, but can also be eaten as a main course.

Serves 4–6
60ml/4 tbsp vegetable oil
2.5ml/½ tsp mustard seeds
2.5ml/½ tsp cumin seeds
2 whole dried red chillies
1.5ml/¼ tsp asafoetida
6–8 curry leaves
2 garlic cloves, crushed
30ml/2 tbsp desiccated (dry unsweetened shredded) coconut
225g/8oz red split lentils, picked, washed and drained
10ml/2 tsp sambhar masala
2.5ml/½ tsp ground turmeric
450ml/¾ pint/scant 2 cups water
450g/1lb mixed vegetables (okra, courgettes/zucchini, cauliflower, shallots and sweet peppers)
15ml/1 tbsp tamarind pulp mixed with 45ml/3 tbsp water, strained, and pulp and seeds discarded
4 firm tomatoes, quartered
60ml/4 tbsp vegetable oil or sunflower oil
2 garlic cloves, finely sliced
a handful coriander (cilantro) leaves, chopped

1 Heat the vegetable oil in a large frying pan. Add the mustard seeds and cumin seeds and fry for 1–2 minutes until they are fragrant and beginning to splutter.

2 Add the chillies, asafoetida, curry leaves, garlic and desiccated coconut to the pan. Cook the mixture over a medium heat, stirring constantly, for about 4–5 minutes until the coconut begins to brown, taking care to avoid it burning.

3 Stir the lentils into the pan, mixing well until combined. Add the sambhar masala and ground turmeric and mix. Pour in the measured water and bring the mixture to the boil.

4 Reduce the heat and simmer gently until the lentils are tender and mushy. Add all the vegetables, tamarind juice and tomatoes to the pan. Bring to the boil, then reduce the heat and simmer gently for about 10–15 minutes, until the vegetables are just tender. They should still retain a little crunch.

5 Transfer the mixture to a large bowl. Fry the garlic slices and coriander. Sprinkle over the lentils and vegetables and serve.

Tarka Dhal Energy 213kcal/898kJ; Protein 11.3g; Carbohydrate 28.2g, of which sugars 2.7g; Fat 7.1g, of which saturates 0.9g; Cholesterol 0mg; Calcium 42mg; Fibre 2.5g; Sodium 18mg.
Chilli Lentils Energy 229kcal/963kJ; Protein 11.5g; Carbohydrate 27.5g, of which sugars 5.4g; Fat 9g, of which saturates 1.2g; Cholesterol 0mg; Calcium 54mg; Fibre 3.2g; Sodium 23mg.

Kidney Bean Curry

This Punjabi dish is a fine example of the area's hearty, robust cuisine. It is widely eaten all over the state, and is even sold by street vendors. Boiled rice makes a good accompaniment.

Serves 4
225g/8oz/1¼ cups dried red
   kidney beans
30ml/2 tbsp vegetable oil
2.5ml/½ tsp cumin seeds
1 onion, thinly sliced
1 fresh green chilli, seeded
   and finely chopped
2 garlic cloves, crushed
2.5cm/1in piece fresh root
   ginger, grated
30ml/2 tbsp curry paste
5ml/1 tsp ground cumin
5ml/1 tsp ground coriander
2.5ml/½ tsp chilli powder
2.5ml/½ tsp salt
400g/14oz can
   chopped tomatoes
30ml/2 tbsp chopped fresh
   coriander (cilantro)

1 Place the kidney beans in a large bowl of cold water and then leave them to soak overnight.

2 Drain the beans and place in a large pan with double the volume of water. Boil vigorously for 10 minutes. Drain, rinse and return the beans to the pan. Add double the volume of water and bring to the boil. Reduce the heat, then cover and cook for 1–1½ hours, or until the beans are soft. This process is essential in order to remove the toxins from the dried kidney beans.

3 Meanwhile, heat the oil in a wok, karahi or large pan and fry the cumin seeds for 2 minutes. Add the onion, chilli, garlic and ginger and fry for 5 minutes. Stir in the curry paste, cumin, coriander, chilli powder and salt, and cook for 5 minutes.

4 Add the tomatoes and simmer for 5 minutes. Add the beans and fresh coriander, reserving a little for the garnish. Cover and cook for 15 minutes adding a little water if necessary. Serve garnished with the reserved coriander.

> **Cook's Tip**
> *Drained and rinsed canned beans can be used instead of dried.*

Fried Spiced Lentils

This simple and spicy supper dish is perfect for a gathering of family or friends. It uses traditional Indian lentils and peas, which can be found in large supermarkets or Asian markets and stores.

Serves 4–6
115g/4oz/½ cup red gram
   (pigeon peas) or green lentils
50g/2oz/¼ cup Bengal gram
4 fresh green chillies
5ml/1 tsp ground turmeric
1 large onion, sliced
400g/14oz can
   chopped tomatoes
60ml/4 tbsp vegetable oil
   or sunflower oil
2.5ml/½ tsp mustard seeds
2.5ml/½ tsp cumin seeds
1 garlic clove, crushed
6 curry leaves
2 dried red chillies
salt
a few curry leaves, to garnish

1 Place the red gram or lentils and bengal gram in a heavy pan and pour in 350ml/12fl oz/1½ cups water. Add the chillies, turmeric and onion slices to the pan and slowly bring to the boil. Reduce the heat and simmer gently, covered, until the gram and lentils are soft and the water has evaporated.

2 Mash the mixture with the back of a spoon. When nearly smooth, add the tomatoes and salt to taste, and mix well. If necessary, thin with a little hot water.

3 Heat the vegetable or sunflower oil in a frying pan. Fry the remaining ingredients until the garlic just begins to brown. Pour the oil and spices over the mixture and cover. After 5 minutes, mix well, garnish, and serve immediately.

> **Cook's Tips**
> • *Red gram, or pigeon peas, are the fruit of a small shrub but are used as a vegetable. They form a staple food in India as well as Africa and the Caribbean, and you will find them in Asian and Caribbean stores and markets.*
> • *Bengal gram, or chana, is a small variety of chickpea, which is commonly used in Indian cuisine.*

Kidney Bean Curry Energy 156kcal/653kJ; Protein 6.4g; Carbohydrate 17g, of which sugars 5.4g; Fat 7.6g, of which saturates 1g; Cholesterol 0mg; Calcium 90mg; Fibre 5.1g; Sodium 236mg.
Fried Spiced Lentils Energy 262kcal/1095kJ; Protein 10.3g; Carbohydrate 26.9g, of which sugars 4.6g; Fat 13.3g, of which saturates 6.2g; Cholesterol 0mg; Calcium 36mg; Fibre 3.1g; Sodium 84mg.

Lentil, Tomato and Aubergine Curry

This curry goes equally well with boiled basmati rice or crusty white bread. Pigeon peas are available from most Asian stores, but green lentils also work well.

Serves 4
225g/8oz/1 cup red gram (pigeon peas) or green lentils
2.5ml/½ tsp ground turmeric
1 large aubergine (eggplant)
7.5ml/1½ tsp salt, or to taste
15ml/1 tbsp coriander seeds
5ml/1 tsp cumin seeds
1–4 dried red chillies, roughly broken up
2.5ml/½ tsp black peppercorns
2.5ml/½ tsp black mustard seeds
225g/8oz fresh tomatoes, chopped
30ml/2 tbsp tamarind juice, made with 15ml/1 tbsp tamarind pulp and 15ml/1 tbsp water, strained and the pulp discarded, or the juice of 1 lime
30ml/2 tbsp fresh coriander (cilantro) leaves and stalks, finely chopped

1 Put the pigeon peas or lentils in a pan and add the turmeric and 1.2 litres/2 pints/5 cups water. Bring the water to the boil, then reduce the heat to medium and cook the lentils for about 3–4 minutes or until all the foam subsides.

2 Reduce the heat to low, cover the pan with a tight-fitting lid and simmer gently for about 20 minutes.

3 Add the aubergine and salt to the pan, re-cover and continue to cook for a further 8–10 minutes or until the aubergine is tender when prodded with a fork.

4 Meanwhile, preheat a small heavy pan over a medium heat. Reduce the heat to low and add the coriander seeds, cumin seeds, chillies, peppercorns and mustard seeds. Stir and roast them for about 30–60 seconds until they begin to splutter and release their aromatic fragrances.

5 Remove them from the pan and leave to cool, then grind finely in a spice grinder, food processor or blender.

6 Add the spice mix to the pigeon peas or lentils, followed by the tomatoes and tamarind or lime juice. Simmer for 2–3 minutes. Add the chopped coriander, remove from the heat and serve.

Spicy Parsnip and Chickpea Stew

The sweet flavour of parsnips goes very well with the spices in this Indian-style vegetable stew.

Serves 4
200g/7oz dried chickpeas, soaked overnight in cold water, then drained
7 garlic cloves, finely chopped
1 small onion, chopped
5cm/2in piece fresh root ginger, chopped
2 green chillies, seeded and chopped
450ml/¾ pint/scant 2 cups plus 75ml/5 tbsp water
60ml/4 tbsp groundnut (peanut) oil
5ml/1 tsp cumin seeds
10ml/2 tsp ground coriander seeds
5ml/1 tsp ground turmeric
2.5–5ml/½–1 tsp chilli powder
50g/2oz cashew nuts, toasted and ground
250g/9oz tomatoes, peeled and chopped
900g/2lb parsnips, cut into chunks
5ml/1 tsp ground roasted cumin seeds
juice of 1 lime, to taste
salt and ground black pepper

To serve
fresh coriander leaves
a few cashew nuts, toasted

1 Put the chickpeas in a pan, cover with cold water and bring to the boil. Boil vigorously for 10 minutes, then reduce the heat to medium and cook for 1–1½ hours, or until tender. Drain.

2 Set 10ml/2 tsp of the garlic aside, then place the remainder in a food processor or blender with the onion, ginger and half the chillies. Add the 75ml/5 tbsp water and process to a paste.

3 Heat the oil in a large frying pan and cook the cumin seeds for 30 seconds. Stir in the coriander seeds, turmeric, chilli powder and the ground cashew nuts. Add the ginger and chilli paste and cook until the liquid begins to evaporate. Add the tomatoes and cook until the mixture turns red-brown in colour.

4 Mix in the chickpeas and parsnips with the remaining water, 5ml/1 tsp salt and plenty of pepper. Bring to the boil, stir, then simmer, uncovered, for 15–20 minutes.

5 Add the ground cumin with more salt and lime juice to taste. Stir in the reserved garlic and green chilli, and cook briefly. Serve immediately, garnished with the coriander and cashew nuts.

Lentil Curry Energy 215kcal/914kJ; Protein 15.5g; Carbohydrate 36.2g, of which sugars 3.1g; Fat 2.1g, of which saturates 0.3g; Cholesterol 0mg; Calcium 69.8mg; Fibre 4.8g; Sodium 28mg.
Parsnips and Chickpeas Energy 495kcal/2079kJ; Protein 17.9g; Carbohydrate 58.4g, of which sugars 17.6g; Fat 22.8g, of which saturates 4.1g; Cholesterol 0mg; Calcium 185mg; Fibre 16.9g; Sodium 84mg.

Red Lentil and Tomato Dhal

This is Indian comfort food at its best – there's nothing like a bowl of dhal spiced with mustard seeds, cumin and coriander to clear away the blues.

Serves 4
30ml/2 tbsp sunflower oil
1 green chilli, halved
2 red onions, halved and
    thinly sliced
10ml/2 tsp finely grated garlic
10ml/2 tsp finely grated fresh
    root ginger
10ml/2 tsp black mustard seeds
15ml/1 tbsp cumin seeds
10ml/2 tsp crushed coriander seeds
10 curry leaves
250g/9oz/generous 1 cup red
    split lentils, rinsed and drained
2.5ml/½ tsp turmeric
2 plum tomatoes, roughly chopped
salt
coriander (cilantro) leaves
    and crispy fried onion,
    to garnish (optional)
natural (plain) yogurt, poppadums
    and griddled flatbread or
    naans, to serve

1 Heat a wok or large pan over a medium heat and add the sunflower oil. When hot add the green chilli and onions, lower the heat and cook gently for 10–12 minutes, until softened.

2 Increase the heat slightly and add the garlic, ginger, mustard seeds, cumin seeds, coriander seeds and curry leaves to the pan. Cook for 2–3 minutes, stirring frequently.

3 Add the lentils to the pan with about 700ml/1 pint 2fl oz/ scant 3 cups water, the turmeric and tomatoes and season with plenty of salt. Stir well and bring the mixture to the boil, cover the pan, reduce the heat and cook very gently for about 25–30 minutes, stirring occasionally.

4 Check the seasoning, then garnish with coriander leaves and crispy fried onion, if you like, and serve with yogurt, poppadums and flatbread or naans.

> **Variation**
> Use yellow split peas in place of the lentils. Like red lentils, they do not need to be soaked before cooking.

Richly Spiced Dhal

Flavoured with spices, coconut milk and tomatoes, this lentil dish makes a filling supper or an excellent side dish to go alongside a dry curry for an Indian banquet. However, warm naan bread and yogurt are all that are needed as accompaniments for a tasty meal.

Serves 4
30ml/2 tbsp vegetable oil
1 large onion, finely chopped
3 garlic cloves, chopped
1 carrot, diced
10ml/2 tsp cumin seeds
10ml/2 tsp yellow mustard seeds
2.5cm/1in piece fresh root
    ginger, grated
10ml/2 tsp ground turmeric
5ml/1 tsp mild chilli powder
5ml/1 tsp garam masala
225g/8oz/1 cup red split lentils
400ml/14fl oz/1⅔ cups water
400ml/14fl oz/1⅔ cups
    coconut milk
5 tomatoes, seeded and chopped
juice of 2 limes
60ml/4 tbsp chopped fresh
    coriander (cilantro)
salt and ground black pepper
25g/1oz/¼ cup flaked (sliced)
    almonds, toasted, to garnish

1 Heat the oil in a large heavy pan. Fry the onion for about 5 minutes until softened, stirring occasionally. Stir the garlic, carrot, cumin and mustard seeds, and ginger into the pan. Cook for about 5 minutes, stirring, until the seeds begin to pop and the carrot has softened slightly.

2 Stir in the ground turmeric, chilli powder and garam masala, and cook for 1 minute or until the flavours begin to mingle, stirring to prevent the spices burning.

3 Add the lentils, water, coconut milk and tomatoes, and season well with salt and black pepper. Bring to the boil, then reduce the heat and simmer, covered, for about 45 minutes, stirring occasionally to prevent the lentils sticking.

4 Stir the lime juice and 45ml/3 tbsp of the fresh coriander into the pan, then check the seasoning.

5 Cook for a further 15 minutes until the lentils soften and become tender. Sprinkle with the remaining coriander and the flaked almonds and serve immediately.

Red Lentil Dhal Energy 295kcal/1242kJ; Protein 16.1g; Carbohydrate 43.7g, of which sugars 8.5g; Fat 7.6g, of which saturates 1g; Cholesterol 0mg; Calcium 71mg; Fibre 4.7g; Sodium 30mg.
Richly Spiced Dhal Energy 295kcal/1242kJ; Protein 16.1g; Carbohydrate 43.7g, of which sugars 8.5g; Fat 7.6g, of which saturates 1g; Cholesterol 0mg; Calcium 71mg; Fibre 4.7g; Sodium 30mg.

Madras Sambal with Chilli and Spices

There are many variations of this dish but it is regularly cooked in one form or another in many Indian homes and served as part of a meal. You can use any combination of vegetables that are in season.

Serves 4
225g/8 oz/1 cup toor dhal or
    yellow split lentils
600ml/1 pint/2½ cups water
2.5ml/½ tsp ground turmeric
2 large potatoes, cut into
    2.5cm/1in chunks
30ml/2 tbsp vegetable oil
2.5ml/½ tsp black
    mustard seeds
1.5ml/¼ tsp fenugreek seeds
4 curry leaves
1 onion, thinly sliced
115g/4oz green beans, cut into
    2.5cm/1in lengths
5ml/1 tsp salt
2.5ml/½ tsp chilli powder
15ml/1 tbsp lemon juice
60ml/4 tbsp desiccated
    (dry unsweetened
    shredded) coconut
toasted coconut pieces,
    to garnish

1 Wash the toor dhal or lentils in several changes of water, picking through to remove any stones. Place in a heavy pan with the measured water and the turmeric. Cover and simmer for about 30–35 minutes, until the lentils are soft.

2 Par-boil the potatoes in a large pan of boiling water for about 10 minutes until they are just tender. Drain well and set aside.

3 Heat the oil in a large frying pan and fry the mustard seeds, fenugreek seeds and curry leaves for 2–3 minutes, stirring constantly, until the seeds begin to splutter.

4 Add the onion and the green beans to the pan and fry for 7–8 minutes. Add the potatoes to the pan and cook, stirring, for a further 2–3 minutes.

5 Stir in the toor dhal or lentils with the salt, chilli powder and lemon juice and simmer for 2 minutes. Stir in the coconut and simmer for about 5 minutes, until the vegetables are tender. Garnish with toasted coconut and serve immediately.

Spicy Mung Bean and Potato Curry

Mung beans are one of the beans that do not require soaking. In this recipe they are cooked with potatoes and traditional Indian spices to give a tasty, healthy curry.

Serves 4
175g/6oz/1 cup mung beans
750ml/1¼ pints/3 cups water
225g/8oz potatoes, cut into
    2cm/¾in chunks
30ml/2 tbsp vegetable oil
2.5ml/½ tsp cumin seeds
1 green chilli, finely chopped
1 garlic clove, crushed
2.5cm/1in piece fresh root ginger,
    finely chopped
1.5ml/¼ tsp ground turmeric
2.5ml/½ tsp chilli powder
5ml/1 tsp salt
5ml/1 tsp sugar
4 curry leaves
5 tomatoes, skinned and diced
15ml/1 tbsp tomato purée (paste)
curry leaves, to garnish
plain boiled basmati rice,
    to serve

1 Wash the beans. Bring to the boil in a large pan with the measured water. Cover the pan, reduce the heat and simmer for about 30 minutes, until the beans are soft.

2 In a separate pan, par-boil the potatoes for about 10 minutes until just tender, then drain well.

3 Heat the oil in a wok or frying pan and fry the cumin seeds until they start to splutter.

4 Add the chilli, garlic and ginger to the pan and fry, stirring constantly, for 3–4 minutes until fragrant. Be careful not to let the garlic burn or it will taste bitter.

5 Add the turmeric, chilli powder, salt and sugar to the pan and cook for about 2 minutes, stirring constantly.

6 Add the curry leaves, tomatoes and tomato purée to the pan, mix well and simmer for 5 minutes until the sauce thickens. Add the tomato sauce and potatoes to the mung beans and mix together. Serve immediately with plain boiled rice, and garnish with the curry leaves.

Madras Sambal Energy 401kcal/1687kJ; Protein 16.7g; Carbohydrate 50.8g, of which sugars 5.1g; Fat 16g, of which saturates 8.9g; Cholesterol 0mg; Calcium 52mg; Fibre 6.7g; Sodium 36mg.
Spicy Mung Beans Energy 265kcal/1118kJ; Protein 13.8g; Carbohydrate 37.4g, of which sugars 5.7g; Fat 7.9g, of which saturates 1.1g; Cholesterol 0mg; Calcium 58mg; Fibre 5.8g; Sodium 34mg.

Toor Dhal with Chilli and Cherry Tomatoes

Toor dhal has a wonderfully rich texture, which is best appreciated if served with plain boiled rice. Fresh fenugreek leaves, which are available from Asian grocers, impart a stunning aroma.

Serves 4
115g/4oz toor dhal
45ml/3 tbsp corn oil
1.5ml/¼ tsp onion seeds
1 medium bunch spring onions (scallions), roughly chopped
5ml/1 tsp crushed garlic
1.5ml/¼ tsp ground turmeric
7.5ml/1½ tsp crushed ginger
5ml/1 tsp chilli powder
30ml/2 tbsp fresh fenugreek leaves
5ml/1 tsp salt
150ml/¼ pint/⅔ cup water
6–8 cherry tomatoes
30ml/2 tbsp fresh coriander (cilantro) leaves
½ green (bell) pepper, seeded and sliced
15ml/1 tbsp lemon juice
shredded spring onion (scallion) tops and fresh coriander (cilantro) leaves, to garnish

1 Cook the toor dhal or lentils in a large pan of boiling water until it is soft and mushy. Set aside.

2 Heat the oil with the onion seeds in a non-stick wok or frying pan for a few seconds until hot. Add the dhal to the wok or frying pan and stir-fry for about 3 minutes.

3 Add the spring onions to the pan followed by the garlic, turmeric, ginger, chilli powder, fenugreek leaves and salt and continue to stir-fry for 5–7 minutes.

4 Pour in enough water to loosen the mixture. Add the cherry tomatoes, coriander, green pepper and lemon juice. Serve garnished with shredded onion tops and coriander leaves.

> **Cook's Tip**
> *Any remaining fresh fenugreek leaves can be frozen in a plastic bag. Use spinach if you cannot get fenugreek.*

Courgettes with Dhal and Aromatic Spices

The nutty flavour of split peas goes particularly well with courgettes and tomatoes, perked up with a selection of aromatic spices. Serve with plain rice or bread for a filling and tasty supper.

Serves 4–6
225g/8oz courgettes (zucchini)
1 large onion
2 garlic cloves
2 fresh green chillies
175g/6oz/⅔ cup mung dhal or yellow split peas
2.5ml/½ tsp ground turmeric
60ml/4 tbsp vegetable oil
2.5ml/½ tsp mustard seeds
2.5ml/½ tsp cumin seeds
1.5ml/¼ tsp asafoetida
a few fresh coriander (cilantro) and mint leaves, chopped
6–8 curry leaves
2.5ml/½ tsp sugar
200g/7oz can chopped tomatoes
60ml/4 tbsp lemon juice
salt

1 Cut the courgettes into wedges. Finely slice the onion and crush the garlic. Chop the green chillies.

2 In a large pan, simmer the dhal or peas and turmeric in 300ml/½ pint/1¼ cups water, until cooked but not mushy. Drain the cooked lentils, retaining the cooking liquid, and set aside while you cook the vegetables.

3 Heat the oil in a frying pan and add the courgette wedges, sliced onion, crushed garlic and chopped chillies. Add the mustard and cumin seeds, asafoetida, fresh coriander and mint, and stir in the curry leaves and sugar. Fry the ingredients together, stirring occasionally, and then add the chopped tomatoes. Mix well and add salt to taste.

4 Cover the pan and cook until the courgettes are nearly tender but still have a little crunch.

5 Fold in the drained dhal or peas and the lemon juice. If the dish is too dry, add some of the reserved cooking water. Reheat thoroughly and serve immediately.

Toor Dhal Energy 192kcal/806kJ; Protein 8.2g; Carbohydrate 20.2g, of which sugars 3.3g; Fat 9.4g, of which saturates 1.4g; Cholesterol 0mg; Calcium 34mg; Fibre 2.3g; Sodium 16mg.
Courgettes with Dhal Energy 196kcal/823kJ; Protein 9.7g; Carbohydrate 24g, of which sugars 4.7g; Fat 7.7g, of which saturates 1g; Cholesterol 0mg; Calcium 72mg; Fibre 3.2g; Sodium 23mg.

Potato, Cauliflower and Broad Bean Curry

This is a hot and spicy vegetable curry, loaded with potatoes, cauliflower and broad beans, and is especially tasty when served with rice, a few poppadums and a raita.

Serves 4

2 garlic cloves, chopped
2.5cm/1in piece fresh root ginger
1 fresh green chilli, seeded and chopped
30ml/2 tbsp vegetable oil
1 onion, sliced
1 large potato, chopped
15ml/1 tbsp curry powder
1 cauliflower, cut into small florets
600ml/1 pint/2½ cups vegetable stock
275g/10oz can broad (fava) beans
juice of ½ lemon (optional)
salt and ground black pepper
fresh coriander (cilantro) sprig, to garnish
plain boiled rice, to serve

1 Blend the chopped garlic, ginger and chopped chilli with 15ml/1 tbsp of the oil in a food processor or blender until the mixture forms a smooth paste.

2 In a large, heavy pan, fry the sliced onion and chopped potato in the remaining oil for 5 minutes, until the onion is soft and the potato is starting to brown, then stir in the spice paste and curry powder. Cook for another minute.

3 Add the cauliflower florets to the onion and potato and stir well until thoroughly combined with the spicy mixture, then pour in the stock and bring to the boil over a high heat.

4 Season well with salt and black pepper, cover and simmer for 10 minutes. Add the beans with the liquid from the can and cook, uncovered, for a further 10 minutes.

5 Check the seasoning and adjust if necessary. Add a good squeeze of lemon juice, if using, and give the curry a final stir.

6 Serve immediately, on warmed plates, garnished with fresh coriander sprigs and accompanied by plain boiled rice.

Chickpea, Sweet Potato and Aubergine Chilli Dhal

Spicy and delicious – this is a great dish to serve when you want a meal that is nutritious and aromatic.

Serves 3–4

45ml/3 tbsp olive oil
1 red onion, chopped
3 garlic cloves, crushed
115g/4oz sweet potatoes, peeled and diced
3 garden eggs or 1 large aubergine (eggplant), diced
425g/15oz can chickpeas, drained
5ml/1 tsp dried tarragon
2.5ml/½ tsp dried thyme
5ml/1 tsp ground cumin
5ml/1 tsp ground turmeric
2.5ml/½ tsp ground allspice
5 canned plum tomatoes, chopped with 60ml/4 tbsp reserved juice
6 ready-to-eat dried apricots
600ml/1 pint/2½ cups well-flavoured vegetable stock
1 green chilli, seeded and finely chopped
30ml/2 tbsp chopped fresh coriander (cilantro)
salt and ground black pepper

1 Heat the olive oil in a large pan. Add the onion, garlic and potatoes and cook until the onion has softened.

2 Stir in the garden eggs or aubergine, then add the chickpeas and the herbs and spices. Stir well to mix and cook over a low heat for a few minutes.

3 Add the tomatoes and their juice, the apricots, stock, chilli and seasoning. Stir well, bring to the boil and cook for 15 minutes.

4 When the sweet potatoes are tender, add the coriander, stir, taste, and adjust the seasoning if necessary. Serve immediately.

Cook's Tip
Garden egg is a small variety of aubergine used in West Africa. It is round and white, which may explain its other name – eggplant. You can peel the aubergine for this dish, if you prefer, but it is not necessary. Either white or orange sweet potatoes can be used and you can add less chickpeas, if you wish.

Broad Bean Curry Energy 194kcal/813kJ; Protein 11.5g; Carbohydrate 20.9g, of which sugars 4.8g; Fat 7.7g, of which saturates 1g; Cholesterol 0mg; Calcium 96mg; Fibre 8.1g; Sodium 40mg.
Chickpea Dhal Energy 322kcal/1356kJ; Protein 12g; Carbohydrate 41.6g, of which sugars 16.6g; Fat 13.5g, of which saturates 1.7g; Cholesterol 0mg; Calcium 107mg; Fibre 9.3g; Sodium 260mg.

Curried Spinach and Potato with Mixed Chillies

This delicious curry, suitable for vegetarians, is mildly spiced with a warming flavour from the fresh and dried chillies.

Serves 4–6
225g/8oz potatoes
60ml/4 tbsp vegetable oil
2.5cm/1in piece fresh root
  ginger, crushed
4 garlic cloves, crushed

1 onion, coarsely chopped
2 green chillies, chopped
2 whole dried red chillies,
  coarsely broken
5ml/1 tsp cumin seeds
225g/8oz fresh spinach, trimmed,
  washed and chopped or
  225g/8oz frozen spinach,
  thawed and drained
salt
2 firm tomatoes, coarsely
  chopped, to garnish

1 Wash the potatoes and cut them into quarters. If using small new potatoes, leave them whole. Heat the vegetable oil in a frying pan and fry the potatoes until evenly brown on all sides. Remove from the pan and set aside.

2 Remove the excess oil leaving 15ml/1 tbsp in the pan. Fry the ginger, garlic, onion, green chillies, dried chillies and cumin seeds until the onion is golden brown.

3 Add the potatoes and salt to the pan and stir well. Cover the pan and cook gently until the potatoes are tender and can be easily pierced with a sharp knife.

4 Add the spinach and stir well. Cook with the pan uncovered until the spinach is tender and all the excess fluids in the pan have evaporated. Transfer the curry to a serving plate, garnish with the chopped tomatoes and serve immediately.

> **Cook's Tip**
> *India is blessed with over 18 varieties of spinach. If you have access to an Indian or Chinese market or grocer, look out for some of the more unusual varieties.*

Masala Chana

Chickpeas are cooked in a variety of ways all over India. Tamarind adds a sharp, tangy flavour to this slowly simmered curry.

Serves 4
225g/8oz/1¼ cups dried
  chickpeas, soaked overnight
  and drained
50g/2oz tamarind pulp
120ml/4fl oz/½ cup boiling water
30ml/2 tbsp vegetable oil
2.5ml/½ tsp cumin seeds

1 onion, finely chopped
2 garlic cloves, crushed
2.5cm/1in piece fresh root
  ginger, grated
1 fresh green chilli, finely chopped
5ml/1 tsp ground cumin
5ml/1 tsp ground coriander
1.5ml/¼ tsp ground turmeric
2.5ml/½ tsp salt
225g/8oz tomatoes, peeled and
  finely chopped
2.5ml/½ tsp garam masala
chopped fresh chillies and
  chopped onion, to garnish

1 Place the chickpeas in a large pan with double the volume of cold water. Bring to the boil and boil vigorously for about 10 minutes. Skim off any scum that has risen to the surface of the liquid, using a slotted spoon. Lower the heat, cover the pan with a tight-fitting lid and simmer for about 1½–2 hours or until the chickpeas are tender.

2 Meanwhile, break up the tamarind and soak in the boiling water for about 15–20 minutes. Rub the tamarind through a sieve (strainer) into a bowl, discarding any stones and fibre that is left behind in the sieve.

3 Heat the oil in a large, heavy pan and fry the cumin seeds for 2 minutes until they splutter. Add the onion, garlic, ginger and chilli, and fry for 5 minutes.

4 Stir in the cumin and coriander, with the turmeric and salt, and fry for 3–4 minutes. Add the chopped tomatoes. Bring to the boil and then simmer for 5 minutes.

5 Drain the chickpeas and add to the tomato mixture together with the garam masala and tamarind pulp. Cover and simmer gently for about 25–30 minutes. Garnish with the chopped chillies and onion before serving.

Masala Chana Energy 256kcal/1075kJ; Protein 13.1g; Carbohydrate 32.2g, of which sugars 4.1g; Fat 9.2g, of which saturates 1.1g; Cholesterol 0mg; Calcium 105mg; Fibre 6.8g; Sodium 285mg.
Curried Spinach Energy 135kcal/560kJ; Protein 3g; Carbohydrate 13.5g, of which sugars 5.9g; Fat 8g, of which saturates 1g; Cholesterol 0mg; Calcium 86mg; Fibre 2.6g; Sodium 62mg.

Black-eyed Bean and Potato Curry

Nutty-flavoured black-eyed beans make a nutritious dish. This hot and spicy combination is ideal for an autumn evening.

Serves 4–6
2 potatoes
225g/8oz/1¼ cups black-eyed beans (peas), soaked overnight and drained
1.5ml/¼ tsp bicarbonate of soda (baking soda)
5ml/1 tsp five-spice powder
1.5ml/¼ tsp asafoetida
2 onions, finely chopped
2.5cm/1in piece fresh root ginger, crushed

a few fresh mint leaves
450ml/¾ pint/scant 2 cups water
60ml/4 tbsp vegetable oil
2.5ml/½ tsp each ground cumin, ground coriander, ground turmeric and chilli powder
4 fresh green chillies, seeded and chopped
75ml/5 tbsp tamarind juice made with 15ml/1 tbsp tamarind pulp mixed with 60ml/4 tbsp water, strained, and pulp and seeds discarded
115g/4oz/4 cups fresh coriander (cilantro), chopped
2 firm tomatoes, chopped
salt

1 Cut the potatoes into bitesize cubes and boil in a large pan of lightly salted water until tender.

2 Place the drained black-eyed beans in a heavy pan and add the bicarbonate of soda, five-spice powder and asafoetida. Add the chopped onions, crushed root ginger, mint leaves and the measured water. Simmer until the beans are soft. Drain and reserve the liquid.

3 Heat the vegetable oil in a frying pan. Gently fry the ground cumin and coriander, the turmeric and chilli powder with the green chillies and tamarind juice, until they are well blended and releasing their fragrances.

4 Pour the spice mixture over the black-eyed beans in the pan and mix well until all the ingredients are well combined.

5 Add the potatoes, fresh coriander, tomatoes and salt. Mix well, and, if necessary, thin with a little reserved water. Reheat for a minute and serve immediately.

Spicy Chickpeas with Potato Cakes and Green Chillies

The potato cakes in this recipe are given a slightly sour-sweet flavour by the addition of amchur, a powder that is made from unripe or green mangoes.

Serves 10–12
30ml/2 tbsp vegetable oil
30ml/2 tbsp ground coriander
30ml/2 tbsp ground cumin
2.5ml/½ tsp ground turmeric
2.5ml/½ tsp salt
2.5ml/½ tsp sugar
30ml/2 tbsp flour, mixed to a paste with a little water
450g/1lb boiled chickpeas, well drained

2 fresh green chillies, chopped
5cm/2in piece fresh root ginger, finely crushed
75g/3oz fresh coriander (cilantro) leaves, chopped
2 firm tomatoes, chopped

For the potato cakes
450g/1lb potatoes, boiled and coarsely mashed
4 green chillies, finely chopped
50g/2oz coriander (cilantro) leaves, finely chopped
7.5ml/1½ tsp ground cumin
5ml/1 tsp amchur (dry mango powder)
salt
vegetable oil, for shallow-frying

1 Make the spicy chickpeas. Heat the oil in a pan and fry the coriander, cumin, turmeric, salt, sugar and flour paste until the water has evaporated and the oil separated.

2 Add the chickpeas, chillies, ginger, fresh coriander and tomatoes to the pan. Mix well and simmer for 5 minutes. Transfer to a serving dish and keep warm.

3 To make the potato cakes, mix the mashed potato in a large mixing bowl with the green chillies, coriander, ground cumin, amchur and salt, to taste. Mix well until all the ingredients in the bowl are thoroughly blended.

4 Using your hands, shape the potato mixture into little cakes. Heat the oil in a shallow frying pan or griddle and fry them on both sides until golden brown. Transfer to a warmed serving dish and serve immediately with the spicy chickpeas.

Black-eyed Bean Curry Energy 266kcal/1118kJ; Protein 11.8g; Carbohydrate 36.8g, of which sugars 8.5g; Fat 9g, of which saturates 1.1g; Cholesterol 0mg; Calcium 110mg; Fibre 8.8g; Sodium 28mg.
Spicy Chickpeas Energy 163kcal/684kJ; Protein 5.2g; Carbohydrate 17.3g, of which sugars 1.6g; Fat 8.8g, of which saturates 1.1g; Cholesterol 0mg; Calcium 68mg; Fibre 3g; Sodium 96mg.

Spicy Chickpea and Aubergine Stew

This is a Lebanese dish, but similar recipes are found all over the Mediterranean. The vegetables have a warm, smoky flavour, subtly enriched with spices. Crunchy fried onion rings provide a contrast of taste and texture. Serve the stew on a bed of rice.

Serves 4
3 large aubergines (eggplants), cut into cubes
200g/7oz/1 cup chickpeas, soaked overnight
60ml/4 tbsp olive oil

3 garlic cloves, chopped
2 large onions, chopped
2.5ml/½ tsp ground cumin
2.5ml/½ tsp ground cinnamon
2.5ml/½ tsp ground coriander
3 × 400g/14oz cans chopped tomatoes
salt and ground black pepper
cooked rice, to serve

For the garnish
30ml/2 tbsp olive oil
1 onion, sliced
1 garlic clove, sliced
sprigs of coriander (cilantro)

1 Place the aubergines in a colander and sprinkle them with salt. Sit the colander in a bowl and leave for 30 minutes, to allow the bitter juices to escape. Rinse with cold water and pat dry using a piece of kitchen paper.

2 Drain the chickpeas and put in a pan with enough water to cover. Bring to the boil, reduce the heat and simmer for about 30 minutes, or until tender. Drain.

3 Heat the oil in a large pan. Add the garlic and onions and cook gently until soft. Add the spices and cook, stirring, for a few seconds. Add the aubergine and stir to coat with the spices and onion. Cook for 5 minutes.

4 Add the tomatoes and chickpeas and season with salt and pepper. Cover and simmer for 20 minutes.

5 To make the garnish, heat the oil in a frying pan and, when very hot, add the sliced onion and garlic. Fry until golden and crisp. Serve the stew with rice, topped with the onion and garlic and garnished with coriander.

Malay Vegetable Curry with Coconut

Originally from southern India, this delicious curry has found its way into many Malay homes. Made with firm vegetables, roots and gourds, all cut into long bitesize pieces, it is substantial and flexible – choose your own assortment of vegetables.

Serves 4
2–3 green chillies, seeded and chopped
25g/1oz fresh root ginger, peeled and chopped
5–10ml/1–2 tsp roasted cumin seeds
10ml/2 tsp sugar

5–10ml/1–2 tsp ground turmeric
1 cinnamon stick
5ml/1 tsp salt
2 carrots, cut into bitesize sticks
2 sweet potatoes, cut into bitesize sticks
2 courgettes (zucchini), partially peeled in strips, seeded and cut into bitesize sticks
1 green plantain, peeled and cut into bitesize sticks
a small coil of yard-long beans or a few green beans, cut into bitesize sticks
a handful fresh curry leaves
1 fresh coconut, grated
250ml/8fl oz/1 cup Greek (US strained plain) yogurt
salt and ground black pepper

1 Using a mortar and pestle or food processor, grind the chillies, ginger, roasted cumin seeds and sugar to a paste.

2 In a heavy pan, bring 450ml/15fl oz/scant 2 cups water to the boil. Stir in the turmeric, cinnamon stick and salt. Add the carrots and cook for 1 minute. Add the sweet potatoes and cook for 2 minutes. Add the courgettes, plantain and beans and cook for a further 2 minutes.

3 Reduce the heat, stir in the spice paste and curry leaves, and cook gently for 4–5 minutes, or until the vegetables are tender but not soft and mushy, and the liquid has greatly reduced.

4 Gently stir in half the coconut. Take the pan off the heat and fold in the yogurt. Season to taste with salt and pepper.

5 Quickly roast the remaining coconut in a heavy pan over a high heat, until nicely browned. Sprinkle a little over the curry in the pan, and serve the rest with the curry and flatbread.

Spicy Chickpea Stew Energy 201kcal/843kJ; Protein 7.1g; Carbohydrate 22.3g, of which sugars 10.4g; Fat 10g, of which saturates 1.4g; Cholesterol 0mg; Calcium 57mg; Fibre 5.9g; Sodium 175mg.
Malay Curry Energy 419kcal/1753kJ; Protein 9.9g; Carbohydrate 47.7g, of which sugars 19.4g; Fat 23g, of which saturates 16.9g; Cholesterol 0mg; Calcium 176mg; Fibre 9g; Sodium 104mg.

Balti Potatoes with Aubergines and Pepper

Choose the smaller variety of aubergines for this curry as they are tastier than the large ones, which contain a lot of water and little flavour. Buy small aubergines from specialist grocers or larger supermarkets.

Serves 4
10–12 baby potatoes
6 small aubergines (eggplants)
1 medium red (bell) pepper
15ml/1 tbsp vegetable oil
2 medium onions, sliced
4–6 curry leaves
2.5ml/½ tsp onion seeds
5ml/1 tsp crushed coriander seeds
2.5ml/½ tsp cumin seeds
5ml/1 tsp grated fresh root ginger
5ml/1 tsp crushed garlic
5ml/1 tsp crushed dried red chillies
15ml/1 tbsp chopped fresh
    fenugreek leaves
5ml/1 tsp chopped fresh
    coriander (cilantro)
15ml/1 tbsp natural (plain)
    low-fat yogurt
fresh coriander (cilantro) leaves,
    to garnish

1 Cook the unpeeled potatoes in a pan of boiling water until they are just tender, but still whole.

2 Cut the aubergines into quarters if very small, or eighths if using slightly larger aubergines.

3 Cut the pepper in half, remove the seeds and ribs and discard, then slice the flesh into thin even strips.

4 Heat the oil in a karahi, wok or large heavy frying pan and fry the sliced onions, curry leaves, onion seeds, crushed coriander seeds and cumin seeds until the onion slices are soft and golden brown, stirring constantly.

5 Add the ginger, garlic, crushed chillies and fenugreek to the pan, followed by the aubergines and potatoes. Stir everything together and cover the pan with a lid. Lower the heat and cook the vegetables for about 5–7 minutes.

6 Remove the lid, add the fresh coriander followed by the yogurt and stir well. Serve garnished with coriander leaves.

Vegetable Curry with Ginger and Chilli

This is a delicious vegetable curry, in which fresh mixed vegetables are cooked in a spicy, aromatic yogurt sauce.

Serves 4
10ml/2 tsp cumin seeds
8 black peppercorns
2 green cardamom pods, seeds only
5cm/2in cinnamon stick
2.5ml/½ tsp grated nutmeg
45ml/3 tbsp vegetable oil
1 green chilli, chopped
2.5cm/1in piece fresh root
    ginger, grated
5ml/1 tsp chilli powder
2.5ml/½ tsp salt
2 large potatoes, cut into
    2.5cm/1in chunks
225g/8oz cauliflower, broken
    into florets
225g/8oz okra, thickly sliced
150ml/¼ pint/⅔ cup natural
    (plain) yogurt
150ml/¼ pint/⅔ cup
    vegetable stock
toasted flaked (sliced) almonds
    and fresh coriander (cilantro)
    sprigs, to garnish

1 Grind the cumin seeds, peppercorns, cardamom seeds, cinnamon stick and nutmeg to a fine powder using a food processor, blender or a mortar and pestle.

2 Heat the oil in a large pan and fry the chopped chilli and ginger for about 2 minutes, stirring all the time.

3 Add the chilli powder, salt and ground spice mixture to the pan and fry for about 2–3 minutes, stirring all the time to prevent the spices from sticking to the pan and burning.

4 Stir the potatoes into the pan, cover, and cook for about 10 minutes over a low heat, stirring occasionally.

5 Add the cauliflower and okra to the pan and mix well to combine the ingredients. Cook for about 5 minutes.

6 Add the yogurt and stock to the pan. Bring to the boil, then reduce the heat. Cover with a lid and simmer for 20 minutes, or until all the vegetables are tender. Garnish with toasted almonds and coriander sprigs, and serve immediately.

Balti Potatoes Energy 273kcal/1142kJ; Protein 6.6g; Carbohydrate 34.9g, of which sugars 23.7g; Fat 13.2g, of which saturates 1.5g; Cholesterol 0mg; Calcium 183mg; Fibre 8.4g; Sodium 114mg.
Vegetable Curry Energy 238kcal/996kJ; Protein 9.1g; Carbohydrate 26.7g, of which sugars 6.9g; Fat 11.6g, of which saturates 1.8g; Cholesterol 1mg; Calcium 202mg; Fibre 4.3g; Sodium 56mg.

Vegetable Curry with Lemon Rice

Fragrant jasmine rice, subtly flavoured with lemon grass and cardamom, is the perfect partner for this richly spiced vegetable curry.

Serves 4

10ml/2 tsp vegetable oil
400ml/14fl oz/1²/₃ cups
    coconut milk
300ml/½ pint/1¼ cups
    vegetable stock
225g/8oz new potatoes, halved
8 baby corn cobs
5ml/1 tsp golden caster
    (superfine) sugar
185g/6½oz broccoli florets
1 red (bell) pepper, seeded and
    sliced lengthways
115g/4oz spinach, tough stalks
    removed, leaves shredded
30ml/2 tbsp chopped fresh
    coriander (cilantro)
salt and ground black pepper

For the spice paste

1 red chilli, seeded and chopped
3 green chillies, seeded
    and chopped
1 lemon grass stalk, outer leaves
    removed and lower 5cm/2in
    finely chopped
2 shallots, chopped
finely grated rind of 1 lime
2 garlic cloves, chopped
5ml/1 tsp ground coriander
2.5ml/½ tsp ground cumin
1cm/½in piece fresh galangal,
    finely chopped
30ml/2 tbsp chopped fresh
    coriander (cilantro)

For the rice

225g/8oz/1¼ cups fragrant
    jasmine rice
6 cardamom pods, bruised
1 lemon grass stalk, outer leaves
    removed, cut into 3 pieces
475ml/16fl oz/2 cups water

1 Make the spice paste. Place all the ingredients in a food processor and blend to a coarse paste. Heat the oil in a large, heavy pan. Stir-fry the paste over a medium heat for 1–2 minutes. Pour in the coconut milk and stock and bring to the boil. Reduce the heat, add the potatoes and simmer for 15 minutes.

2 Meanwhile, put the rice, cardamom pods, lemon grass and water in a pan. Bring to the boil, reduce the heat, cover, and cook for 10–15 minutes. Remove the cardamom and lemon grass.

3 Add the corn to the curry, season and cook for 2 minutes. Add the sugar, broccoli and pepper, and cook for 5 minutes. Stir in the spinach and half the coriander. Cook for 2 minutes, then serve with the rice and garnished with the remaining coriander.

Spiced Indian Rice with Spinach, Tomatoes and Cashew Nuts

This all-in-one rice dish is simple to prepare in a slow cooker and makes a delicious, nutritious meal for all the family. It can also be served as a tasty accompaniment to a spicy meat curry.

Serves 4

30ml/2 tbsp sunflower oil
15ml/1 tbsp ghee or
    unsalted butter
1 onion, finely chopped
2 garlic cloves, crushed

3 tomatoes, peeled, seeded
    and chopped
275g/10oz/1½ cups easy-cook
    (converted) brown rice
5ml/1 tsp each ground coriander
    and ground cumin, or 10ml/
    2 tsp dhana jeera powder
2 carrots, coarsely grated
750ml/1¼ pints/3 cups boiling
    vegetable stock
175g/6oz baby spinach
    leaves, washed
salt and ground black pepper
50g/2oz/½ cup unsalted cashew
    nuts, toasted, to garnish

1 Heat the oil and ghee or butter in a heavy pan, add the onion and fry gently for 6–7 minutes, until soft. Add the garlic and chopped tomatoes and cook for a further 2 minutes.

2 Rinse the rice in a sieve (strainer) under cold running water, drain well and transfer to the pan. Add the ground coriander and cumin or dhana jeera powder and stir for a few seconds. Turn off the heat and transfer the mixture from the pan to a slow cooker.

3 Stir the carrots into the cooking pot, then pour in the stock, season with salt and pepper, and stir to mix. Switch the slow cooker on to high. Cover and cook for 1 hour.

4 Lay the spinach on the surface of the rice, replace the lid and cook for a further 30–40 minutes, or until the spinach has wilted and the rice is cooked and tender.

5 Stir the spinach into the rice in the pot and check the seasoning, adding a little more salt and pepper, if necessary. Sprinkle the cashew nuts over the rice and serve immediately.

Vegetable Curry Energy 279kcal/1161kJ; Protein 9.8g; Carbohydrate 17.4g, of which sugars 13.3g; Fat 19.4g, of which saturates 3.6g; Cholesterol 5mg; Calcium 99mg; Fibre 3.3g; Sodium 824mg.
Spiced Rice Energy 473kcal/1989kJ; Protein 10.1g; Carbohydrate 72.1g, of which sugars 9.2g; Fat 18g, of which saturates 4.5g; Cholesterol 8mg; Calcium 111mg; Fibre 4.8g; Sodium 349mg.

Sweet Rice with Spiced Chickpeas

This delicious rice dish combines the sweet flavour of the rice with the hot and sour taste of the chickpeas.

Serves 6

350g/12oz/1²⁄₃ cups dried chickpeas, soaked overnight
60ml/4 tbsp vegetable oil
1 large onion, very finely chopped
225g/8oz tomatoes, peeled and finely chopped
15ml/1 tbsp ground coriander
15ml/1 tbsp ground cumin
5ml/1 tsp ground fenugreek
5ml/1 tsp ground cinnamon
1–2 fresh hot green chillies, seeded and finely sliced
2.5cm/1in piece of fresh root ginger, grated
60ml/4 tbsp lemon juice
salt and ground black pepper
15ml/1 tbsp chopped fresh coriander (cilantro), to garnish

For the rice

40g/1½oz/3 tbsp ghee or butter
4 green cardamom pods
4 cloves
650ml/22fl oz/2³⁄₄ cups boiling water
350g/12oz/1³⁄₄ cups basmati rice, soaked and drained
5–10ml/1–2 tsp sugar
5–6 saffron strands, soaked in warm water

1 Drain the chickpeas and place in a large pan. Pour in water to cover and bring to the boil. Simmer, covered, for 1–1¼ hours until tender. Drain the chickpeas, reserving the cooking liquid.

2 Heat the oil in a pan. Reserve 30ml/2 tbsp of the onion and add the remainder to the pan. Fry for 4–5 minutes, stirring frequently. Add the tomatoes. Cook for 5–6 minutes, until soft.

3 Stir in the coriander, cumin, fenugreek and cinnamon. Cook for 30 seconds, then add the chickpeas and 350ml/12fl oz/ 1½ cups of the reserved cooking liquid. Season with salt, then cover and simmer for 15–20 minutes, stirring occasionally.

4 Meanwhile, melt the ghee or butter in a pan and fry the cardamom pods and cloves for 2 minutes. Pour in the boiling water and stir in the rice. Cover and cook for 10 minutes.

5 Add the sugar and saffron liquid to the rice. Mix the reserved onion with the chillies, ginger and lemon juice, and add to the chickpeas. Garnish with the coriander and serve with the rice.

Oven-baked Pumpkin Stuffed with Apricot Pilaff

Serves 4–6

1 pumpkin, weighing about 1.2kg/2½lb
225g/8oz/generous 1 cup long grain rice, well rinsed
30–45ml/2–3 tbsp olive oil
15ml/1 tbsp butter
a few saffron threads
5ml/1 tsp coriander seeds
2–3 strips of orange peel, pith removed and finely sliced
45–60ml/3–4 tbsp shelled pistachio nuts
30–45ml/2–3 tbsp dried cranberries, soaked in boiling water for 5 minutes and drained
175g/6oz/³⁄₄ cup ready-to-eat dried apricots, sliced or chopped
1 bunch of fresh basil, leaves torn
1 bunch each of fresh coriander (cilantro), mint and flat leaf parsley, coarsely chopped
salt and ground black pepper
lemon wedges and thick natural (plain) yogurt, to serve

1 Preheat the oven to 200°C/400°F/Gas 6. Wash the pumpkin and cut off the stalk end to use as a lid. Scoop all the seeds out of the middle with a spoon, and pull out the stringy fibres. Replace the lid, put the pumpkin on a baking tray and bake for 1 hour.

2 Meanwhile, put the rice in a pan and pour in enough water to cover. Add a pinch of salt and bring to the boil, then partially cover the pan and simmer for 10–12 minutes, until the water has been absorbed and the rice is cooked but still has a bite.

3 Heat the oil and butter in a heavy pan. Stir in the saffron, coriander seeds, orange peel, pistachios, cranberries and apricots, then stir in the cooked rice. Season with salt and pepper. Turn off the heat, cover the pan with a dish towel, followed by the lid, and leave the pilaff to steam for 10 minutes, then toss in the herbs.

4 Spoon the pilaff into the cavity in the pumpkin. Put the lid back on and bake in the oven for a further 20 minutes.

5 To serve, remove the lid and slice a round off the top of the pumpkin. Place the ring on a plate and spoon some pilaff in the middle. Prepare the rest in the same way. Serve with lemon wedges and a bowl of yogurt.

Sweet Rice Energy 834kcal/3491kJ; Protein 27.3g; Carbohydrate 126.9g, of which sugars 12.3g; Fat 25.2g, of which saturates 7.1g; Cholesterol 21mg; Calcium 196mg; Fibre 11.3g; Sodium 104mg.
Pumpkin Energy 345kcal/1443kJ; Protein 9.9g; Carbohydrate 50.1g, of which sugars 18.6g; Fat 12g, of which saturates 2.6g; Cholesterol 5mg; Calcium 299mg; Fibre 9.6g; Sodium 93mg.

Vegetable Biryani

This is a good-tempered dish made from everyday ingredients, and thus indispensable for the cook catering for an unexpected vegetarian guest.

Serves 4–6
175g/6oz/scant 1 cup long-grain rice, rinsed
2 whole cloves
seeds from 2 cardamom pods
450ml/³⁄4 pint/scant 2 cups vegetable stock
2 garlic cloves
1 small onion, roughly chopped

5ml/1 tsp cumin seeds
5ml/1 tsp ground coriander
2.5ml/¹⁄2 tsp ground turmeric
2.5ml/¹⁄2 tsp chilli powder
1 large potato, cut into 2.5cm/1in cubes
2 carrots, sliced
¹⁄2 cauliflower, broken into bitesize florets
50g/2oz green beans, cut into 2.5cm/1in lengths
30ml/2 tbsp chopped fresh coriander (cilantro), plus extra to garnish
30ml/2 tbsp lime juice
salt and ground black pepper

1 Put the rice, cloves and cardamom seeds into a large, heavy pan. Pour over the vegetable stock and bring to the boil. Reduce the heat, cover the pan and simmer for 20 minutes or until all the stock has been absorbed.

2 Meanwhile, put the garlic cloves, onion, cumin seeds, ground coriander, turmeric, chilli powder and seasoning into a blender or food processor together with about 30ml/2 tbsp water. Blend until a smooth paste forms. Scrape the paste into a large flameproof casserole.

3 Preheat the oven to 180°C/350°F/Gas 4. Cook the spicy paste in the casserole over a low heat for 2 minutes, stirring occasionally. Add the potato cubes, carrots, cauliflower, beans and 90ml/6 tbsp water. Cover and cook over a low heat for 12 minutes, stirring occasionally. Add the chopped fresh coriander.

4 Remove the cloves from the rice. Spoon the rice over the vegetables. Sprinkle with the lime juice. Cover and cook in the oven for 25 minutes or until the vegetables are tender. Fluff up the rice with a fork before serving, garnished with the extra chopped fresh coriander.

Rice Layered with Bengal Gram

This rice and lentil dish is served with a gourd curry, or palida, which is prominently flavoured with fenugreek and soured with dried mangosteen.

Serves 4–6
175g/6oz/²⁄3 cup Bengal gram or lentils of your choice
600ml/1 pint/2¹⁄2 cups water
2.5ml/¹⁄2 tsp ground turmeric
50g/2oz deep-fried onions, crushed
45ml/3 tbsp green masala paste
a few fresh mint and coriander (cilantro) leaves, chopped
350g/12oz/1³⁄4 cups basmati rice, cooked
30ml/2 tbsp ghee
salt

For the curry
60ml/4 tbsp vegetable oil
1.5ml/¹⁄4 tsp fenugreek seeds
15g/¹⁄2oz dried fenugreek leaves
2 garlic cloves, crushed
5ml/1 tsp ground coriander
5ml/1 tsp cumin seeds
5ml/1 tsp chilli powder
60ml/4 tbsp gram flour mixed with 60ml/4 tbsp water
450g/1lb bottle gourd, peeled, pith and seeds removed and cut into bitesize pieces, or marrow (large zucchini) or firm courgettes (zucchini) prepared in the same way
175ml/6fl oz/³⁄4 cup tomato juice
juice of 3 lemons
salt

1 For the rice, boil the Bengal gram in the water with the turmeric, for 15 minutes or until the grains are soft. Drain and reserve the water. Toss the Bengal gram gently with the deep-fried onions, masala paste, mint and coriander. Add salt to taste.

2 Grease a heavy pan and place a layer of rice in the bottom. Add the Bengal gram mixture and another layer of the remaining rice. Place small knobs (pats) of ghee on top, sprinkle with a little water and heat until steam rises from the mixture. Keep warm.

3 To make the curry, heat the oil in a pan and fry the fenugreek seeds and leaves and the garlic until the garlic turns golden.

4 Mix the ground coriander, cumin and chilli powder to a paste with a little water. Add to the pan and simmer until all the water has evaporated. Add the gram-flour paste, gourd, marrow or courgettes and the tomato juice. Add the lemon juice and salt. Cook until the gourd is soft. Serve immediately with the rice.

Vegetable Biryani Energy 260kcal/1089kJ; Protein 5.7g; Carbohydrate 50.4g, of which sugars 11.3g; Fat 4.1g, of which saturates 0.6g; Cholesterol 0mg; Calcium 49mg; Fibre 3g; Sodium 27mg.
Rice with Bengal Gram Energy 326kcal/1367kJ; Protein 11.3g; Carbohydrate 39.6g, of which sugars 2.9g; Fat 14.8g, of which saturates 3.7g; Cholesterol 0mg; Calcium 62mg; Fibre 2.3g; Sodium 82mg.

Tomato Biryani

Although generally served as an accompaniment to meat, poultry or fish dishes, this tasty rice dish can also be eaten as a complete meal on its own.

Serves 4

400g/14oz/2 cups basmati rice
15ml/1 tbsp vegetable oil
2.5ml/½ tsp onion seeds
1 medium onion, sliced
2 medium tomatoes, sliced
1 orange or yellow (bell) pepper, seeded and sliced
5ml/1 tsp grated fresh root ginger
5ml/1 tsp crushed garlic
5ml/1 tsp chilli powder
30ml/2 tbsp chopped fresh coriander (cilantro)
1 medium potato, diced
7.5ml/1½ tsp salt
50g/2oz/½ cup frozen peas
750ml/1¼ pints/3 cups water

1 Wash the rice well under cold running water and leave it to soak in water for about 30 minutes.

2 Heat the oil in a heavy pan and fry the onion seeds for about 1 minute. Add the sliced onion to the pan and fry for about 5–7 minutes, stirring occasionally to prevent the slices from sticking to the pan and burning.

3 Add the sliced tomatoes and pepper, ginger, garlic and chilli powder. Stir-fry for 2 minutes.

4 Add the fresh coriander, potato, salt and peas and stir-fry over a medium heat for a further 5 minutes.

5 Transfer the rice to a colander and drain. Add it to the spiced tomato and potato mixture and stir-fry for 1–2 minutes.

6 Pour in the water and bring to the boil, then lower the heat to medium. Cover and cook the rice for 12–15 minutes. Leave to stand for 5 minutes and then serve.

> **Cook's Tip**
> *Plain rice can look a bit dull; it is greatly enhanced by adding colourful ingredients such as tomatoes, peppers and peas.*

Basmati Rice with Potato

Rice is eaten at all meals in Indian and Pakistani homes. There are several ways of cooking rice, and mostly whole spices are used. Always choose a good-quality basmati rice.

Serves 4

300g/11oz/1½ cups basmati rice
15ml/1 tbsp vegetable oil
1 small cinnamon stick
1 bay leaf
1.5ml/¼ tsp black cumin seeds
3 green cardamom pods
1 medium onion, sliced
5ml/1 tsp grated fresh root ginger
5ml/1 tsp crushed garlic
1.5ml/¼ tsp ground turmeric
7.5ml/1½ tsp salt
1 large potato, roughly diced
475ml/16fl oz/2 cups water
15ml/1 tbsp chopped fresh coriander (cilantro)

1 Wash the rice well under cold running water and leave it to soak in water for 20 minutes.

2 Heat the oil in a heavy pan, add the cinnamon, bay leaf, black cumin seeds, cardamom pods and onion and cook for about 2 minutes, stirring constantly.

3 Add the ginger, garlic, turmeric, salt and potato to the pan, and cook for a further 1 minute.

4 Drain the rice thoroughly. Add it to the potato and spices in the pan and stir well to combine the ingredients.

5 Pour the water into the pan and then stir in the coriander. Cover the pan with a lid and cook for 15–20 minutes.

6 Remove the pan from the heat and leave to stand, still covered, for 5–10 minutes before serving.

> **Cook's Tip**
> *It is important to observe the full standing time for this dish before serving. Use a slotted spoon to serve the rice and potato mixture and handle it carefully to avoid breaking or damaging the delicate grains of rice.*

Tomato Biryani Energy 475kcal/1990kJ; Protein 11.5g; Carbohydrate 102.9g, of which sugars 9g; Fat 1.9g, of which saturates 0.3g; Cholesterol 0mg; Calcium 47mg; Fibre 3.5g; Sodium 18mg.
Basmati Rice with Potato Energy 355kcal/1483kJ; Protein 7.2g; Carbohydrate 70.5g, of which sugars 1.5g; Fat 4.8g, of which saturates 0.6g; Cholesterol 0mg; Calcium 28mg; Fibre 0.7g; Sodium 745mg.

Aubergine Pilaff with Cinnamon

This North African rice dish varies from region to region, but all recipes include meaty chunks of aubergine.

Serves 4–6
2 large aubergines (eggplants)
30–45ml/2–3 tbsp olive oil
30–45ml/2–3 tbsp pine nuts
1 large onion, finely chopped
5ml/1 tsp coriander seeds
30ml/2 tbsp currants, soaked for
   5–10 minutes and drained
10–15ml/2–3 tsp sugar
15–30ml/1–2 tbsp
   ground cinnamon
15–30ml/1–2 tbsp dried mint
1 small bunch of fresh dill,
   finely chopped
3 tomatoes, skinned, seeded and
   finely chopped
350g/12oz/generous 1¾ cups
   long or short grain rice, well
   rinsed and drained
sunflower oil, for deep-frying
juice of ½ lemon
salt and ground black pepper
fresh mint and lemon, to garnish

1 Quarter the aubergines lengthways, then slice each quarter into chunks and place in a large bowl of salted water. Leave to soak for at least 30 minutes.

2 Meanwhile, heat the olive oil in a heavy pan, stir in the pine nuts and cook until they turn golden. Add the onion and cook until soft, then stir in the coriander seeds and currants. Add the sugar, cinnamon, mint and dill and stir in the tomatoes.

3 Add the rice, stirring until well coated, then pour in 900ml/1½ pints/3¾ cups water, season with salt and pepper and bring to the boil. Lower the heat, partially cover the pan, and simmer for 10–12 minutes, until almost all the liquid has been absorbed. Turn off the heat, cover with a dish towel and the lid and leave the rice to steam for about 15 minutes.

4 Heat enough oil for deep-frying in a wok. Drain the aubergines and squeeze them dry, then deep-fry them in batches until golden brown. Lift out and drain on kitchen paper.

5 Transfer the rice into a warmed serving bowl and toss the aubergine chunks through it with the lemon juice. Garnish with the fresh mint and serve the pilaff either warm or cold, with lemon wedges for squeezing over.

Basmati and Nut Pilaff with Mixed Spices

Vegetarians will love this simple spicy pilaff.

Serves 4
15–30ml/1–2 tbsp sunflower oil
   or vegetable oil
1 onion, chopped
1 garlic clove, crushed
1 large carrot, coarsely grated
225g/8oz/generous 1 cup
   basmati rice, soaked for 1 hour
5ml/1 tsp cumin seeds
10ml/2 tsp ground coriander
10ml/2 tsp black mustard
   seeds (optional)
4 green cardamom pods
450ml/¾ pint/scant 2 cups
   vegetable stock or water
1 bay leaf
75g/3oz/¾ cup unsalted walnuts
   and cashew nuts
salt and ground black pepper
fresh parsley or coriander
   (cilantro) sprigs, to garnish

1 Heat the oil in a large pan and gently fry the onion, garlic and carrot for 3–4 minutes. Drain the rice and then add to the pan with the spices. Cook for 1–2 minutes more, stirring to coat the grains in oil.

2 Pour in the stock or water, add the bay leaf and season well. Bring to the boil, lower the heat, cover the pan with a lid and simmer very gently for 10–12 minutes.

3 Remove the pan from the heat without lifting the lid. Leave to stand for about 5 minutes, then check the rice. If it is cooked, there will be small steam holes on the surface of the rice. Remove and discard the bay leaf and the cardamom pods.

4 Stir in the nuts and check the seasoning. Spoon on to a warmed serving platter, garnish with the fresh parsley or coriander sprigs and serve immediately.

> **Cook's Tip**
> Use whichever nuts you prefer in this dish – even unsalted peanuts taste good, although almonds, cashew nuts or pistachios are more exotic.

Aubergine Pilaff Energy 369kcal/1539kJ; Protein 6.1g; Carbohydrate 52.2g, of which sugars 11g; Fat 15.2g, of which saturates 1.8g; Cholesterol 0mg; Calcium 38mg; Fibre 2.7g; Sodium 8mg.
Basmati and Nut Pilaff Energy 376kcal/1562kJ; Protein 7.5g; Carbohydrate 50g, of which sugars 4g; Fat 16g, of which saturates 1.4g; Cholesterol 0mg; Calcium 42mg; Fibre 1.6g; Sodium 7mg.

Spicy Courgettes with Tomato Rice and Fresh Herbs

This slow-cooked rice dish is first simmered on the stove and then finished off in the oven.

Serves 4–8

1kg/2¼lb courgettes (zucchini)
60ml/4 tbsp olive oil
3 onions, finely chopped
3 garlic cloves, crushed
5ml/1 tsp chilli powder
400g/14oz can chopped tomatoes
200g/7oz/1 cup risotto or
   short grain rice
600–750ml/1–1¼ pints/
   2½–3 cups vegetable or
   chicken stock
30ml/2 tbsp chopped
   fresh parsley
30ml/2 tbsp chopped fresh dill
salt and ground white pepper
sprigs of dill and olives, to garnish
thick natural (plain) yogurt,
   to serve

1 Preheat the oven to 190°C/375°F/Gas 5. Top and tail the courgettes and slice into large chunks.

2 Heat half the oil in a large pan and cook the onions and garlic until just soft. Stir in the chilli powder and tomatoes and simmer for about 5 minutes.

3 Add the courgettes and salt to taste. Cook over a low to medium heat for 10–15 minutes, before adding the rice.

4 Add the stock to the pan, cover and simmer for 25 minutes, or until the rice is tender. Stir the mixture occasionally.

5 Season with pepper, and stir in the parsley and dill. Transfer to an ovenproof dish and bake in the oven for about 45 minutes.

6 Halfway through cooking, brush the remaining oil over the courgette mixture. Garnish with the dill and olives, then serve.

> **Cook's Tip**
> *Add extra liquid, as necessary, while simmering the rice on the stove to prevent the mixture from sticking to the pan.*

Vegetarian Kedgeree

This spicy lentil and rice dish is a delicious variation of the original Indian version of kedgeree, known as kitchiri. You can serve it as it is, or topped with quartered hard-boiled eggs. It is also good with grilled mushrooms.

Serves 4

50g/2oz/¼ cup red split
   lentils, rinsed
1 bay leaf
225g/8oz/1 cup basmati
   rice, rinsed
4 cloves
50g/2oz/4 tbsp butter
5ml/1 tsp curry powder
2.5ml/½ tsp mild chilli powder
30ml/2 tbsp chopped fresh flat
   leaf parsley
salt and ground black pepper
4 hard-boiled eggs, quartered, to
   serve (optional)

1 Put the lentils in a pan, add the bay leaf and cover with cold water. Bring to the boil, skim off any foam, then reduce the heat. Cover and simmer for 25–30 minutes, until tender. Drain, then discard the bay leaf.

2 Meanwhile, place the rice in a pan and cover with about 475ml/16fl oz/2 cups boiling water. Add the cloves and a pinch of salt. Cook, covered, for 10–15 minutes, until all the water is absorbed and the rice is tender. Discard the cloves.

3 Melt the butter over a gentle heat in a large frying pan, then add the curry and chilli powders and cook for 1 minute.

4 Stir the lentils and rice into the pan and mix well until they are coated in the spiced butter.

5 Season with salt and pepper and cook for 1–2 minutes until heated through. Stir in the fresh parsley and serve immediately with the hard-boiled eggs, if using.

> **Cook's Tip**
> *Rice is a high-carbohydrate food that provides sustained amounts of energy, making it a perfect food to start the day. Rice can also help to ease diarrhoea and stomach upsets.*

Spicy Courgettes Energy 201kcal/837kJ; Protein 5.6g; Carbohydrate 30.1g, of which sugars 8g; Fat 6.6g, of which saturates 1g; Cholesterol 0mg; Calcium 72mg; Fibre 3g; Sodium 10mg.
Vegetarian Kedgeree Energy 481kcal/2015kJ; Protein 14.8g; Carbohydrate 72.6g, of which sugars 4.1g; Fat 15.2g, of which saturates 3.5g; Cholesterol 0mg; Calcium 65mg; Fibre 2.8g; Sodium 82mg.

Garlic and Ginger Rice

This rice dish goes well with vegetable or meat curries.

Serves 4–6
15ml/1 tbsp vegetable oil
2–3 garlic cloves, finely chopped
25g/1oz fresh root ginger, finely chopped
225g/8oz/generous 1 cup long grain rice, rinsed in several bowls of water and drained
900ml/1½ pints/3¾ cups chicken stock
a bunch of fresh coriander (cilantro) leaves, finely chopped

1 Heat the oil in a heavy pan. Stir in the garlic and ginger and fry until golden. Stir in the rice and allow it to absorb the flavours for 1–2 minutes. Pour in the stock and stir well. Bring the stock to the boil, then reduce the heat.

2 Sprinkle the coriander over the surface of the stock, cover the pan, and leave to cook gently for 20–25 minutes, until the rice has absorbed all the liquid. Turn off the heat and fluff up the rice, cover and leave for 10 minutes before serving.

Fragrant Coconut Rice

The addition of coconut milk makes this rice deliciously creamy.

Serves 4
1 litre/1¾ pints/4 cups coconut milk
450g/1lb/2¼ cups short grain rice, thoroughly washed and drained
1 pandanus (screwpine) leaf, tied in a loose knot
salt

1 Heat the coconut milk in a heavy pan and stir in the rice with a little salt. Add the pandanus leaf and bring to the boil. Reduce the heat and simmer for about 15 minutes or until the liquid has been absorbed.

2 Remove from the heat and cover the pan with a dish towel and the lid. Leave the rice to steam for a further 15–20 minutes, then fluff it up with a fork and serve.

Pilau Rice with Whole Spices

This fragrant rice dish makes an excellent accompaniment to any curry meal.

Serves 4
generous pinch of saffron strands
600ml/1 pint/2½ cups hot chicken stock
50g/2oz/¼ cup butter
1 onion, chopped
1 garlic clove, crushed
½ cinnamon stick
6 green cardamom pods
1 bay leaf
250g/9oz/1⅓ cups basmati rice
50g/2oz/⅓ cup sultanas (golden raisins)
15ml/1 tbsp sunflower oil or vegetable oil
50g/2oz/½ cup cashew nuts

1 Add the saffron strands to a jug (pitcher) containing the hot chicken stock. Stir well to release the colour of the saffron, and set aside while cooking the other ingredients.

2 Heat the butter in a pan and fry the chopped onion and crushed garlic for 5 minutes. Stir in the cinnamon stick, cardamoms and bay leaf and cook for a further 2 minutes.

3 Add the rice and cook, stirring, for 2 minutes more. Pour in the saffron-flavoured stock and add the sultanas.

4 Bring to the boil, stir, then lower the heat, cover with a tight-fitting lid and cook gently for about 8 minutes or until the rice is tender and all the liquid has been absorbed.

5 Meanwhile, heat the oil in a frying pan and fry the cashew nuts until browned. Drain on kitchen paper. Sprinkle the browned cashew nuts evenly over the rice and serve.

Cook's Tip
Don't be tempted to use black cardamoms in this dish. They are coarser and more strongly flavoured than green cardamoms and are only used in highly spiced dishes that are cooked for a long time. When using cardamoms of any colour, make sure they are fresh or the dish will taste musty.

Garlic and Ginger Rice Energy 151kcal/632kJ; Protein 3g; Carbohydrate 30g, of which sugars 0g; Fat 2g, of which saturates 0.3g; Cholesterol 0mg; Calcium 9mg; Fibre 0.1g; Sodium 124mg.
Fragrant Coconut Rice Energy 459kcal/1927kJ; Protein 9.1g; Carbohydrate 102g, of which sugars 12.3g; Fat 1.3g, of which saturates 0.5g; Cholesterol 0mg; Calcium 94mg; Fibre 0g; Sodium 275mg.
Pilau Rice Energy 302kcal/1258kJ; Protein 5.8g; Carbohydrate 46.4g, of which sugars 1g; Fat 10.1g, of which saturates 1.1g; Cholesterol 0mg; Calcium 49mg; Fibre 0.8g; Sodium 2mg.

Brown Rice with Lime

It is unusual to find brown rice in Chinese recipes, but the nutty flavour of the grains is enhanced by the fragrance of limes, coriander and lemon grass in this delicious dish.

Serves 4
2 limes
1 lemon grass stalk
225g/8oz/generous 1 cup brown long grain rice
15ml/1 tbsp olive oil
1 onion, chopped
2.5cm/1in piece fresh root ginger, peeled and finely chopped
7.5ml/1½ tsp coriander seeds
7.5ml/1½ tsp cumin seeds
750ml/1¼ pints/3 cups vegetable stock
60ml/4 tbsp chopped fresh coriander (cilantro)
spring onion (scallion) green and toasted coconut strips, to garnish
1 lime cut into 4 wedges, to serve

1 Pare the limes, using a cannelle knife (zester) or fine grater, taking care to avoid cutting into the bitter pith. Set the rind aside. Finely chop the lower bulbous portion of the lemon grass stalk and set it aside.

2 Rinse the rice in plenty of cold running water until the water runs clear. Transfer it into a sieve (strainer) and drain thoroughly.

3 Heat the oil in a large pan. Add the onion, ginger, coriander and cumin seeds, lemon grass and lime rind to the pan and cook over low heat for 2–3 minutes.

4 Add the rice to the pan and cook, stirring constantly, for 1 minute, then pour in the stock and bring to the boil. Reduce the heat to very low and cover the pan.

5 Cook gently for 30 minutes, then check the rice. If it is still crunchy, cover the pan and cook for a further 3–5 minutes. Remove the pan from the heat.

6 Stir in the fresh coriander, fluff up the rice grains with a fork, cover the pan and leave to stand for 10 minutes. Transfer to a warmed dish, garnish with spring onion green and toasted coconut strips, and serve with lime wedges.

Saffron Rice with Cardamoms

The addition of aromatic green cardamom pods, cloves, milk and saffron gives this dish both a delicate flavour and colour. It is the perfect dish to accompany a simple chicken or lamb curry and would also go well with a spicy vegetable dish or dhal.

Serves 6
450g/1lb/2⅓ cups basmati rice
750ml/1¼ pints/3 cups water
3 green cardamom pods
2 cloves
5ml/1 tsp salt
45ml/3 tbsp semi-skimmed (low-fat) milk
2.5ml/½ tsp saffron strands, crushed

1 Wash the rice under cold water and leave to soak in water for 20 minutes. Drain the rice well and place it in a pan. Pour the measured water into the pan.

2 Add the cardamoms, cloves and salt. Stir, then bring to the boil. Lower the heat, cover the pan tightly and simmer the rice for about 5 minutes so that it starts to cook.

3 Meanwhile, place the milk in a small heavy pan. Add the saffron strands and heat gently.

4 Add the saffron milk to the rice and stir. Cover again and continue cooking over low heat for 5–6 minutes. Remove the pan from the heat without lifting the lid. Leave the rice to stand for about 5 minutes before serving.

Cook's Tips
• *The saffron milk can be heated in the microwave. Mix the milk and saffron strands in a suitable jug (pitcher) or bowl and warm them for 1 minute on Low.*
• *The rice can be coloured and flavoured with a generous pinch of ground turmeric instead of saffron. The effect will not be as subtle, but the results will still be very satisfactory.*
• *Just before serving the rice, remove the cardamom pods and whole cloves, or warn guests to look out for them.*

Saffron Rice Energy 348kcal/1452kJ; Protein 6.7g; Carbohydrate 71g, of which sugars 0.9g; Fat 3.6g, of which saturates 2g; Cholesterol 8mg; Calcium 21mg; Fibre 0.2g; Sodium 515mg.
Brown Rice with Lime Energy 235kcal/996kJ; Protein 4.3g; Carbohydrate 47.3g, of which sugars 1.9g; Fat 4.5g, of which saturates 0.8g; Cholesterol 0mg; Calcium 35mg; Fibre 1.9g; Sodium 6mg.

Lemon-laced Rice

Lemon-laced rice is very popular all over India – its mildly acidic flavour is a perfect backdrop for any spicy curry. The dish also looks beautiful, with a pale yellow background for black mustard seeds, curry leaves and roasted cashew nuts. If you don't eat nuts, try adding a handful of toasted sunflower or pumpkin seeds instead.

Serves 4
225g/8oz/1¼ cups
   basmati rice
30ml/2 tbsp sunflower oil or
   olive oil
2.5ml/½ tsp black mustard seeds
10–12 curry leaves,
   preferably fresh
25g/1oz cashew nuts, broken
2.5ml/½ tsp ground turmeric
5ml/1 tsp salt, or to taste
30ml/2 tbsp lemon juice

1 Wash and rinse the rice two or three times in cold water, or until the water runs clear. Soak it for 15–20 minutes, rinse and drain it in a colander.

2 Heat the oil in a non-stick pan over a medium heat. When it is hot, but not smoking, add the mustard seeds, curry leaves and cashew nuts. Let them sizzle for 15–20 seconds.

3 Add the rice, turmeric and salt to the pan. Stir-fry the rice for 2–3 minutes, then add 475ml/16fl oz/2 cups hot water and the lemon juice.

4 Stir the pan once, bring to the boil and continue to boil for about 2 minutes. Cover the pan tightly, reduce the heat and simmer gently for an additional 7–8 minutes.

5 Remove the pan from the heat and leave to stand, undisturbed, for 6–7 minutes. Fork through the rice, and serve immediately as an accompaniment to curry.

Variation
Replace the lemon juice with 15ml/1 tbsp lime juice and add 50g/2oz/⅓ cup raisins for a fruity variation on this theme.

Pineapple Fried Rice

This dish is ideal to prepare for a special occasion meal. Served in the pineapple skin shells, it is sure to be the talking point of the dinner.

Serves 4–6
1 pineapple
30ml/2 tbsp vegetable oil
1 small onion, finely chopped
2 fresh green chillies, seeded
   and chopped
225g/8oz lean pork, cut into strips

115g/4oz cooked, peeled
   prawns (shrimp)
675–900g/1½–2lb/3–4 cups
   plain boiled rice, cooked and
   completely cold
50g/2oz/⅓ cup roasted
   cashew nuts
2 spring onions (scallions), chopped
30ml/2 tbsp fish sauce
15ml/1 tbsp soy sauce
2 fresh red chillies, sliced, and
   10–12 fresh mint leaves,
   to garnish

1 Using a sharp knife, cut the pineapple in half. Remove the flesh from both halves by cutting around inside the skin. Reserve the pineapple skin shells for serving the rice.

2 Slice the pineapple flesh and chop it into small even cubes. You will need about 115g/4oz of pineapple in total. Any remaining fruit can be reserved for use in a dessert.

3 Heat the oil in a wok or large pan. Add the onion and chillies and fry for about 3–5 minutes until softened. Add the strips of pork and cook until they have browned on all sides.

4 Stir in the prawns and rice and toss them well together. Continue to stir-fry until the rice is thoroughly heated.

5 Add the chopped pineapple, cashew nuts and spring onions. Season to taste with fish sauce and soy sauce. Spoon into the pineapple shells and garnish with the chillies and mint leaves.

Cook's Tip
When buying a pineapple, look for a sweet-smelling fruit with an even brownish/yellow skin. Tap the base – a dull sound means the fruit is ripe. It should also give slightly when pressed.

Wild Rice Pilaff

Wild rice isn't a rice at all, but is actually a type of wild grass. Call it what you will, it has a wonderful nutty flavour and combines well with long grain rice in this fruity mixture. Serve as a side dish.

Serves 6
200g/7oz/1 cup wild rice
40g/1 ½ oz/3 tbsp butter
½ onion, finely chopped
200g/7oz/1 cup long grain rice
475ml/16fl oz/2 cups
   chicken stock
75g/3oz/¾ cup flaked
   (sliced) almonds
115g/4oz/⅔ cup sultanas
   (golden raisins)
30ml/2 tbsp chopped fresh
   parsley
salt and ground black pepper

1 Bring a large pan of water to the boil. Add the wild rice and 5ml/1 tsp salt. Lower the heat, cover and simmer gently for 45–60 minutes, until the rice is tender. Drain well.

2 Meanwhile, melt 15g/½oz/1 tbsp of the butter in another pan. Add the onion and cook over medium heat for about 5 minutes until it is just softened. Stir in the long grain rice and cook for 1 minute more.

3 Stir in the stock and bring to the boil. Cover the pan with a lid and simmer gently for 30–40 minutes, until the rice is tender and the liquid has been absorbed.

4 Melt the remaining butter in a small pan. Add the almonds and cook until they are just golden. Set aside.

5 Put the rice mixture in a bowl and add the almonds, sultanas and half the parsley. Stir to mix. Taste and adjust the seasoning if necessary. Transfer to a warmed serving dish, sprinkle with the remaining parsley and serve immediately.

> **Cook's Tip**
> A well-flavoured stock will make a big difference to the end result. If you haven't time to make your own stock, use a carton or can of good-quality stock.

Saigon Chilli Rice

Although plain steamed rice is served at almost every meal in Vietnam, many families like to sneak in a little spice too. A burst of chilli for fire, turmeric for colour, and coriander for its cooling flavour, are all that's needed.

Serves 4
15ml/1 tbsp vegetable oil
2–3 green or red Thai chillies,
   seeded and finely chopped
2 garlic cloves, finely chopped
2.5cm/1in fresh root
   ginger, chopped
5ml/1 tsp sugar
10–15ml/2–3 tsp
   ground turmeric
225g/8oz/generous 1 cup long
   grain rice
30ml/2 tbsp nuoc cham
   (Vietnamese fish sauce)
600ml/1 pint/2 ½ cups water
   or stock
1 bunch of fresh coriander
   (cilantro), stalks removed, leaves
   finely chopped
salt and ground black pepper

1 Heat the oil in a heavy pan. Stir in the chillies, garlic and ginger with the sugar. As they begin to colour, stir in the turmeric. Add the rice, coating it well, then pour in the nuoc mam and the water or stock – the liquid should sit about 2.5cm/1in above the rice.

2 Season with salt and ground black pepper and bring the liquid to the boil. Reduce the heat, cover and simmer for about 25 minutes, or until the water has been absorbed.

3 Remove from the heat and leave the rice to steam for a further 10 minutes before serving.

4 Transfer the rice on to a serving dish. Add some of the coriander and lightly toss together using a fork. Garnish with the remaining fresh coriander.

> **Cook's Tip**
> This rice goes well with grilled and stir-fried fish and shellfish dishes, but you can serve it as an alternative to plain rice. Add extra chillies, if you like it hotter.

Saigon Chilli Rice Energy 252kcal/1066kJ; Protein 5g; Carbohydrate 51g, of which sugars 1g; Fat 5g, of which saturates 1g; Cholesterol 0mg; Calcium 24mg; Fibre 0.3g; Sodium 500mg.
Wild Rice Pilaff Energy 424kcal/1769kJ; Protein 8.4g; Carbohydrate 68.3g, of which sugars 14.5g; Fat 13g, of which saturates 4g; Cholesterol 14mg; Calcium 69mg; Fibre 1.7g; Sodium 48mg.

Pea and Mushroom Pilau

Tiny white button mushrooms and sweet petits pois, or baby peas, add an attractive splash of colour and flavour to this delectable rice dish.

Serves 6
450g/1lb/2¼ cups basmati rice
15ml/1 tbsp vegetable oil or
   sunflower oil
2.5ml/½ tsp cumin seeds
2 black cardamom pods
2 cinnamon sticks
3 garlic cloves, sliced
5ml/1 tsp salt
1 medium tomato, sliced
50g/2oz/⅔ cup button (white)
   mushrooms
75g/3oz/¾ cup petits pois
   (baby peas)
750ml/1¼ pints/3 cups water

1 Wash the rice well under cold running water and leave it to soak in water for 30 minutes.

2 In a medium, heavy pan or wok, heat the vegetable or sunflower oil and add the cumin seeds, cardamom pods, cinnamon sticks, garlic and salt.

3 Add the tomato and mushrooms to the pan and cook for about 2–3 minutes, stirring constantly.

4 Transfer the rice to a sieve (strainer) and drain it thoroughly. Add it to the pan with the peas. Stir gently, making sure that you do not break up the grains of rice.

5 Add the water to the pan and bring it to the boil. Lower the heat, cover tightly and continue to cook for about 15–20 minutes. Just before serving, remove the lid from the pan and fluff up the rice with a fork. Spoon into a warmed serving dish and serve immediately.

Cook's Tip
Petits pois are small green peas, picked when very young. The tender, sweet peas inside the immature pods are ideal for this delicately flavoured rice dish. However, if you can't find petits pois, garden peas can be used instead.

Basmati Rice and Peas

This is a very simple rice dish, but it can make a useful quick accopmpaniment to a main course.

Serves 4
300g/11oz/1½ cups basmati rice
15ml/1 tbsp vegetable oil
6–8 curry leaves
1.5ml/¼ tsp mustard seeds
1.5ml/¼ tsp onion seeds
30ml/2 tbsp fresh
   fenugreek leaves
5ml/1 tsp crushed garlic
5ml/1 tsp grated fresh root ginger
5ml/1 tsp salt
115g/4oz/1 cup frozen peas
475ml/16fl oz/2 cups water

1 Wash the rice well under cold running water and leave it to soak in a bowl of water for 30 minutes.

2 Heat the oil in a heavy pan and add the curry leaves, mustard seeds, onion seeds, fenugreek leaves, garlic, ginger and salt and stir-fry for 2–3 minutes.

3 Drain the rice thoroughly, and add it to the pan with the other ingredients. Stir gently to combine.

4 Add the frozen peas and water and bring to the boil. Lower the heat, cover with a lid and cook for 15–20 minutes. Remove from the heat and leave to stand, still covered, for 10 minutes.

5 When ready to serve, fluff up the rice with a fork. Spoon the mixture on to serving plates and serve immediately.

Colourful Pilau Rice

This lightly spiced rice makes an extremely attractive accompaniment to many balti dishes, and is easily made.

Serves 4–6
450g/1lb/2¼ cups
   basmati rice
75g/3oz/6 tbsp unsalted butter
4 cloves
4 green cardamom pods
1 bay leaf
5ml/1 tsp salt
1 litre/1¾ pints/4 cups water
a few drops each of yellow,
   green and red food
   colouring

1 Wash the basmati rice twice under cold running water, drain well and set aside in a sieve (strainer).

2 Melt the butter in a medium pan, and add the cloves, cardamoms, bay leaf and salt. Lower the heat and add the rice. Fry for about 1 minute, stirring constantly.

3 Add the water to the rice and spices and bring to the boil. As soon as it has boiled, cover the pan and reduce the heat. Cook for 10–15 minutes. Taste a grain of rice after 10 minutes; it should be slightly *al dente* (soft but with a bite in the centre).

4 Just before you are ready to serve the rice, pour a few drops of each colouring at different sides of the pan. Leave to stand for 5 minutes so that the colours can 'bleed' into the rice. Mix gently with a fork and serve immediately.

Pea and Mushroom Pilau Energy 304kcal/1272kJ; Protein 6.9g; Carbohydrate 62.2g, of which sugars 0.3g; Fat 2.8g, of which saturates 0.3g; Cholesterol 0mg; Calcium 22mg; Fibre 0.7g; Sodium 1mg.
Basmati Rice and Peas Energy 329kcal/1373kJ; Protein 8.1g; Carbohydrate 64.4g, of which sugars 0.7g; Fat 4.1g, of which saturates 0.5g; Cholesterol 0mg; Calcium 27mg; Fibre 1.4g; Sodium 493mg.
Colourful Rice Energy 362kcal/1509kJ; Protein 5.6g; Carbohydrate 59.9g, of which sugars 0.1g; Fat 10.7g, of which saturates 6.5g; Cholesterol 27mg; Calcium 17mg; Fibre 0g; Sodium 403mg.

Rice with Seeds and Spices

Toasted sunflower and sesame seeds impart a rich, nutty flavour to rice spiced with turmeric, cardamom and coriander, for this delicious change from plain boiled rice, and a colourful accompaniment to serve with spicy curries.

Serves 4

5ml/1 tsp sunflower oil
2.5ml/¹/ tsp ground turmeric
6 cardamom pods, lightly crushed
5ml/1 tsp coriander seeds, lightly crushed
1 garlic clove, crushed
200g/7oz/1 cup basmati rice
400ml/14fl oz/1²/₃ cups vegetable stock
115g/4oz/¹/₂ cup natural (plain) yogurt
15ml/1 tbsp toasted sunflower seeds
15ml/1 tbsp toasted sesame seeds
salt and ground black pepper
coriander (cilantro) leaves, to garnish

1 Heat the oil in a non-stick frying pan or wok and fry the turmeric, cardamom pods, coriander seeds and garlic for about 1 minute, stirring constantly.

2 Add the rice and stock, bring to the boil, then cover and simmer for 15 minutes, or until just tender.

3 Stir in the yogurt and the toasted sunflower and sesame seeds. Season with salt and ground black pepper and serve immediately, garnished with coriander leaves.

Cook's Tip
Seeds are particularly rich in minerals, so they are a good addition to all kinds of dishes. Light toasting in a frying pan or oven will improve their fine flavour.

Variation
Basmati rice gives the best texture and flavour for this dish, but you can also use ordinary long grain rice in place of the basmati rice, if you prefer.

Rice with Cinnamon and Star Anise

Originating from China, this thick rice porridge or 'congee', known as bubur in Malaysia and Indonesia, has become popular all over South-east Asia. The basic recipe is nourishing but rather bland, and the joy of the dish is derived from the ingredients that are added.

Serves 4–6

25g/1oz fresh root ginger, peeled and sliced
1 cinnamon stick
2 star anise
2.5ml/¹/₂ tsp salt
115g/4oz/¹/₂ cup short grain rice, thoroughly washed and drained

1 Bring 1.2 litres/2 pints/5 cups water to the boil in a heavy pan. Stir in the spices, the salt and the rice.

2 Reduce the heat, cover the pan, and simmer gently for 1 hour, or longer if you prefer a thicker, smoother consistency. Serve the rice while piping hot.

Variations
With the addition of pickles, strips of omelette and braised dishes, this cinnamon and star anise rice dish is popular for supper in Singapore. In Malaysia, it is enjoyed for breakfast with fried or grilled fish, chicken and beef, as well as with pickles. Often flavoured with ginger, cinnamon and star anise, it is usually cooked until it is thick but the grains are still visible, whereas some of the Chinese versions are cooked for longer, so that the rice breaks down completely and the texture is quite smooth. The consistency varies from family to family: some people like it soupy and eat it with a spoon.

Cook's Tip
This dish is often eaten for breakfast, in Malaysia, and some domestic rice cookers have a 'congee' setting, which allows the dish to be prepared the night before and slowly cooked overnight, in order to be ready in the morning.

Rice with Seeds Energy 310kcal/1294kJ; Protein 8.3g; Carbohydrate 53.5g, of which sugars 2.8g; Fat 6.7g, of which saturates 0.9g; Cholesterol 0mg; Calcium 117mg; Fibre 0.7g; Sodium 31mg.
Rice with Cinnamon Energy 235kcal/996kJ; Protein 4.3g; Carbohydrate 47.3g, of which sugars 1.9g; Fat 4.5g, of which saturates 0.8g; Cholesterol 0mg; Calcium 35mg; Fibre 1.9g; Sodium 6mg.

Mushroom Pilau

This dish is simplicity itself. Serve with any Indian dish or with roast lamb or chicken.

Serves 4

30ml/2 tbsp vegetable oil
2 shallots, finely chopped
1 garlic clove, crushed
3 green cardamom pods
25g/1oz/2 tbsp ghee or butter

175g/6oz/2½ cups button
 (white) mushrooms, sliced
225g/8oz/generous 1 cup
 basmati rice, soaked
5ml/1 tsp grated fresh
 root ginger
good pinch of garam masala
450ml/¾ pint/scant 2 cups water
15ml/1 tbsp chopped fresh
 coriander (cilantro)
salt

1 Heat the vegetable oil in a flameproof casserole and fry the shallots, garlic and cardamom pods over medium heat for about 3–4 minutes, stirring frequently, until the shallots have softened and are beginning to brown.

2 Add the ghee or butter. When it has melted, add the mushrooms and fry for 2–3 minutes more.

3 Add the rice, ginger and garam masala. Cook over low heat for 2–3 minutes, stirring constantly, then stir in the water and a little salt. Bring to the boil, then cover tightly and simmer over very low heat for 10 minutes.

4 Remove the casserole from the heat. Leave to stand, covered, for 5 minutes. Add the chopped fresh coriander and fork it through the rice. Spoon the rice into a warmed serving bowl and serve immediately.

Variation
For a nuttier pilau, fry 1.5ml/¼ tsp cumin seeds with the cardamom pods at step 1. When the rice has almost cooked, drain it and gently stir in a pinch of saffron threads and 15ml/1 tbsp ground almonds. Leave the rice to stand for a few minutes before serving. Alternatively, you could stir in a handful of toasted cashew nuts when the rice is ready.

Aromatic Indian Rice with Peas

This versatile rice dish is often served at elaborate meals for Indian festivals, which include meat and vegetable curries, a yogurt dish, and chutneys.

Serves 4

350g/12oz/1¾ cups basmati rice
45ml/3 tbsp ghee or 30ml/2 tbsp
 vegetable oil and a small
 amount of butter

1 cinnamon stick
6–8 cardamom pods, crushed
4 cloves
1 onion, halved lengthways
 and sliced
25g/1oz fresh root ginger, peeled
 and grated
5ml/1 tsp sugar
130g/4½oz fresh peas, shelled,
 or frozen peas
5ml/1 tsp salt

1 Rinse the rice and put it in a bowl. Cover with plenty of water and leave to soak for 30 minutes. Drain thoroughly.

2 Heat the ghee, or oil and butter, in a heavy pan. Stir in the cinnamon stick, cardamom and cloves.

3 Add the onion, ginger and sugar to the pan, and fry until golden, stirring frequently. Add the peas, followed by the rice, and stir for 1 minute to coat the rice in ghee.

4 Pour in 600ml/1 pint/2½ cups water. Add the salt, stir once and bring the liquid to the boil. Reduce the heat and allow to simmer for 15–20 minutes, until the liquid has been absorbed.

5 Turn off the heat, cover the pan with a clean dish towel and the lid, and leave the rice to steam for a further 10 minutes. Spoon the rice on to a serving dish.

Variations
• This dish also works with diced carrot or beetroot (beet), or chickpeas. You can also add a little tomato purée (paste) to give the rice a red tinge.
• Sprinkle the rice with chopped fresh mint and coriander (cilantro), if you like, or with roasted chilli and coconut.

Sweet-and-Sour Rice

This popular Middle Eastern rice dish is flavoured with fruit and spices. Zereshk are small dried berries – use cranberries as a substitute.

Serves 4
50g/2oz/½ cup zereshk or
    fresh cranberries
45g/1½oz/3 tbsp butter

50g/2oz/⅓ cup raisins
50g/2oz/¼ cup sugar
5ml/1 tsp ground cinnamon
5ml/1 tsp ground cumin
350g/12oz/1¾ cups basmati
    rice, soaked
2–3 saffron strands, soaked in
    15ml/1 tbsp boiling water
pinch of salt

1 Thoroughly wash the zereshk or cranberries in cold water at least four or five times to rinse off any bits of grit. Drain well. Melt 15g/½oz/1 tbsp of the butter in a heavy frying pan and fry the raisins for 1–2 minutes.

2 Add the zereshk or cranberries, fry for a few seconds, and then add the sugar, with half of the cinnamon and cumin. Cook briefly and then set aside.

3 Drain the rice, then put it in a pan with plenty of boiling, lightly salted water. Bring back to the boil, reduce the heat and simmer for 4 minutes. Drain and rinse once again.

4 Melt half the remaining butter in the cleaned rice pan, add 15ml/1 tbsp water and stir in half the rice. Sprinkle with half the raisin mixture and top with all but 45ml/3 tbsp of the rice. Sprinkle over the remaining raisin mixture.

5 Mix the remaining cinnamon and cumin with the reserved rice, and sprinkle this mixture evenly over the layered mixture. Melt the remaining butter, drizzle it over the surface, then cover the pan with a clean dish towel. Cover with a tight-fitting lid, lifting the corners of the cloth back over the lid. Steam the rice over a very low heat for 20–30 minutes.

6 Just before serving, mix 45ml/3 tbsp of the rice with the saffron water. Spoon the sweet and sour rice on to a large, flat serving dish and sprinkle the saffron rice over the top, to garnish.

Tanzanian Vegetable Rice

Serve this tasty dish with baked chicken or fish. Add the vegetables near the end of cooking so that they remain crisp.

Serves 4
350g/12oz/1¾ cups basmati rice
45ml/3 tbsp vegetable oil
1 onion, chopped

2 garlic cloves, crushed
750ml/1¼ pints/3 cups vegetable
    stock or water
115g/4oz/⅔ cup fresh or drained
    canned corn kernels
½ red or green (bell) pepper,
    seeded and chopped
1 large carrot, grated
fresh chervil sprigs,
    to garnish

1 Rinse the rice in a sieve (strainer) under cold running water until the water runs clear. Set it aside in the sieve to drain thoroughly for about 15 minutes.

2 Heat the oil in a large pan or wok and fry the chopped onion for a few minutes over a medium heat, stirring frequently, until it starts to soften.

3 Add the rice to the pan and fry for about 10 minutes, stirring constantly to prevent the rice sticking to the bottom of the pan. Then stir in the crushed garlic.

4 Pour the stock or water into the pan and stir well. Bring to the boil, then lower the heat, cover the pan with a tight-fitting lid and simmer for 10 minutes.

5 Sprinkle the corn kernels over the rice, then spread the chopped pepper on top. Sprinkle over the grated carrot.

6 Cover the pan tightly. Steam over a low heat for about 15 minutes or until the rice is tender, then mix with a fork, pile on to a platter and garnish with chervil. Serve immediately.

Variation
You can replace the corn with the same quantity of fresh or frozen peas, if you prefer.

Sweet and Sour Rice Energy 465kcal/1943kJ; Protein 7g; Carbohydrate 87g, of which sugars 17.2g; Fat 9.8g, of which saturates 5.9g; Cholesterol 24mg; Calcium 32mg; Fibre 0.6g; Sodium 77mg.
Tanzanian Rice Energy 552kcal/2305kJ; Protein 12.7g; Carbohydrate 108.3g; of which sugars 4.8g; Fat 7g; of which saturates 1g; Cholesterol 0mg; Calcium 43mg; Fibre 3g; Sodium 10mg.

Naan

Probably the most popular bread enjoyed with an Indian curry is naan, which was introduced from Persia. Traditionally, naan is not rolled, but patted and stretched until the teardrop shape is achieved. You can, of course, roll it out to a circle, then gently pull the lower end, which will give you the traditional shape.

Makes 3

225g/8oz/2 cups unbleached
  strong white bread flour
2.5ml/½ tsp salt
15g/½ oz fresh yeast
60ml/4 tbsp milk, heated
  until lukewarm
15ml/1 tbsp vegetable oil
30ml/2 tbsp natural (plain) yogurt
1 egg, beaten
30–45ml/2–3 tbsp melted ghee
  or butter, for brushing

1 Sift the flour and salt together into a large bowl. In a smaller bowl, cream the yeast with the milk. Set aside for 15 minutes.

2 Add the yeast and milk mixture, vegetable oil, yogurt and egg to the flour. Combine the mixture using your hands until it forms a soft dough. Add a little lukewarm water if the dough is too dry.

3 Turn the dough out on to a lightly floured surface and knead for about 10 minutes, or until it feels smooth. Return the dough to the bowl, cover and leave in a warm place for about 1 hour, or until it has doubled in size. Preheat the oven to its highest setting – it should not be any lower than 230°C/450°F/Gas 8.

4 Turn out the dough back on to the floured surface and knead for a further 2 minutes. Divide into three equal pieces, shape into balls and roll out into teardrop shapes 25cm/10in long, 13cm/5in wide and 5mm–8mm/¼–⅓in thick.

5 Preheat the grill (broiler) to its highest setting. Meanwhile, place the naan on preheated baking sheets and bake for 3–4 minutes, or until puffed up.

6 Place under the hot grill for a few seconds until the tops brown. Brush with ghee or butter and serve warm.

Garlic and Coriander Naan

Traditionally cooked in a very hot clay oven known as a tandoor, naan are usually eaten with dry meat or vegetable dishes.

Makes 3

275g/10oz/2½ cups unbleached
  strong white bread flour
5ml/1 tsp salt

5ml/1 tsp dried yeast
60ml/4 tbsp natural (plain) yogurt
15ml/1 tbsp melted butter or
  ghee, plus 30–45ml/2–3 tbsp
  for brushing
1 garlic clove, finely chopped
5ml/1 tsp black onion seeds
15ml/1 tbsp chopped fresh
  coriander (cilantro)
10ml/2 tsp clear honey, warmed

1 Sift the flour and salt together into a large bowl. In a smaller bowl, cream the yeast with the yogurt. Set aside for 15 minutes. Add the yeast mixture to the flour with the smaller quantity of melted butter or ghee, and add the chopped garlic, black onion seeds and chopped coriander, mixing to a soft dough.

2 Transfer the dough on to a lightly floured surface and knead for about 10 minutes until smooth and elastic. Place in a lightly oiled bowl, cover with lightly oiled clear film (plastic wrap) and leave to rise in a warm place for about 45 minutes, or until the dough has doubled in bulk.

3 Preheat the oven to 230°C/450°F/Gas 8. Place three heavy baking sheets in the oven to heat. Turn the dough out on to a lightly floured surface and knock back (punch down). Divide into three equal pieces and shape each into a ball.

4 Cover two of the balls of dough with oiled clear film and roll out the third into a teardrop shape about 25cm/10in long, 13cm/5in wide and about 5mm–8mm/¼–⅓in thick. Preheat the grill (broiler) to its highest setting. Place the single naan on a hot baking sheet and bake for about 3–4 minutes, or until it has puffed up.

5 Remove the naan from the oven, brush with honey and grill for a few seconds or until browned slightly. Wrap in a clean dish towel to keep warm while you roll out and cook the remaining naan. Brush with melted butter or ghee and serve warm.

Naan Energy 315kcal/1334kJ; Protein 9.4g; Carbohydrate 58.5g, of which sugars 1.5g; Fat 6.5g, of which saturates 1.1g; Cholesterol 63mg; Calcium 123mg; Fibre 2.3g; Sodium 356mg.
Garlic Naan Energy 374kcal/1585kJ; Protein 10.4g; Carbohydrate 74.2g, of which sugars 2.9g; Fat 6.1g, of which saturates 3g; Cholesterol 11mg; Calcium 176mg; Fibre 2.8g; Sodium 706mg.

Red Lentil Pancakes

This is a type of *dosa*, which is essentially a pancake from southern India, but it is used in a similar fashion to north Indian bread.

Makes 6

150g/5oz/³/₄ cup long
  grain rice
50g/2oz/¹/₄ cup red split lentils
250ml/8fl oz/1 cup warm water
5ml/1 tsp salt
2.5ml/¹/₂ tsp ground turmeric
2.5ml/¹/₂ tsp ground black pepper
30ml/2 tbsp chopped fresh
  coriander (cilantro)
vegetable oil, for frying
  and drizzling

1 Place the rice and lentils in a large bowl, cover with the warm water, cover and soak for at least 8 hours or overnight.

2 Drain off the water and reserve. Place the rice and lentils in a food processor or blender and blend until smooth. Blend in the reserved soaking water. Scrape into a bowl, cover tightly with clear film (plastic wrap) and leave in a warm place to ferment for about 24 hours.

3 Stir the salt, turmeric, black pepper and coriander into the rice mixture. Heat a heavy frying pan over medium heat for a few minutes until hot. Smear the pan with oil and add about 30–45ml/2–3 tbsp of the batter mixture.

4 Using the rounded base of a soup spoon, gently spread the batter out, using a circular motion, to make a pancake that is about 15cm/6in in diameter.

5 Cook in the pan for 1¹/₂–2 minutes, or until set. Drizzle a little oil over the pancake and around the edges. Turn over and cook for about 1 minute, or until golden brown. Keep the cooked pancakes warm in a low oven or on a plate over simmering water while cooking the remaining pancakes. Serve warm.

> **Variation**
> *Add 60ml/4 tbsp grated coconut to the batter just before cooking to create a richer flavour.*

Missi Rotis

These delicious unleavened breads are a speciality from Punjab in India. Gram flour, also known as besan, is made from ground chickpeas and is combined here with the traditional wheat flour.

Makes 4

115g/4oz/1 cup gram flour
115g/4oz/1 cup wholemeal
  (whole-wheat) flour
1 fresh green chilli, seeded
  and chopped
¹/₂ onion, finely chopped
15ml/1 tbsp chopped fresh
  coriander (cilantro)
2.5ml/¹/₂ tsp ground turmeric
2.5ml/¹/₂ tsp salt
15ml/1 tbsp vegetable oil or
  melted butter
120–150ml/4–5fl oz/¹/₂– ²/₃ cup
  lukewarm water
30–45ml/2–3 tbsp melted
  unsalted butter or ghee

1 Mix the two types of flour, chilli, onion, coriander, turmeric and salt together in a large mixing bowl. Stir in the 15ml/1 tbsp vegetable oil or melted butter.

2 Mix sufficient water into the mixture to make a pliable soft dough. Turn out the dough on to a lightly floured surface and knead with your hands until smooth.

3 Place in a lightly oiled bowl, cover with lightly oiled clear film (plastic wrap) and leave to rest for 30 minutes.

4 Turn the dough out on to a lightly floured surface. Divide the dough into four equal pieces and shape into balls in the palms of your hands. Roll out each ball into a thick round about 15–18cm/6–7in in diameter.

5 Heat a griddle or heavy frying pan over medium heat for a few minutes until hot. Brush both sides of one roti with some melted butter or ghee. Add it to the griddle or frying pan and cook for about 2 minutes, turning after 1 minute.

6 Brush the cooked roti lightly with melted butter or ghee again, slide it on to a plate and keep warm in a low oven while cooking the remaining rotis in the same way. Serve the rotis immediately while still warm.

Red Lentil Pancakes Energy 153kcal/641kJ; Protein 4.1g; Carbohydrate 25.1g, of which sugars 0.3g; Fat 4.1g, of which saturates 0.4g; Cholesterol 0mg; Calcium 21mg; Fibre 0.7g; Sodium 333mg.
Missi Rotis Energy 298kcal/1267kJ; Protein 8.5g; Carbohydrate 65.8g, of which sugars 1.6g; Fat 2g, of which saturates 0.3g; Cholesterol 0mg; Calcium 114mg; Fibre 3.2g; Sodium 3mg.

Stuffed Indian Bananas with Coriander and Cumin

Bananas are cooked with spices including coriander and cumin in many different ways in India. Green bananas are available from Indian stores or use plantains or unripe eating bananas.

Serves 4
4 green bananas or plantains
30ml/2 tbsp ground coriander
15ml/1 tbsp ground cumin
5ml/1 tsp chilli powder
2.5ml/½ tsp salt
1.5ml/¼ tsp ground turmeric
5ml/1 tsp sugar
15ml/1 tbsp gram flour
45ml/3 tbsp chopped fresh coriander (cilantro), plus extra sprigs to garnish
90ml/6 tbsp vegetable oil
1.5ml/¼ tsp cumin seeds
1.5ml/¼ tsp black mustard seeds
warm chapatis, to serve

1 Trim the bananas or plantains and cut each crossways into three pieces, leaving the skin on. Make a lengthwise slit along each piece, without cutting all the way through the flesh.

2 On a plate, mix together the ground coriander, cumin, chilli powder, salt, turmeric, sugar, gram flour, chopped fresh coriander and 15ml/1 tbsp of the oil. Use your fingers to combine well. Carefully stuff each piece of banana with the spice mixture, taking care not to break the bananas in half.

3 Heat the remaining oil in a wok, karahi or large pan, and fry the cumin and mustard seeds for 2 minutes or until they begin to splutter and release their fragrances.

4 Add the bananas and toss gently in the oil. Cover and simmer over a low heat for 15 minutes, stirring from time to time, until the bananas are soft but not mushy. Garnish with the fresh coriander sprigs, and serve with warm chapatis, if you like.

Variation
Baby courgettes (zucchini) would make a delicious alternative to bananas in this dish.

Stuffed Okra with Ginger, Cumin and Chilli

The Gujarati community excels in the art of vegetarian cooking. Stuffed okra is easy to make.

Serves 4–6
225g/8oz large okra
15ml/1 tbsp amchur (dry mango powder)
2.5ml/½ tsp ground ginger
2.5ml/½ tsp ground cumin
2.5ml/½ tsp hot chilli powder (optional)
2.5ml/½ tsp ground turmeric
vegetable oil or groundnut (peanut) oil, for frying and mixing
30ml/2 tbsp cornflour (cornstarch), placed in a plastic bag
salt

1 Wash the okra, and trim off the tips and discard. Make a slit lengthwise in the centre of each okra, taking care not to cut all the way through the pod.

2 In a bowl, mix the amchur, ginger, cumin, chilli, if using, turmeric and salt with a few drops of vegetable oil. Leave the mixture to rest for 1–2 hours or refrigerate overnight.

3 Using your fingers, part the slit of each okra carefully without opening it all the way and, using a small spoon, fill each with as much filling as possible. Put all the okra into the plastic bag with the cornflour, hold the top closed and shake the bag carefully to cover all the okra evenly.

4 Fill a wok, karahi or large pan with enough oil to sit 2.5cm/1in deep. Heat the oil and fry the okra in small batches for 5–8 minutes or until they are brown and slightly crisp. Serve hot with any meat, poultry or fish curry.

Cook's Tip
When buying okra, choose pods without any blemishes or damage. Wash them thoroughly, rubbing each one gently with a soft vegetable brush or your fingertips.

Stuffed Indian Bananas Energy 268kcal/1122kJ; Protein 3.1g; Carbohydrate 39.6g, of which sugars 26.3g; Fat 11.9g, of which saturates 1.5g; Cholesterol 0mg; Calcium 30mg; Fibre 1.8g; Sodium 3mg.
Stuffed Okra Energy 176kcal/734kJ; Protein 1.7g; Carbohydrate 15.5g, of which sugars 1.4g; Fat 12.4g, of which saturates 1.6g; Cholesterol 0mg; Calcium 92mg; Fibre 2.3g; Sodium 12mg.

Sweet-and-sour Pineapple

This may sound like a Chinese recipe, but it is a traditional Bengali dish. The predominant flavour is ginger, and the pieces of golden pineapple, dotted with plump, juicy raisins, have plenty of visual appeal with a taste to match.

Serves 4
800g/1¾lb pineapple rings or
  chunks in natural juice

15ml/1 tbsp vegetable oil or
  sunflower oil
2.5ml/½ tsp black mustard seeds
2.5ml/½ tsp cumin seeds
2.5ml/½ tsp onion seeds
10ml/2 tsp grated fresh
  root ginger
5ml/1 tsp crushed dried chillies,
  seeds removed (optional)
50g/2oz/⅓ cup seedless raisins
115g/4oz/generous ½ cup sugar
7.5ml/1½ tsp salt

1 Drain the pineapple in a sieve (strainer) and reserve the juice. Chop the pineapple rings or chunks finely (you should have approximately 500g/1¼lb).

2 Heat the vegetable oil in a wok, karahi or large pan over a medium heat and immediately add the mustard seeds. As soon as they pop, add the cumin seeds, then the onion seeds. Add the ginger and chillies and stir-fry the spices briskly for 30 seconds until they release their flavours.

3 Add the pineapple, raisins, sugar and salt to the pan. Pour in about 300ml/½ pint/1¼ cups of the juice (make up with cold water if necessary) and add to the pineapple.

4 Bring the mixture to the boil, reduce the heat to medium and cook, uncovered, for 20–25 minutes. Serve hot.

Variation
Two or three mangoes can be used for this dish instead of the pineapple, if you prefer. Choose ripe fruits that will be full of flavour. To prepare, cut off both sides of the fruit, keeping close to the stone (pit), then peel off the skin and chop the flesh into chunks. Canned mangoes in natural juice could also be used.

Chilli and Mustard Pineapple

Pineapple is cooked with coconut milk and a blend of spices in this South Indian dish, which could be served with any meat, fish or vegetable curry. The chilli adds heat, and the mustard seeds lend a nutty flavour that complements the sweet pineapple.

Serves 4
1 pineapple
50ml/2fl oz/¼ cup water
150ml/¼ pint/⅔ cup
  coconut milk

2.5ml/½ tsp ground turmeric
2.5ml/½ tsp crushed dried
  red chillies
5ml/1 tsp salt
10ml/2 tsp sugar
15ml/1 tbsp groundnut
  (peanut) oil or vegetable oil
2.5ml/½ tsp mustard seeds
2.5ml/½ tsp cumin seeds
1 small onion or ½ large onion,
  finely chopped
1–2 dried red chillies, seeded
  and broken up
6–8 curry leaves

1 Halve the pineapple lengthways and cut each half into two, so that you end up with four boat-shaped pieces. Peel them and remove the eyes and the central core and discard. Cut the flesh into bitesize pieces.

2 Put the pineapple in a wok, karahi or large pan and add the measured water, with the coconut milk, turmeric and crushed chillies. Bring to a slow simmer over a low heat, and cook, covered, for 10–12 minutes, or until the pineapple is just soft, but do not let it go mushy.

3 Add the salt and sugar to the pineapple, and cook, uncovered, until the sauce thickens.

4 Heat the oil in a second pan, and add the mustard seeds. As soon as they begin to pop, add the cumin seeds and the onion. Fry for 6–7 minutes, stirring regularly, until the onion is soft.

5 Add the broken up dried red chillies and the curry leaves to the pan. Fry for about 1–2 minutes and pour the entire contents over the pineapple. Stir well, then remove from the heat. Serve hot or cold, but not chilled.

Sweet-and-sour Pineapple Energy 215kcal/915kJ; Protein 1.2g; Carbohydrate 55.7g, of which sugars 55.6g; Fat 0.1g, of which saturates 0g; Cholesterol 0mg; Calcium 38mg; Fibre 1.4g; Sodium 5mg.
Chilli Pineapple Energy 138kcal/584kJ; Protein 1.5g; Carbohydrate 26.7g, of which sugars 25.5g; Fat 3.6g, of which saturates 0.5g; Cholesterol 0mg; Calcium 57mg; Fibre 2.6g; Sodium 47mg.

Mixed Vegetables in a Spicy Coconut Broth

There are many ways to make a vegetable curry, but this recipe, in which the vegetables are simmered in coconut milk, is typical of South India. This cross between a soup and stew is perfect for a vegetarian lunch, with warm naan bread or soft chapatis as an accompaniment.

Serves 4

225g/8oz potatoes, cut into
   5cm/2in cubes
125g/4oz/³⁄4 cup green beans
150g/5oz carrots, cut into chunks
500ml/17fl oz/2¹⁄4 cups
   vegetable stock or water
1 small aubergine (eggplant),
   about 225g/8oz,
   quartered lengthwise
75g/3oz coconut milk powder
5ml/1 tsp salt, or to taste
30ml/2 tbsp vegetable oil
6–8 fresh or 8–10 dried
   curry leaves
1–2 dried red chillies, chopped
   into small pieces
5ml/1 tsp ground cumin
5ml/1 tsp ground coriander
2.5ml/¹⁄2 tsp ground turmeric

1 Put the potatoes, beans and carrots in a large pan and add 300ml/¹⁄2 pint/1¹⁄4 cups of the stock or water. Bring to the boil. Reduce the heat a little, cover the pan and cook for 5 minutes.

2 Cut the aubergine quarters into pieces about 5cm/2in thick and add them to the pan.

3 Blend the coconut milk powder with the remaining hot water and add it to the soup with the salt. Bring to a slow simmer, cover and cook for 6–7 minutes.

4 In a small pan, heat the vegetable oil over a medium heat and add the curry leaves and the chillies. Immediately follow with the cumin, coriander and turmeric. Cook the spices for about 30–40 seconds, stirring frequently.

5 Pour the entire contents of the pan over the vegetables. Stir to distribute the spices evenly and remove the pan from the heat. Ladle the soup into warmed bowls and serve piping hot, with any naan bread or soft chapatis.

Masala Beans with Fenugreek and Coriander

The term masala refers to the blending of several spices to achieve a distinctive taste, with different spice-combinations being used to complement specific ingredients.

Serves 4

1 onion
5ml/1 tsp ground cumin
5ml/1 tsp ground coriander
5ml/1 tsp sesame seeds
5ml/1 tsp chilli powder
2.5ml/¹⁄2 tsp crushed garlic
1.5ml/¹⁄4 tsp ground turmeric
5ml/1 tsp salt
30ml/2 tbsp vegetable oil
1 tomato, quartered
225g/8oz/1¹⁄2 cups green
   beans, blanched
1 bunch fresh fenugreek leaves,
   stems discarded
60ml/4 tbsp chopped fresh
   coriander (cilantro)
15ml/1 tbsp lemon juice

1 Roughly chop the onion. Mix together the cumin and coriander, sesame seeds, chilli powder, garlic, turmeric and salt.

2 Put the chopped onion and spice mixture into a food processor or blender, and process for about 30–45 seconds until you have a rough paste.

3 In a wok, karahi or large pan, heat the oil over a medium heat and fry the spice paste for 5 minutes, stirring occasionally.

4 Add the tomato quarters, blanched green beans, fresh fenugreek and chopped coriander.

5 Stir-fry the contents of the pan for about 5 minutes, then sprinkle in the lemon juice and serve.

Variation
Instead of fresh fenugreek, you can also use 15ml/1 tbsp dried fenugreek for this recipe. Dried fenugreek is readily available from Indian stores and markets. It may be sold by its Indian name, kasuri methi.

Vegetables in Coconut Energy 80kcal/335kJ; Protein 1.2g; Carbohydrate 5.6g, of which sugars 5.3g; Fat 6.1g, of which saturates 0.9g; Cholesterol 0mg; Calcium 29mg; Fibre 2.3g; Sodium 71mg.
Masala Beans Energy 72kcal/295kJ; Protein 1.6g; Carbohydrate 2.9g, of which sugars 2.4g; Fat 6g, of which saturates 0.9g; Cholesterol 0mg; Calcium 47mg; Fibre 2.1g; Sodium 6mg.

Spicy Glazed Pumpkin with Coconut Sauce

Pumpkins, butternut squash and winter melons can all be cooked in this way. Throughout Vietnam and Cambodia, variations of this sweet, mellow dish are often served as an accompaniment to rice or a spicy curry.

Serves 4
200ml/7fl oz/scant 1 cup
  coconut milk
15ml/1 tbsp nuoc mam or
  tuk trey
30ml/2 tbsp palm sugar (jaggery)
30ml/2 tbsp groundnut
  (peanut) oil
4 garlic cloves, finely chopped
25g/1oz fresh root ginger, peeled
  and finely shredded
675g/1½lb pumpkin flesh, cubed
ground black pepper
a handful of curry or basil leaves,
  to garnish
chilli oil, for drizzling
fried onion rings, to garnish
plain boiled or coconut rice,
  to serve

1 In a bowl, beat the coconut milk and the nuoc mam or tuk trey with the sugar, until it has dissolved. Set aside.

2 Heat the oil in a wok or heavy pan and stir in the garlic and ginger. Stir-fry until they begin to colour, then stir in the pumpkin cubes, mixing well to combine.

3 Pour in the coconut milk and mix well. Reduce the heat, cover and simmer for about 20 minutes, until the pumpkin is tender and the sauce has reduced.

4 Season with pepper and garnish with curry or basil leaves and fried onion rings. Serve hot with plain or coconut rice, drizzled with a little chilli oil.

> **Cook's Tip**
> *Nuoc mam is a fish sauce popular in Vietnam and Cambodia. It is made from salted and fermented small fish. Tuk trey is another fish sauce from the region featuring other ingredients such as vinegar, lime juice, sugar and garlic.*

Malay Pak Choi in Spiced Coconut Milk

The abundant vegetables of Malaysia are often cooked in coconut milk. The style of this dish is sweet and rich, with plentiful use of shrimp paste, which is a key ingredient. For this dish, you could use green beans, curly kale, or any type of cabbage, all of which are delicious served with steamed, braised or spicy fish dishes.

Serves 4
4 shallots, chopped
2 garlic cloves, peeled and
  finely chopped
1 lemon grass stalk, trimmed
  and chopped
25g/1oz fresh root ginger, peeled
  and chopped
2 red chillies, seeded and
  finely chopped
5ml/1 tsp shrimp paste
5ml/1 tsp ground turmeric
5ml/1 tsp palm sugar (jaggery)
15ml/1 tbsp sesame or groundnut
  (peanut) oil
400ml/14fl oz/1⅔ cups
  coconut milk
450g/1lb pak choi (bok choy),
  separated into leaves
salt and ground black pepper

1 Using a mortar and pestle or food processor, grind the shallots, garlic, lemon grass, ginger and chillies to a paste. Beat in the shrimp paste, turmeric and sugar.

2 Heat the oil in a wok or heavy pan, and stir in the spice paste. Cook for 2 minutes until fragrant and beginning to colour.

3 Pour in the coconut milk, mix well, and let it bubble away over a medium to high heat until it thickens.

4 Drop in the cabbage leaves, coating them in the coconut milk, and cook for a minute or two until wilted. Season to taste with salt and pepper and serve immediately.

> **Variation**
> *Make the dish using Chinese leaves (Chinese cabbage) or kale, cut into thick ribbons, or a mixture of the two.*

Fiery Bean Stew with Chillies and Coconut Milk

This curry is from the Philippines, which is well renowned for its fiery food. In typical style, this rich, pungent dish is hot, and it is served with extra chillies to chew on.

Serves 3–4

30–45ml/2–3 tbsp coconut or groundnut (peanut) oil
1 onion, finely chopped
2–3 garlic cloves, finely chopped
40g/1½oz fresh root ginger, finely chopped
1 lemon grass stalk, finely chopped
4–5 red chillies, seeded and finely chopped

15–30ml/1–2 tbsp bagoong or 15ml/1 tbsp shrimp paste
15–30ml/1–2 tbsp tamarind paste
15–30ml/1–2 tbsp palm sugar (jaggery)
2 x 400g/14oz cans unsweetened coconut milk
4 kaffir lime leaves
500g/1¼lb yard-long beans
salt and ground black pepper
1 bunch of fresh coriander (cilantro) leaves, roughly chopped, to garnish

To serve

cooked rice
raw chillies

1 Heat the oil in a wok or large, heavy frying pan that has a lid. Stir in the onion, garlic, ginger, lemon grass and chillies and fry until fragrant and beginning to colour. Add the bagoong or shrimp paste, tamarind paste and sugar to the pan and stir in the coconut milk and lime leaves.

2 Bring the mixture to the boil, reduce the heat and toss in the whole beans. Partially cover the pan and cook the beans gently for 6–8 minutes until tender. Season the stew with salt and pepper to taste and sprinkle with chopped coriander to garnish. Serve with rice and extra chillies to chew on.

> **Cook's Tip**
> If you prefer, you can reduce the quantity of chillies used in the recipe to suit your taste buds and you do not have to serve the stew with extra chillies if you don't want to.

Corn on the Cob in Onion Curry Sauce

Corn is grown extensively in the Punjab region, where it is used in many delicacies. Here, corn is cooked in a thick rich onion sauce in this classic Punjabi dish. It is excellent served with naan bread or other Indian breads on the side.

Serves 4–6

4 corn cobs, thawed if frozen
vegetable oil, for frying

1 large onion, finely chopped
2 cloves garlic, crushed
5cm/2in piece fresh root ginger, crushed
2.5ml/½ tsp ground turmeric
2.5ml/½ tsp onion seeds
2.5ml/½ tsp cumin seeds
2.5ml/½ tsp five-spice powder
6–8 curry leaves
2.5ml/½ tsp sugar
200ml/7fl oz/scant 1 cup natural (plain) yogurt
chilli powder, to taste

1 Cut each corn cob in half, using a heavy knife or cleaver to make clean cuts. Heat the oil in a wok, karahi or large pan and fry the corn until golden brown, stirring occasionally. Remove the corn from the pan and keep warm.

2 Remove any excess oil, leaving about 30ml/2 tbsp in the wok. Grind the onion, garlic and ginger to a paste using a mortar and pestle, a food processor or a blender.

3 Transfer the onion paste to a bowl and add the spices, chilli powder, curry leaves and sugar. Mix well to ensure all the ingredients are combined.

4 Heat the oil gently and fry the onion paste mixture for about 8–10 minutes until all the spices have blended well and the oil separates from the sauce.

5 Set aside the mixture to cool a little and then fold in the yogurt. Mix to a smooth sauce.

6 Reheat the sauce over a low heat for about 10–12 minutes. Place the corn in a warmed serving dish and pour the sauce over it. Serve immediately while hot.

Fiery Bean Stew Energy 200kcal/840kJ; Protein 5.5g; Carbohydrate 24.4g, of which sugars 22.9g; Fat 9.7g, of which saturates 1.5g; Cholesterol 19mg; Calcium 158mg; Fibre 3.4g; Sodium 384mg.
Corn on the Cob Energy 164kcal/689kJ; Protein 4.2g; Carbohydrate 20.1g, of which sugars 4g; Fat 8g, of which saturates 1.1g; Cholesterol 0mg; Calcium 19mg; Fibre 2g; Sodium 44mg.

Stir-fried Crispy Tofu with Asparagus

Asparagus is not only elegant but also delicious. This fabulous Thai dish is the perfect side dish to serve at a dinner party.

Serves 2

250g/9oz deep-fried tofu cubes
30ml/2 tbsp groundnut (peanut) oil
15ml/1 tbsp Thai green
   curry paste
30ml/2 tbsp light soy sauce
2 kaffir lime leaves, rolled into
   cylinders and then thinly sliced
30ml/2 tbsp sugar
150ml/¼ pint/⅔ cup
   vegetable stock
250g/9oz Asian asparagus,
   trimmed and sliced into
   5cm/2in lengths
30ml/2 tbsp roasted peanuts,
   finely chopped

1 Preheat the grill (broiler) to medium. Place the tofu cubes in a grill pan and grill (broil) for 2–3 minutes, then turn them over and continue to cook until they are crisp and golden brown all over. Watch them carefully; they must not be allowed to burn.

2 Heat the oil in a wok or heavy frying pan. Add the green curry paste and cook over a medium heat, stirring constantly, for 1–2 minutes, until it gives off its aroma.

3 Stir the soy sauce, lime leaves, sugar and vegetable stock into the wok or pan and mix well. Bring to the boil, then reduce the heat to low so that the mixture is just simmering.

4 Add the asparagus and simmer gently for 5 minutes. Meanwhile, chop each piece of tofu into four pieces, then add to the pan along with the peanuts.

5 Toss to coat all the ingredients in the sauce, then spoon into a warmed dish and serve immediately.

> **Variation**
> Substitute slim carrot batons, baby leeks or small broccoli florets for the Asian asparagus, if you like.

Southern Thai Curried Vegetables with Coconut

Rich curry flavours are found in the food of Thailand, where many dishes are made with coconut milk and spiced with turmeric.

Serves 4

90g/3½oz Chinese leaves
   (Chinese cabbage), shredded
90g/3½oz beansprouts
90g/3½oz/scant 1 cup green
   beans, trimmed
100g/3½oz broccoli florets
15ml/1 tbsp sesame
   seeds, toasted

For the sauce
60ml/4 tbsp coconut cream
5ml/1 tsp Thai red curry paste
90g/3½oz/1¼ cups oyster
   mushrooms or field (portabello)
   mushrooms, sliced
60ml/4 tbsp coconut milk
5ml/1 tsp ground turmeric
5ml/1 tsp thick tamarind juice,
   made by mixing tamarind
   paste with a little warm water
juice of ½ lemon
60ml/4 tbsp light soy sauce
5ml/1 tsp palm sugar (jaggery) or
   light muscovado (brown) sugar

1 Blanch the shredded Chinese leaves, beansprouts, green beans and broccoli in boiling water for 1 minute per batch. Drain, place in a bowl and leave to cool.

2 To make the sauce, pour the coconut cream into a wok or frying pan and heat gently for 2–3 minutes, until it separates. Stir in the red curry paste. Cook over a low heat for 30 seconds.

3 Increase the heat, add the mushrooms and cook for a further 2–3 minutes. Pour in the coconut milk and stir in the turmeric, tamarind juice, lemon juice, soy sauce and sugar.

4 Pour the mixture over the prepared vegetables and toss well to combine. Sprinkle with the toasted sesame seeds and serve.

> **Cook's Tip**
> To make coconut cream use a carton or can of coconut milk. Skim the cream off the top and cook 60ml/4 tbsp of it before adding the paste. Add the measured milk later, as in the recipe.

Stir-fried Tofu Energy 287kcal/1195kJ; Protein 14.3g; Carbohydrate 20.3g, of which sugars 19.5g; Fat 17g, of which saturates 2.1g; Cholesterol 0mg; Calcium 682mg; Fibre 2.2g; Sodium 1075mg.
Southern Thai Vegetables Energy 162kcal/672kJ; Protein 5g; Carbohydrate 6.3g, of which sugars 5.4g; Fat 13.2g, of which saturates 9.4g; Cholesterol 0mg; Calcium 75mg; Fibre 2.5g; Sodium 1096mg.

Spiced Pumpkin Wedges and Sautéed Spinach

Warmly spiced roasted pumpkin, combined with creamy spinach and the fire of chilli, makes a lovely accompaniment for curries, grills and roasts.

Serves 4–6
10ml/2 tsp coriander seeds
5ml/1 tsp cumin seeds
5ml/1 tsp fennel seeds
5–10ml/1–2 tsp cinnamon
2 dried red chillies, chopped
coarse salt
2 garlic cloves
30ml/2 tbsp olive oil
1 medium pumpkin, halved,
   seeded, cut into 6–8 wedges

For the sautéed spinach
30–45ml/2–3 tbsp pine nuts
30–45ml/2–3 tbsp olive oil
1 red onion, halved and sliced
1–2 dried red chillies, finely sliced
1 apple, peeled, cored and sliced
2 garlic cloves, crushed
5–10ml/1–2 tsp ground
   roasted cumin
10ml/2 tsp clear honey
450g/1lb spinach, steamed and
   roughly chopped
60–75ml/4–5 tbsp double
   (heavy) cream
salt and ground black pepper
a handful of fresh spinach leaves,
   to garnish

1 Preheat the oven to 200°C/400°F/Gas 6. Grind the coriander, cumin and fennel seeds, cinnamon and chillies with a little coarse salt in a mortar with a pestle. Add the garlic and a little of the olive oil and pound to form a paste. Rub the spice mixture over the pumpkin segments and place them, skin side down, in an ovenproof dish or roasting pan. Bake the spiced pumpkin for 35–40 minutes, or until tender.

2 To make the spinach, roast the pine nuts in a dry frying pan until golden, then transfer on to a plate. Add the olive oil to the pan. Sauté the onion with the chilli until soft, then stir in the apple and garlic. Once the apple begins to colour, stir in most of the pine nuts, most of the cumin and the honey.

3 Toss in the spinach and, once it has heated through, stir in most of the cream. Season to taste and remove from the heat. Swirl the last of the cream on top, sprinkle with the reserved pine nuts and roasted cumin, and spinach leaves. Serve hot.

Spiced Coconut Mushrooms

Here is a simple and delicious way to cook mushrooms. They can be served with almost any Indian meal as well as with traditional grilled or roasted meats and poultry.

Serves 4
30ml/2 tbsp groundnut
   (peanut) oil
2 garlic cloves, finely chopped

2 fresh red chillies, seeded
   and sliced into rings
3 shallots or 1 small onion,
   finely chopped
225g/8oz/3 cups brown cap
   (cremini) mushrooms,
   thickly sliced
150ml/¼ pint/⅔ cup
   coconut milk
30ml/2 tbsp chopped fresh
   coriander (cilantro)
salt and ground black pepper

1 Heat a karahi, wok or heavy frying pan until hot, add the groundnut oil and swirl it around. Add the garlic and chillies, then stir-fry for a few seconds.

2 Add the chopped shallots or onion and cook them for about 2–3 minutes, stirring constantly, until softened. Add the mushrooms and stir-fry for 3 minutes.

3 Pour the coconut milk into the pan and bring to the boil. Boil rapidly over high heat until the liquid has reduced by about half and has thickened to coat the mushrooms. Season to taste with salt and black pepper.

4 Sprinkle over the chopped fresh coriander and toss the mushrooms gently to mix. Serve immediately.

Variations
• You can use chopped fresh chives instead of chopped fresh coriander (cilantro), if you wish.
• White (button) mushrooms or field (portabello) mushrooms would also work well in this dish instead of the brown cap (cremini) mushrooms.
• Sprinkle some chopped toasted cashew nuts over the mushrooms before serving, if you like.

Pumpkin Energy 456kcal/1897kJ; Protein 18.9g; Carbohydrate 22.1g, of which sugars 17.1g; Fat 31.9g, of which saturates 13.2g; Cholesterol 45mg; Calcium 635mg; Fibre 10g; Sodium 337mg.
Spiced Mushrooms Energy 76kcal/313kJ; Protein 2g; Carbohydrate 3.4g, of which sugars 3g; Fat 6.1g, of which saturates 0.8g; Cholesterol 0mg; Calcium 26mg; Fibre 0.8g; Sodium 46mg.

Spiced Aubergine with Chilli Sauce and Sesame Seeds

Chunks of aubergine are coated in a rich sauce and sprinkled with sesame seeds to make an unusual side dish that is quick to cook. This straightforward yet versatile vegetarian dish can be served hot, warm or cold, as the occasion demands.

Serves 4–6

2 aubergines, total weight about 600g/1lb 6oz, cut into large chunks
15ml/1 tbsp salt
5ml/1 tsp chilli powder, or to taste
75–90ml/5–6 tbsp sunflower oil or vegetable oil
15ml/1 tbsp rice wine or medium-dry sherry
100ml/3½fl oz/scant ½ cup water
75ml/5 tbsp chilli bean sauce (see Cook's Tip)
salt and ground black pepper
a few toasted sesame seeds, to garnish

1 Place the aubergine chunks on a plate, sprinkle them with the salt and leave to stand for 15–20 minutes. Rinse well, drain and pat dry thoroughly with kitchen paper. Toss the aubergine cubes in the chilli powder.

2 Heat a wok or large frying pan and add the sunflower or vegetable oil. When the oil is hot, add the aubergine chunks, with the rice wine or sherry. Stir constantly until the aubergine chunks start to turn a little brown.

3 Stir the measured water into the pan, cover with a lid and steam for 2–3 minutes. Add the chilli bean sauce and cook for 2 minutes. Season to taste, then spoon on to a serving dish, sprinkle with sesame seeds and serve.

> **Cook's Tip**
> If you can't get hold of chilli bean sauce, use 15–30ml/
> 1–2 tbsp chilli paste mixed with 2 crushed garlic cloves,
> 15ml/1 tbsp each dark soy sauce and rice vinegar, and
> 10ml/2 tsp light soy sauce.

Roasted Root Vegetables with Spices

These spiced vegetables can be roasted alongside a joint of meat or a whole chicken. They will virtually look after themselves and make a delicious side dish.

Serves 4

3 parsnips, peeled
3 potatoes, peeled
3 carrots, peeled
3 sweet potatoes, peeled
60ml/4 tbsp olive oil
8 shallots, peeled
2 garlic cloves, sliced
10ml/2 tsp white mustard seeds
10ml/2 tsp coriander seeds, lightly crushed
5ml/1 tsp cumin seeds
2 bay leaves
salt and ground black pepper

1 Preheat the oven to 190°C/375°F/Gas 5. Bring a pan of lightly salted water to the boil. Cut the parsnips, potatoes, carrots and sweet potatoes into chunks.

2 Add the mixed vegetable chunks to the pan and bring the water back to the boil. Boil for about 2–3 minutes, then drain the vegetables thoroughly.

3 Pour the olive oil into a large, heavy roasting pan and place over a medium heat. When the oil is hot add the drained vegetables together with the whole shallots and garlic. Fry, tossing the vegetables over the heat, until they have turned pale golden at the edges.

4 Add the mustard, coriander and cumin seeds and the bay leaves. Cook for 1 minute, then season with salt and pepper.

5 Transfer the roasting pan to the oven and roast for about 45 minutes, turning the vegetables occasionally, until they are crisp and golden and cooked through. Serve immediately.

> **Variation**
> You can vary the selection of vegetables according to what is available. Try using swede (rutabaga) or pumpkin instead of, or as well as, the vegetables suggested.

Spiced Aubergine Energy 173kcal/719kJ; Protein 6g; Carbohydrate 10.6g, of which sugars 6.6g; Fat 12.4g, of which saturates 2g; Cholesterol 95mg; Calcium 62mg; Fibre 3.2g; Sodium 44mg.
Roasted Vegetables Energy 290kcal/1213kJ; Protein 11.5g; Carbohydrate 32.5g, of which sugars 13.3g; Fat 13.6g, of which saturates 1.6g; Cholesterol 0mg; Calcium 175mg; Fibre 9.1g; Sodium 271mg.

Balti Corn with Cauliflower and Chilli

This quick, tasty and nutritious vegetable dish is a great side dish to serve with a more substantial curry. It will also make a delicious main course if served with plain boiled rice, a dhal-based dish or simply with some Indian bread such as naan, chapati or paratha.

Serves 4
30ml/2 tbsp corn oil
4 curry leaves
1.5ml/¼ tsp onion seeds
2 medium onions, diced
1 red chilli, seeded and chopped
175g/6oz frozen corn
½ small cauliflower, cut into
   small florets
3–7 mint leaves

1 Heat the corn oil in a wok or large frying pan. Add the curry leaves and the onion seeds and cook, stirring constantly, for about 30 seconds.

2 Add the diced onions to the pan and fry them for about 5–8 minutes until golden brown.

3 Add the chilli, corn and cauliflower to the pan and cook, stirring frequently, for 5–8 minutes.

4 Finally, add the mint leaves and heat for 2–3 minutes until the vegetables are tender. Serve immediately.

Variation
Using frozen corn means this dish is very quick and simple to prepare, but, if you prefer, use fresh corn that has been sliced from a couple of cooked cobs.

Cook's Tip
It is best to cook this dish just before you are ready to serve, as the flavours tend to diminish if it is kept warm for too long.

Balti Mushrooms in a Garlic and Chilli Sauce

This is a simple and delicious Balti recipe which could be accompanied by bread or one of the rice side dishes from this book.

Serves 4
350g/12oz/4½ cups button
   (white) mushrooms
15ml/1 tbsp vegetable oil
1 bay leaf

3 garlic cloves, roughly chopped
2 fresh green chillies, seeded
   and chopped
225g/8oz/1 cup low-fat fromage
   frais or ricotta cheese
15ml/1 tbsp chopped fresh mint
15ml/1 tbsp chopped fresh
   coriander (cilantro)
5ml/1 tsp salt
fresh mint and coriander (cilantro)
   leaves, to garnish

1 Cut the button mushrooms in half if small, or in quarters if they are large, and set aside.

2 Heat the oil in a karahi, wok or large, heavy frying pan, then add the bay leaf, chopped garlic and chillies, and quickly cook for about 1 minute, stirring frequently.

3 Add the chopped mushrooms to the pan. Cook for about 2 minutes, stirring frequently.

4 Remove from the heat and stir in the fromage frais or ricotta cheese, followed by the mint, coriander and salt.

5 Return the pan to the heat and stir-fry for 2–3 minutes, then transfer to a warmed serving dish and garnish with the fresh mint and coriander leaves before serving.

Cook's Tip
Balti curries have their origins in Baltistan, the area that is now North Pakistan. They are traditionally aromatic but not heavily flavoured with chilli, and Indian bread is usually used to scoop up the food rather than utensils. However, plain boiled or steamed rice also goes well with all the dishes.

Balti Corn Energy 124kcal/519kJ; Protein 4g; Carbohydrate 19g, of which sugars 4g; Fat 4g, of which saturates 1g; Cholesterol 0mg; Fibre 3g; Sodium 120mg.
Balti Mushrooms Energy 153kcal/633kJ; Protein 5.4g; Carbohydrate 3.1g, of which sugars 2.8g; Fat 13.3g, of which saturates 4.4g; Cholesterol 5mg; Calcium 90mg; Fibre 1.5g; Sodium 28mg.

Courgettes with Mushrooms in a Spicy Sauce

When cream and mushrooms are cooked together they complement each other beautifully. Though this dish sounds very rich, by using single cream and very little oil you can keep the fat content to a minimum.

Serves 4

30ml/2 tbsp vegetable oil
1 medium onion, roughly chopped
5ml/1 tsp ground coriander
5ml/1 tsp ground cumin
5ml/1 tsp salt
2.5ml/½ tsp chilli powder
225g/8oz/3 cups mushrooms, thickly sliced
2 medium courgettes (zucchini), thickly sliced
45ml/3 tbsp single (light) cream
15ml/1 tbsp chopped fresh coriander (cilantro), to garnish (optional)

1 Heat the oil in a large frying pan and fry the chopped onion for 6–8 minutes until golden brown.

2 Lower the heat to medium, add the ground coriander, cumin, salt and chilli powder to the pan and stir together well.

3 Once the onions and the spices are well blended, add the mushrooms and courgettes and cook gently, stirring frequently, for about 5 minutes until soft. If the mixture seems too dry just add a little water to loosen.

4 Finally pour the cream into the pan and mix in well to combine with the vegetables. Garnish with fresh chopped coriander, if you wish, and serve immediately.

Cook's Tip
Choose whichever mushrooms are available for this dish. White (button) mushrooms, field (portabello) mushrooms and brown cap (cremini) mushrooms all work well. More exotic mushrooms such as chanterelles, oyster mushrooms and morel mushrooms will also be delicious cooked in this way.

Stir-fried Vegetable Florets with Hazelnuts

A rich hazelnut dressing turns crunchy cauliflower and broccoli into a very special vegetable dish. It works well as a side dish to a vegetarian or meat curry but can equally be eaten on its own with some freshly baked Indian breads.

Serves 4

175g/6oz/1½ cups bitesize cauliflower florets
175g/6oz/1½ cups bitesize broccoli florets
15ml/1 tbsp sunflower oil
50g/2oz/½ cup hazelnuts, finely chopped
¼ red chilli, finely chopped, or 5ml/1 tsp chilli powder (optional)
60ml/4 tbsp crème fraîche or fromage frais
salt and ground black pepper
chilli powder, to garnish

1 Make sure the cauliflower and broccoli florets are all of an even size so that they cook at the same time. Heat the sunflower oil in a pan or wok and toss the florets over a high heat for about 1 minute.

2 Reduce the heat and continue cooking the vegetables for another 5 minutes, stirring frequently.

3 Add the chopped hazelnuts and fresh chilli or chilli powder, if using, to the pan. Stir well to combine the ingredients. Season with salt and ground black pepper.

4 When the cauliflower is crisp and nearly tender, stir in the crème fraîche or fromage frais. Continue to cook for about 2 minutes until heated through. Serve immediately, sprinkled with a little chilli powder.

Cook's Tip
The crisper these florets are the better, so cook them just long enough to make them piping hot, and give them time to absorb all the flavours.

Courgettes with Mushrooms Energy 90kcal/374kJ; Protein 5g; Carbohydrate 7.5g, of which sugars 3.4g; Fat 4.9g, of which saturates 0.7g; Cholesterol 0mg; Calcium 69mg; Fibre 1.7g; Sodium 16mg.
Stir-fried Florets Energy 205kcal/849kJ; Protein 3.9g; Carbohydrate 20.1g, of which sugars 17.4g; Fat 12.5g, of which saturates 2.1g; Cholesterol 0mg; Calcium 61mg; Fibre 5.8g; Sodium 93mg.

Vegetables and Beans with Curry Leaves

This spicy mix of vegetables and beans is quite a dry curry, so it is ideal to serve alongside a saucy meat curry or dhal. It is quite a hot dish, so feel free to reduce the amount of dried red chillies to suit your taste.

Serves 4
30ml/2 tbsp vegetable oil
6 curry leaves
3 garlic cloves, sliced
3 dried red chillies
1.5ml/¼ tsp onion seeds
1.5ml/¼ tsp fenugreek seeds
3 fresh green chillies, seeded and chopped
10ml/2 tsp desiccated (dry unsweetened shredded) coconut, plus extra to garnish (optional)
115g/4oz/½ cup canned red kidney beans, drained
1 medium carrot, cut into strips
50g/2oz green beans, diagonally sliced
1 medium red (bell) pepper, cut into strips
5ml/1 tsp salt
30ml/2 tbsp lemon juice

1 Heat the vegetable oil in a wok, karahi or deep frying pan. Add the curry leaves, garlic cloves, dried chillies, and onion and fenugreek seeds and cook over a medium heat for about 5–6 minutes, stirring frequently.

2 When the spices in the pan turn a shade darker, add the remaining ingredients and stir well to combine.

3 Lower the heat, cover the pan with a lid and cook for about 5 minutes, stirring occasionally.

4 Transfer the curry to a warmed serving dish and serve garnished with extra coconut, if you wish.

> **Cook's Tip**
> Fresh curry leaves are extremely aromatic and there really is no substitute for them. Fresh curry leaves also freeze well, but if necessary you can use dried ones.

Vegetable Chilli

This spicy chilli is packed with healthy vegetables and is sure to go down a treat with the whole family.

Serves 8
50ml/2fl oz/¼ cup olive oil or vegetable oil
2 onions, chopped
75g/3oz celery, finely sliced
2 carrots, cut in 1cm/½in cubes
2 garlic cloves, crushed
2.5ml/½ tsp celery seeds
1.5ml/¼ tsp cayenne
5ml/1 tsp ground cumin
45ml/3 tbsp chilli powder
400g/14oz canned chopped plum tomatoes with their juice
250ml/8fl oz/1 cup vegetable stock or water
2.5ml/½ tsp fresh or dried thyme
1 bay leaf
350g/12oz cauliflower florets
3 courgettes (zucchini), cut into 1cm/½in cubes
300g/11oz can corn, drained
400g/14oz can kidney or pinto beans, drained
hot pepper sauce (optional)
salt

1 Heat the oil in a large flameproof casserole or heavy pan and add the onions, celery, carrots, and garlic. Cover the casserole and cook over a low heat for 8–10 minutes stirring from time to time, until the onions are softened.

2 Stir in the celery seeds, cayenne, cumin, and chilli powder. Mix well. Add the tomatoes, stock or water, salt, thyme and bay leaf. Stir. Cook for 15 minutes, uncovered.

3 Add the cauliflower and courgettes to the pan. Cover and cook for a further 10 minutes.

4 Add the corn and kidney or pinto beans, stir well, and cook for 10 minutes more, uncovered. Check the seasoning, and add a dash of hot pepper sauce if desired. Serve with freshly boiled rice or baked potatoes, if you like.

> **Variation**
> This dish is a great way to use up any left over vegetables in the kitchen cupboard – try broccoli, aubergines (eggplants), butternut squash or sweet potato.

Middle Eastern Vegetable Stew

A spiced dish of mixed vegetables makes a delicious and filling vegetarian side dish. Children may prefer less chilli.

Serves 4–6
45ml/3 tbsp vegetable stock
1 green (bell) pepper, seeded
 and sliced
2 medium courgettes
 (zucchini), sliced
2 medium carrots, sliced
2 celery sticks, sliced
2 medium potatoes, diced
400g/14oz can
 chopped tomatoes
5ml/1 tsp chilli powder
30ml/2 tbsp chopped fresh mint
15ml/1 tbsp ground cumin
400g/14oz can cooked
 chickpeas, drained
salt and black pepper
mint sprigs, to garnish

1 Heat the vegetable stock in a large flameproof casserole until boiling, then add the sliced pepper, courgettes, carrots, and celery. Stir over a high heat for 2–3 minutes, until the vegetables are just beginning to soften.

2 Add the potatoes, tomatoes, chilli powder, mint, and cumin. Add the chickpeas and bring to the boil.

3 Reduce the heat, cover the casserole, and simmer for about 30 minutes, or until all the vegetables are tender. Season to taste with salt and black pepper and serve immediately while hot, garnished with the mint sprigs.

> **Cook's Tip**
> Chickpeas are traditional in this type of Middle Eastern dish. If you prefer you can use dried chickpeas, which need to be soaked and cooked, instead of the pre-cooked canned variety.

> **Variation**
> Other vegetables can be substituted for those in the recipe, if you prefer, just use whatever you have to hand – try swede (rutabaga), sweet potato or parsnips.

Gujarati Stuffed Vegetables with a Spicy Tomato Sauce

In this fabulous recipe from Gujarat in India, two different vegetables are stuffed with an irresistible blend of spices and peanuts.

Serves 4
12 small potatoes
8 baby aubergines (eggplants)
single (light) cream, to
 garnish (optional)

For the stuffing
15ml/1 tbsp sesame seeds
30ml/2 tbsp ground coriander
30ml/2 tbsp ground cumin
2.5ml/½ tsp salt
1.5ml/¼ tsp chilli powder
2.5ml/½ tsp ground turmeric
10ml/2 tsp sugar
1.5ml/¼ tsp garam masala
15ml/1 tbsp peanuts,
 roughly crushed
15ml/1 tbsp gram flour
2 garlic cloves, crushed
15ml/1 tbsp lemon juice
30ml/2 tbsp chopped fresh
 coriander (cilantro)

For the sauce
30ml/2 tbsp vegetable oil
2.5ml/½ tsp black
 mustard seeds
400g/14oz can
 chopped tomatoes
30ml/2 tbsp chopped fresh
 coriander (cilantro)
150ml/¼ pint/⅔ cup water

1 Preheat the oven to 200°C/400°F/Gas 6. Make slits in the potatoes and aubergines, without cutting right through.

2 Mix all the ingredients for the stuffing together in a bowl. Using a small spoon, carefully stuff the potatoes and aubergines with the spice mixture. Place the stuffed vegetables, evenly spaced, in a greased ovenproof dish.

3 Heat the oil in a pan and fry the mustard seeds for 2 minutes until they begin to splutter, then add the tomatoes, coriander and any leftover stuffing, together with the water. Simmer for 5 minutes until the sauce thickens.

4 Pour the sauce over the potatoes and aubergines. Cover and bake for 25–30 minutes until the vegetables are soft. Garnish with single cream, if using. Serve with any Indian bread or with a meat or chicken curry of your choice.

Middle Eastern Stew Energy 149kcal/630kJ; Protein 7.8g; Carbohydrate 24.9g, of which sugars 6.8g; Fat 2.7g, of which saturates 0.4g; Cholesterol 0mg; Calcium 66mg; Fibre 5.7g; Sodium 172mg.
Gujarati Vegetables Energy 302kcal/1260kJ; Protein 7.2g; Carbohydrate 35.2g, of which sugars 9.6g; Fat 14.9g, of which saturates 3g; Cholesterol 9mg; Calcium 75mg; Fibre 2.3g; Sodium 191mg.

Aloo Saag

Traditional Indian spices – mustard seed, ginger and chilli – give a really good kick to potatoes and spinach in this delicious, authentic curry.

Serves 4
450g/1lb spinach
30ml/2 tbsp vegetable oil
5ml/1 tsp black mustard seeds
1 onion, thinly sliced
2 garlic cloves, crushed
2.5cm/1in piece fresh root ginger, finely chopped
675g/1½lb firm potatoes, cut into 2.5cm/1in chunks
5ml/1 tsp chilli powder
5ml/1 tsp salt
120ml/4fl oz/½ cup water

1 Wash the spinach in several changes of water then blanch it in a little boiling water for 3–4 minutes.

2 Drain the spinach thoroughly and set aside to cool slightly. When it is cool enough to handle, use your hands to squeeze out all the remaining liquid.

3 Heat the oil in a large pan and fry the mustard seeds for 2 minutes, stirring, until they begin to splutter.

4 Add the onion, garlic and ginger to the pan and cook for 5 minutes, stirring frequently.

5 Stir in the potatoes, chilli powder, salt and water and cook for about 8 minutes, stirring occasionally.

6 Finally, add the spinach to the pan. Cover and simmer for 10–15 minutes until the spinach is very soft and the potatoes are tender. Serve immediately while hot.

Cook's Tip
To make certain that the spinach is dry before adding it to the potatoes, put it in a clean dish towel, roll up tightly and squeeze gently to remove any excess liquid. Choose a firm waxy variety of potato or a baby salad potato so the pieces do not break up during cooking.

Masala Mashed Potatoes

This delightfully simple variation on the popular Western side dish can be used as an accompaniment to just about any main course dish, not just Indian spicy dishes and curries.

Serves 4
3 medium potatoes
15ml/1 tbsp chopped fresh mint and coriander (cilantro), mixed
5ml/1 tsp mango powder (amchur)
5ml/1 tsp salt
5ml/1 tsp crushed black peppercorns
1 fresh red chilli, seeded and chopped
1 fresh green chilli, seeded and chopped
50g/2oz/¼ cup butter

1 Put the potatoes in a large pan. Add enough water to cover and bring to the boil, then simmer for about 15 minutes, or until the potatoes are tender, but do not allow them to get too soft.

2 Drain thoroughly and leave to cool slightly, then mash them down using a masher or potato ricer.

3 Stir all the remaining ingredients together in a small mixing bowl until well combined.

4 Stir the herb and spice mixture into the mashed potatoes. Mix together thoroughly with a fork and transfer to a warmed serving dish. Serve immediately.

Cook's Tip
Mango powder, also known as amchur, is the unripe green fruit of the mango tree ground to a powder. The sour mangoes are sliced and dried in the sun, turning a light brown, before they are ground. Mango powder adds a fruity sharpness and a slightly resinous bouquet to a dish. It is widely used with vegetables and is usually added towards the end of the cooking time. If mango powder is unavailable, the nearest substitute is lemon or lime juice, but it will not taste quite the same.

Aloo Saag Energy 201kcal/845kJ; Protein 6.2g; Carbohydrate 30.2g, of which sugars 4.7g; Fat 6.9g, of which saturates 0.9g; Cholesterol 0mg; Calcium 205mg; Fibre 4.3g; Sodium 668mg.
Masala Potatoes Energy 219kcal/919kJ; Protein 3.1g; Carbohydrate 28.9g, of which sugars 3g; Fat 10.9g, of which saturates 6.7g; Cholesterol 27mg; Calcium 13mg; Fibre 1.8g; Sodium 600mg.

Spinach with Spicy Chickpeas

This richly flavoured side dish makes an excellent accompaniment to a dry curry or a rice-based stir-fry. It is particularly good served drizzled with a little plain yogurt – the sharp, creamy flavour complements the complex spices perfectly.

Serves 4
200g/7oz dried chickpeas
30ml/2 tbsp sunflower oil
2 onions, halved and
    thinly sliced
10ml/2 tsp ground coriander
10ml/2 tsp ground cumin
5ml/1 tsp hot chilli powder
2.5ml/½ tsp ground turmeric
15ml/1 tbsp medium or hot
    curry powder
400g/14oz can
    chopped tomatoes
5ml/1 tsp caster
    (superfine) sugar
30ml/2 tbsp chopped fresh
    mint leaves
115g/4oz baby leaf spinach
salt and ground black pepper

1 Soak the chickpeas in cold water overnight. Drain, rinse and place in a large pan. Cover with water and bring to the boil. Reduce the heat and simmer for 45 minutes to 1¼ hours, or until just tender. Drain and set aside.

2 Heat the oil in a wok or frying pan, add the onions and cook over a low heat for 15 minutes, until lightly golden.

3 Add the ground coriander and cumin, chilli powder, turmeric and curry powder to the onions in the pan and cook for about 2–3 minutes, stirring frequently.

4 Add the tomatoes, sugar and 105ml/7 tbsp water to the pan and bring to the boil. Cover, reduce the heat and simmer gently for 15 minutes, stirring occasionally.

5 Add the chickpeas to the pan, season well and cook gently for 8–10 minutes. Stir in the chopped mint.

6 Divide the spinach leaves between shallow bowls, top with the chickpea mixture and serve immediately with a main course of curry or stir-fry.

Spicy Tamarind Chickpeas

Chickpeas make a good base for many vegetarian curries cooked in a slow cooker. Here, they are tossed with sharp tamarind and spices to make a light lunch or side dish.

Serves 4
225g/8oz/1¼ cups dried chickpeas
50g/2oz tamarind pulp
45ml/3 tbsp vegetable oil
2.5ml/½ tsp cumin seeds
1 onion, very finely chopped
2 garlic cloves, crushed
2.5cm/1in piece of fresh root
    ginger, peeled and grated
5ml/1 tsp ground cumin
5ml/1 tsp ground coriander
1.5ml/¼ tsp ground turmeric
1 fresh green chilli, finely chopped
2.5ml/½ tsp salt
225g/8oz tomatoes, chopped
2.5ml/½ tsp garam masala
chopped fresh chillies and
    chopped red onion, to garnish

1 Put the chickpeas in a large bowl and pour over cold water to cover. Leave to soak for at least 8 hours, or overnight.

2 Drain the chickpeas and put in a pan with at least double the volume of cold water. Bring the water to the boil and boil vigorously for at least 10 minutes. Skim off any scum, then drain the chickpeas and transfer into a slow cooker.

3 Pour 750ml/1¼ pints/3 cups of near-boiling water over the chickpeas and switch the slow cooker to high. Cover with the lid and cook for 4–5 hours, or until the chickpeas are just tender.

4 Meanwhile, break up the tamarind with a fork. Pour over 120ml/4fl oz/½ cup of boiling water and leave to soak for 15 minutes. Transfer into a sieve (strainer) and discard the water. Rub the pulp through, discarding any stones and fibre.

5 Heat the oil in a large pan, add the cumin seeds and fry for 2 minutes, until they splutter. Add the onion, garlic and ginger and fry for 5 minutes. Add the cumin, coriander, turmeric, chilli and salt and fry for 3–4 minutes. Add the tomatoes, garam masala and tamarind pulp and bring to the boil.

6 Stir the tamarind mixture into the chickpeas, cover and cook for a further 1 hour. Serve garnished with the chilli and onion.

Spicy Chickpeas Energy 277kcal/1164kJ; Protein 12.8g; Carbohydrate 32.6g, of which sugars 5.3g; Fat 11.5g, of which saturates 1.3g; Cholesterol 0mg; Calcium 103mg; Fibre 7.1g; Sodium 274mg.
Spinach with Chickpeas Energy 267kcal/1122kJ; Protein 13.3g; Carbohydrate 35.5g, of which sugars 10.2g; Fat 9g, of which saturates 1.1g; Cholesterol 0mg; Calcium 170mg; Fibre 8.2g; Sodium 83mg.

Karahi Potatoes with Whole Spices and Mixed Chillies

The potato is transformed into something quite exotic when it is cooked as part of a dish like this.

Serves 4

15ml/1 tbsp vegetable oil
5ml/1 tsp cumin seeds
3 curry leaves
5ml/1 tsp crushed dried red chillies
2.5ml/½ tsp mixed onion, mustard and fenugreek seeds
2.5ml/½ tsp fennel seeds
3 garlic cloves, sliced
2.5cm/1in piece fresh root ginger, grated
2 onions, sliced
6 new potatoes, thinly sliced
15ml/1 tbsp chopped fresh coriander (cilantro)
1 fresh red chilli, seeded and sliced
1 fresh green chilli, seeded and sliced

1 Heat the oil in a karahi, wok or heavy pan. Lower the heat slightly and add the cumin seeds, curry leaves, dried red chillies, mixed onion, mustard and fenugreek seeds, fennel seeds, garlic slices and ginger. Fry for 1 minute.

2 Add the onions to the pan and fry for a further 5 minutes, or until the onions are golden brown.

3 Add the potatoes, fresh coriander and red and green chillies and mix well. Cover the pan tightly with a lid or foil; if using foil, make sure that it does not touch the food. Cook over a very low heat for about 7 minutes or until the potatoes are tender.

4 Remove the pan from the heat, and take off the lid or foil cover. Serve hot straight from the pan.

Cook's Tip
Choose a waxy variety of new potato for this fairly hot vegetable dish; if you use a very soft potato, it will not be possible to cut it into thin slices without it breaking up. Suitable varieties are often labelled 'salad potatoes' when sold at supermarkets. Leave the skin on for a tastier result.

Baby Potatoes with Red Chillies and Coriander

When new potatoes are in season and plentiful, there really is no better way to enjoy them than in this classic spicy side dish. Enjoy it as an accompaniment to a curry main course or simply on its own with some chutneys or pickles.

Serves 4

12–14 baby new potatoes, peeled and halved
30ml/2 tbsp vegetable oil
2.5ml/½ tsp crushed dried red chillies
2.5ml/½ tsp white cumin seeds
2.5ml/½ tsp fennel seeds
2.5ml/½ tsp crushed coriander seeds
15ml/1 tbsp salt
1 medium onion, sliced
1–4 fresh red chillies, chopped
15ml/1 tbsp chopped fresh coriander (cilantro)

1 Cook the baby potatoes in a large pan of boiling water until soft but still firm. Remove the pan from the heat and drain off all the water.

2 In a wok or deep frying pan, heat the vegetable oil, then turn down the heat to medium. Then add the crushed chillies, cumin, fennel and coriander seeds and salt to the pan and fry, stirring frequently, for 30–40 seconds.

3 Add the sliced onion to the pan and fry for 6–7 minutes, stirring frequently, until golden brown. Then add the potatoes, red chillies and fresh coriander.

4 Cover the pan with a lid and cook for a further 5–7 minutes over a very low heat. Serve immediately.

Variation
The quantity of red chillies used here may be too fiery for some palates, particularly children. For a milder version, either seed the chillies, use fewer or substitute them with 1 roughly chopped red (bell) pepper.

Karahi Potatoes Energy 152kcal/641kJ; Protein 3.8g; Carbohydrate 27.5g, of which sugars 6g; Fat 3.9g, of which saturates 0.5g; Cholesterol 0mg; Calcium 46mg; Fibre 2.6g; Sodium 19mg.
Potatoes with Red Chillies Energy 101kcal/421kJ; Protein 1.4g; Carbohydrate 11.4g, of which sugars 1.8g; Fat 5.8g, of which saturates 0.7g; Cholesterol 0mg; Calcium 20mg; Fibre 1.2g; Sodium 501mg.

Bombay Potatoes

This authentic dish is most closely linked to the Gujarati, a totally vegetarian community and the largest population group in the city of Mumbai.

Serves 4–6

2 onions
2 fresh green chillies
50g/2oz/2 cups fresh
   coriander (cilantro)
450g/1lb new potatoes
5ml/1 tsp turmeric
60ml/4 tbsp vegetable oil
2 dried red chillies
6–8 curry leaves
1.5ml/¼ tsp asafoetida
2.5ml/½ tsp each cumin,
   mustard, onion, fennel and
   nigella seeds
lemon juice, to taste
salt

1 Chop the onions and chillies finely, and coarsely chop the coriander. Scrub the potatoes under cold running water and cut them into small pieces.

2 Cook the potatoes in a large pan of boiling water with a little salt and 2.5ml/½ tsp of the turmeric for 10–15 minutes, or until tender. Drain the potatoes well, then mash them with a potato masher and set aside.

3 Heat the vegetable oil in a frying pan and fry the dried chillies and curry leaves over a medium-high heat, stirring frequently, until the chillies are nearly burnt.

4 Add the chopped onions, green chillies, fresh coriander and remaining turmeric to the pan and fry for 2 minutes, until the onions are starting to soften.

5 Add the asafoetida, cumin, mustard, onion, fennel and nigella seeds to the pan. Cook, stirring occasionally, until the onions are soft and translucent but not brown.

6 Fold the potatoes into the pan and add a few drops of water if the mixture is a little dry. Cook over a low heat for about 10–12 minutes, stirring well to ensure the spices are evenly mixed throughout the dish. Stir the lemon juice into the potatoes to taste, and serve immediately.

Indian Potatoes with Poppy Seeds

Poppy seeds are used in Indian cooking as thickening agents, and to lend a nutty taste to sauces. It is the creamy white variety of poppy seed that is used here, rather than the ones with a blue-grey hue that are used for baking.

Serves 4

45ml/3 tbsp white poppy seeds
45–60ml/3–4 tbsp vegetable oil
675g/1½lb potatoes, peeled and
   cut into 1cm/½in cubes
2.5ml/½ tsp black mustard seeds
2.5ml/½ tsp onion seeds
2.5ml/½ tsp cumin seeds
2.5ml/½ tsp fennel seeds
1–2 dried red chillies, chopped or
   broken into small pieces
2.5ml/½ tsp ground turmeric
2.5ml/½ tsp salt
150ml/¼ pint/⅔ cup
   warm water
chopped fresh coriander (cilantro),
   to garnish
pooris and natural (plain) yogurt,
   to serve

1 Preheat a wok, karahi or large pan over a medium heat. When the pan is hot, reduce the heat slightly and add the poppy seeds. Stir them around in the pan until they are just a shade darker. Remove from the pan and allow to cool.

2 In the pan, heat the vegetable oil over a medium heat and fry the cubes of potatoes until they are light brown. Remove them with a slotted spoon and drain on kitchen paper.

3 To the same oil, add the mustard seeds. As soon as they begin to pop, add the onion, cumin and fennel seeds and the chillies. Let the chillies blacken.

4 Stir in the turmeric and follow quickly with the fried potatoes and salt. Stir well and add the warm water. Bring to the boil, cover the pan with the lid and reduce the heat to low. Cook for 8–10 minutes, or until the potatoes are tender.

5 Grind the poppy seeds with a mortar and pestle or in a spice grinder. Stir the ground seeds into the potatoes. They should form a thick paste which clings to the potatoes. If there is too much liquid, continue to stir over medium heat. Transfer to a serving dish. Garnish with coriander and serve with pooris and yogurt.

Bombay Potatoes Energy 143kcal/595kJ; Protein 2.1g; Carbohydrate 17.4g, of which sugars 4.7g; Fat 7.7g, of which saturates 0.9g; Cholesterol 0mg; Calcium 21mg; Fibre 1.7g; Sodium 10mg.
Indian Potatoes Energy 179kcal/748kJ; Protein 2.6g; Carbohydrate 21.8g, of which sugars 5.9g; Fat 9.7g, of which saturates 1.2g; Cholesterol 0mg; Calcium 27mg; Fibre 2.1g; Sodium 13mg.

Fresh Coriander Relish

Delicious as an accompaniment to kebabs, samosas and bhajias, this relish can also be used as a spread for cucumber or tomato sandwiches.

Makes about 450g/1lb/ 2 cups

30ml/2 tbsp vegetable oil
1 dried red chilli
1.5ml/¼ tsp each cumin, fennel
  and onion seeds
1.5ml/¼ tsp asafoetida
4 curry leaves
115g/4oz/1⅓ cups desiccated
  (dry unsweetened
  shredded) coconut
10ml/2 tsp sugar
3 fresh green chillies, seeded
  and chopped
175–225g/6–8oz fresh coriander
  (cilantro), chopped
60ml/4 tbsp mint sauce
juice of 3 lemons
salt

1 Heat the oil in a frying pan and add the dried chilli, the cumin, fennel and onion seeds, the asafoetida, curry leaves, desiccated coconut, sugar and salt to taste. Fry, stirring often, until the coconut turns golden brown. Transfer into a bowl and set aside to cool.

2 Grind the spice mixture with the green chillies, fresh coriander and mint sauce in a food processor or blender or with a mortar and pestle. Moisten with lemon juice. Scrape into a bowl and chill before serving.

> **Cook's Tip**
> This may seem like a lot of coriander, but it is compacted when it is ground with the spices.

> **Variation**
> For Coriander and Walnut Relish, put 90ml/6 tbsp fresh coriander leaves, 2 garlic cloves, 50g/2oz chopped onion and 60ml/4 tbsp sugar into a food processor and grind until thick. Add 50g/2oz/½ cup chopped walnuts and mix well. Add salt and ground black pepper to taste.

Sesame Seed and Chilli Chutney

This is an extremely versatile Indian chutney, which doubles as a delicious dip for poppadums, pakora or bhajias. It also makes a tasty sandwich filling with cucumber.

Serves 4

175g/6oz sesame seeds
5ml/1 tsp salt
120–150ml/4–5fl oz/½–⅔
  cup water
2 green chillies, seeded and diced
60ml/4 tbsp chopped fresh
  coriander (cilantro)
15ml/1 tbsp chopped fresh
  mint leaves
15ml/1 tbsp tamarind paste
30ml/2 tbsp sugar
5ml/1 tsp corn oil
1.5ml/¼ tsp onion seeds
4 curry leaves
6 onion rings, 1 green chilli, seeded
  and sliced, 1 red chilli,
  seeded and sliced, and
  15ml/1 tbsp fresh coriander
  (cilantro) leaves, to garnish

1 Dry-roast the sesame seeds and leave to cool. Place them in a spice grinder and grind to a grainy powder, or grind the seeds using a mortar and pestle.

2 Transfer the sesame powder to a bowl. Add the salt, water, diced chillies, coriander, mint, tamarind paste and sugar and, using a fork, mix everything together.

3 Taste and adjust the seasoning if necessary: the mixture should have a sweet-and-sour flavour.

4 Heat the oil in a heavy pan and fry the onion seeds and curry leaves, stirring constantly, for 2–3 minutes until the seeds begin to splutter and release their fragrances.

5 Add the sesame seed paste to the pan and fry the mixture for about 45 seconds, stirring constantly to avoid it sticking to the base of the pan and burning. Transfer the mixture to a warmed serving dish.

6 Garnish the chutney with onion rings, sliced green and red chillies and the fresh coriander leaves. If it is not to be eaten immediately, cover the chutney tightly and store it in the refrigerator until it is required.

Apple and Sultana Chutney

Use wine or cider vinegar for this stovetop chutney to give it a subtle and mellow flavour. The chutney is perfect served with Indian food or cheeses and freshly made bread.

Makes about 900g/2lb

350g/12oz cooking apples
115g/4oz/⅔ cup sultanas
  (golden raisins)
50g/2oz onion
25g/1oz/¼ cup
  almonds, blanched
5ml/1 tsp white peppercorns
2.5ml/½ tsp coriander seeds
175g/6oz/scant 1 cup sugar
10ml/2 tsp salt
5ml/1 tsp ground ginger
450ml/¾ pint/scant 2 cups cider
  vinegar or wine vinegar
1.5ml/¼ tsp cayenne pepper
red chillies (optional)

1 Peel, core and chop the apples. Chop the sultanas, onion and almonds. Tie the peppercorns and coriander seeds in muslin (cheesecloth), using a long piece of string, and then tie to the handle of a preserving pan or stainless steel pan.

2 Put the sugar, salt, ground ginger and vinegar into the pan, with the cayenne pepper to taste. Heat the mixture gently, stirring, until the sugar has completely dissolved.

3 Add the chopped fruit to the pan. Bring the mixture to the boil and then lower the heat. Simmer for about 1½–2 hours, or until most of the liquid has evaporated.

4 Spoon the chutney into warmed sterilized jars and place one whole fresh chilli in each jar, if using. Leave until cold, then cover and seal the jars and attach a label to each one.

5 Store in a cool, dark place. The chutney is best left for a month to mature before eating and will keep for at least 6 months, if it is correctly stored.

Variation
For a mild chutney, add only a little cayenne pepper. For a spicier one, increase the quantity to taste.

Lime Pickle

Sharp lime pickle is one of the best-known Indian relishes. For this recipe, you will need ripe limes, with a yellow tinge on the skin.

Makes about 900g/2lb/
4 cups

10–12 limes
15ml/1 tbsp salt
120ml/4fl oz/½ cup malt vinegar
250ml/8fl oz/1 cup vegetable oil
5ml/1 tsp asafoetida
10–12 garlic cloves, crushed
2.5cm/1in piece of fresh root
  ginger, grated
10–12 curry leaves
30ml/2 tbsp black mustard seeds,
  finely ground
15ml/1 tbsp cumin seeds,
  finely ground
10ml/2 tsp fenugreek seeds,
  finely ground
10ml/2 tsp ground turmeric
10ml/2 tsp chilli powder
10 green chillies, halved
20ml/4 tsp salt
20ml/4 tsp sugar

1 Wash the limes and dry them with a cloth. Trim them, then cut them into quarters. Sprinkle the quarters with the salt and put them in a colander over a bowl. Set aside for 2 hours, then transfer them to another bowl and add the vinegar. Stir until any remaining salt is dissolved and drain in the colander again.

2 Heat the oil in a pan over a medium heat and add the asafoetida, followed by the garlic, ginger and curry leaves. Allow them to brown in the pan slightly.

3 Add the ground seeds, turmeric and chilli powder, and stir-fry for 1 minute, then add the green chillies, salt and sugar. Stir-fry for 1 minute longer before adding the limes. Remove the pan from the heat and allow to cool completely.

4 Store the lime pickle in sterilized, airtight jars. Leave the pickle in the jar for 4–5 weeks to mature before eating. The pickle will keep for 10–12 months.

Cook's Tip
To sterilize jars for bottling pickles or chutneys, boil them in water for a minimum of 10 minutes.

Apple Chutney Energy 1299kcal/5525kJ; Protein 10.9g; Carbohydrate 299.5g, of which sugars 297.7g; Fat 14.9g, of which saturates 1.1g; Cholesterol 0mg; Calcium 254mg; Fibre 10.4g; Sodium 3.97g.
Lime Pickle Energy 120kcal/492kJ; Protein 0.1g; Carbohydrate 0.3g, of which sugars 0.2g; Fat 13.1g, of which saturates 1.6g; Cholesterol 0mg; Calcium 9mg; Fibre 0.1g; Sodium 436mg.

Green Chilli Pickle

Southern India is the source of some of the hottest curries and pickles. You might imagine that eating them would be a case of going for the burn, but they actually help to cool the body in the heat of the Indian sun.

Makes 450–550g/1–1¼lb/ 2–2½ cups
50g/2oz/4 tbsp yellow mustard seeds, crushed
50g/2oz/4 tbsp freshly ground cumin seeds
25g/1oz/¼ cup ground turmeric
50g/2oz garlic cloves, crushed, plus 20 small garlic cloves, peeled but left whole
150ml/¼ pint/⅔ cup white vinegar
75g/3oz/6 tbsp sugar
10ml/2 tsp salt
150ml/¼ pint/⅔ cup mustard oil
450g/1lb small or medium fresh green chillies

1 Mix together the mustard and cumin seeds, the turmeric, crushed garlic, white vinegar, sugar and salt in a sterilized glass bowl until the ingredients are well blended.

2 Cover the bowl with a clean cloth and leave to rest in a cool place for 24 hours. This enables the spices to infuse (steep) and the sugar and salt to dissolve.

3 Heat the mustard oil in a frying pan and gently fry the spice mixture for about 5 minutes. (Keep a window open while cooking with mustard oil as it is very pungent and the smoke from it may irritate the eyes.)

4 Add the whole, peeled garlic cloves to the pan and fry for a further 5 minutes, stirring frequently.

5 Halve each fresh green chilli, washing your hands carefully afterwards to avoid irritating sensitive skin. Add the chillies and cook gently until tender but still green in colour. This will take about 30 minutes over a low heat.

6 Cool thoroughly, then pour into sterilized jars, ensuring that the oil is evenly distributed if you are using more than one jar. Leave to rest for a week before serving.

Red Hot Relish

Make this tangy, stovetop relish during the summer months when tomatoes and peppers are plentiful.

Makes about 1.3kg/3lb
800g/1¾lb ripe tomatoes, skinned and quartered
450g/1lb red onions, chopped
3 red (bell) peppers, chopped
3 fresh red chillies, seeded and finely sliced
200g/7oz/1 cup sugar
200ml/7fl oz/scant 1 cup red wine vinegar
30ml/2 tbsp mustard seeds
10ml/2 tsp celery seeds
15ml/1 tbsp paprika
5ml/1 tsp salt

1 Put the tomatoes, onions, peppers and chillies in a preserving pan, cover with a lid and simmer over a very low heat for about 10 minutes, stirring once or twice, until the tomato juices run.

2 Add the sugar and vinegar and slowly bring to the boil until the sugar has dissolved completely. Add the mustard seeds, celery seeds, paprika and salt, and stir well to combine.

3 Increase the heat slightly and cook the relish, uncovered, for 30 minutes, or until the mixture has a thick, moist consistency.

4 Spoon the relish into warmed sterilized jars, cover and seal. Store in a cool, dark place and leave for at least 2 weeks before eating. Use the relish within 1 year of making.

Papaya and Lemon Relish

This chunky relish is best made in a slow cooker. Serve with roast meats.

Makes 450g/1lb
1 large unripe papaya
1 onion, very thinly sliced
175ml/6fl oz/generous ¾ cup red wine vinegar
juice of 2 lemons
165g/5½oz/¾ cup golden caster (superfine) sugar
1 cinnamon stick
1 bay leaf
2.5ml/½ tsp hot paprika
2.5ml/½ tsp salt
150g/5oz/1 cup sultanas (golden raisins)

1 Peel the papaya and cut it in half lengthways. Remove the seeds then cut the flesh into small even chunks.

2 Place the papaya chunks in the ceramic cooking pot, add the onion slices and stir in the vinegar. Switch the slow cooker to the high setting, cover with the lid and cook for 2 hours.

3 Add the lemon juice, sugar, cinnamon stick, bay leaf, paprika, salt and sultanas to the ceramic cooking pot. Gently stir the mixture until all of the sugar has completely dissolved.

4 Cook the chutney for a further 1 hour. Leave the cover of the slow cooker off to allow some of the liquid to evaporate and the mixture to reduce. It should be fairly thick and syrupy.

5 Ladle the chutney into hot sterilized jars. Seal and store the chutney for 1 week to allow it to mature. Use within a year but. opened jars should be chilled and consumed within 2 weeks.

Green Chilli Pickle Energy 1953kcal/8134kJ; Protein 51.5g; Carbohydrate 176.9g, of which sugars 95.2g; Fat 123.3g, of which saturates 14.7g Cholesterol 0mg; Calcium 488mg; Fibre 8.2g; Sodium 96mg.
Red Hot Relish Energy 1270kcal/5392kJ; Protein 17.8g; Carbohydrate 306.2g, of which sugars 294.1g; Fat 5.6g, of which saturates 1.4g; Cholesterol 0mg; Calcium 320mg; Fibre 23.5g; Sodium 121mg.
Papaya Relish Energy 1294kcal/5511kJ; Protein 8.4g; Carbohydrate 332.7g, of which sugars 332.7g; Fat 1.4g, of which saturates 0g; Cholesterol 0mg; Calcium 272mg; Fibre 16.1g; Sodium 111mg.

Tomato Relish

This is a simple relish that can be served with most meals. It provides a contrast to hot curries, with its crunchy texture and refreshing ingredients.

Serves 4–6
2 small fresh green chillies
2 limes
2.5ml/½ tsp sugar, or to taste
2 onions, finely chopped
4 firm tomatoes, seeded and
   finely chopped
½ cucumber, finely chopped
a few fresh coriander (cilantro)
   leaves, chopped
salt and ground black pepper
a few fresh mint leaves,
   to garnish

1 Using a sharp knife, cut both the green chillies in half. Scrape out the seeds and discard, then chop the chillies finely and place them in a small bowl.

2 Squeeze the limes. Pour the juice into a glass bowl and add the sugar, with salt and pepper to taste. Set aside until the sugar and salt have dissolved, stirring the mixture occasionally.

3 Add the chopped chillies to the bowl, with the chopped onions, tomatoes, cucumber and fresh coriander leaves. Mix well to combine the ingredients.

4 Cover the bowl with clear film (plastic wrap) and place in the refrigerator for at least 3 hours, so that the flavours blend. Just before serving, taste the relish and add more salt, pepper or sugar if needed. Garnish with mint and serve.

Cook's Tip
If you find that preparing chillies irritates your skin then wear a pair of kitchen gloves or cover your hands with a plastic bag.

Variation
For a milder-flavoured relish, use just one chilli, or dispense with them altogether and substitute with a green (bell) pepper.

Onion, Mango and Peanut Chaat

Chaats are spiced relishes of vegetables and nuts served with Indian meals. Amchur adds a deliciously fruity sourness to this mixture of onions and mango.

Serves 4
90g/3½oz/scant 1 cup
   unsalted peanuts
15ml/1 tbsp groundnut
   (peanut) oil
1 onion, chopped
10cm/4in piece cucumber, seeded
   and cut into 5mm/¼in dice
1 mango, peeled, stoned (pitted)
   and diced
1 green chilli, seeded and chopped
30ml/2 tbsp chopped fresh
   coriander (cilantro)
15ml/1 tbsp chopped fresh mint
15ml/1 tbsp lime juice, or to taste
light muscovado (brown) sugar,
   to taste

For the chaat masala
10ml/2 tsp ground toasted
   cumin seeds
2.5ml/½ tsp cayenne pepper
5ml/1 tsp mango
   powder (amchur)
2.5ml/½ tsp garam masala
pinch of ground asafoetida
salt and ground black pepper

1 To make the chaat masala, mix all the spices together, then season with 2.5ml/½ tsp each of salt and pepper.

2 Fry the peanuts in the oil until lightly browned, stirring frequently, then drain on kitchen paper until cool.

3 Put the onion in a mixing bowl with the cucumber, mango, chilli, fresh coriander and mint. Sprinkle in 5ml/1 tsp of the chaat masala and mix well to thoroughly combine.

4 Stir in the peanuts and then add lime juice and/or sugar to taste. Set the mixture aside for 20–30 minutes to give the flavours time to develop. Transfer the mixture into a serving bowl, sprinkle another 5ml/1 tsp of the chaat masala over the top and serve immediately.

Cook's Tip
Any remaining chaat masala can be placed in a sealed jar and kept in a cool place for 4–6 weeks.

Tomato Relish Energy 530kcal/2262kJ; Protein 3.7g; Carbohydrate 134.1g, of which sugars 134.1g; Fat 1.4g, of which saturates 0.5g; Cholesterol 0mg; Calcium 93mg; Fibre 4.5g; Sodium 2012mg.
Onion Chaat Energy 189kcal/788kJ; Protein 6.9g; Carbohydrate 9.8g, of which sugars 6.6g; Fat 14g, of which saturates 2.4g; Cholesterol 0mg; Calcium 41mg; Fibre 2.4g; Sodium 4mg.

Tomato and Fresh Chilli Chutney

This fresh-tasting and invigorating chutney is the perfect partner to liven up a simple curry or dhal.

Makes about 475ml/ 16fl oz/2 cups
1 red (bell) pepper
4 tomatoes, chopped

2 fresh green chillies, chopped
1 garlic clove, crushed
1.5ml/¼ tsp salt
2.5ml/½ tsp sugar
5ml/1 tsp chilli powder
45ml/3 tbsp tomato
    purée (paste)
15ml/1 tbsp chopped fresh
    coriander (cilantro)

1 Halve the red pepper and remove the core and seeds. Roughly chop the red pepper halves into chunks.

2 Process the pepper with the tomatoes, chillies, garlic, salt, sugar, chilli powder, tomato purée and coriander with 30ml/ 2 tbsp water in a food processor until smooth. Transfer to a sterilized jar, cover and chill until needed.

Mint and Coconut Chutney

This chutney is made using fresh mint leaves and desiccated coconut, all bound together with yogurt.

Makes about 350ml/ 12fl oz/1½ cups
50g/2oz fresh mint leaves

90ml/6 tbsp desiccated
    (dry unsweetened
    shredded) coconut
15ml/1 tbsp sesame seeds
1.5ml/¼ tsp salt
175ml/6fl oz/¾ cup natural
    (plain) yogurt

1 Finely chop the fresh mint leaves, using a sharp kitchen knife or a specialist herb chopper.

2 Put the mint with the coconut, sesame seeds, salt and yogurt into a food processor or blender and process until smooth.

3 Transfer the chutney to a sterilized jar, cover and chill in the refrigerator until needed.

Squash, Apricot and Almond Chutney

Coriander seeds and ground turmeric add a deliciously spicy touch to this rich, slow-cooker chutney. It is ideal spooned on to little savoury canapés or with melting cubes of mozzarella cheese; it is also good in sandwiches, helping to spice up a variety of fillings.

Makes about 1.8kg/4lb
1 small butternut squash,
    weighing about 800g/1¾lb

400g/14oz/2 cups golden sugar
300ml/½ pint/1¼ cups
    cider vinegar
2 onions, finely chopped
225g/8oz/1 cup ready-to-eat
    dried apricots, chopped
finely grated rind and juice of
    1 orange
2.5ml/½ tsp turmeric
15ml/1 tbsp coriander seeds
15ml/1 tbsp salt
115g/4oz/1 cup flaked
    (sliced) almonds

1 Halve the butternut squash and scoop out the seeds. Peel off the skin, then cut the flesh into 1cm/½in cubes.

2 Put the sugar and vinegar in the ceramic cooking pot of the cooker and switch to high. Heat for 30 minutes, then stir until the sugar has completely dissolved.

3 Add the butternut squash, onions, apricots, orange rind and juice, turmeric, coriander seeds and salt to the slow cooker pot and stir well until the ingredients are well combined.

4 Cover the slow cooker with the lid and cook for about 5–6 hours, stirring occasionally during that time.

5 After about 5 hours the chutney should be a fairly thick consistency with relatively little liquid. If it is still quite runny at this stage, cook uncovered for the final hour. Stir the flaked almonds into the chutney.

6 Spoon the chutney into warmed sterilized jars, cover and seal. Store in a cool, dark place and allow the chutney to mature for at least 1 month before eating. It should be used within 2 years. Once opened, store jars of the chutney in the refrigerator and use within 2 months.

Tomato and Chilli Chutney Energy 187kcal/794kJ; Protein 9.7g; Carbohydrate 33.2g, of which sugars 30g; Fat 2.5g, of which saturates 0.5g; Cholesterol 0mg; Calcium 175mg; Fibre 7.5g; Sodium 157mg.
Mint and Coconut Chutney Energy 753kcal/3117kJ; Protein 18.6g; Carbohydrate 21.7g, of which sugars 18.9g; Fat 66.6g, of which saturates 50.2g; Cholesterol 2mg; Calcium 559mg; Fibre 13.5g; Sodium 181mg.
Squash Chutney Energy 2770kcal/11,723kJ; Protein 41.7g; Carbohydrate 532.6g, of which sugars 524.1g; Fat 67.3g, of which saturates 5.9g; Cholesterol 0mg; Calcium 807mg; Fibre 31.6g; Sodium 5967mg.

Sweet and Hot Dried-fruit Chutney

This rich, thick and slightly sticky preserve of spiced dried fruit is simple to make in the slow cooker. It is a wonderful way to enliven cold roast turkey left over from your Christmas or Thanksgiving dinner.

Makes about 1.5kg/3lb 6oz

350g/12oz/1½ cups ready-to-eat dried apricots
225g/8oz/1½ cups dried dates, stoned (pitted)
225g/8oz/1⅓ cups dried figs
50g/2oz/⅓ cup glacé (candied) citrus peel
150g/5oz/1 cup raisins
50g/2oz/½ cup dried cranberries
75ml/2½fl oz/⅓ cup cranberry juice
300ml/½ pint/1¼ cups cider vinegar
225g/8oz/1 cup caster (superfine) sugar
finely grated rind of 1 lemon
5ml/1 tsp mixed (apple pie) spice
5ml/1 tsp ground coriander
5ml/1 tsp cayenne pepper
5ml/1 tsp salt

1 Chop the apricots, dates, figs and citrus peel, and put all the dried fruit in the ceramic cooking pot. Pour over the cranberry juice, stir, then cover the slow cooker and switch to low. Cook for 1 hour, or until the fruit has absorbed most of the juice.

2 Add the cider vinegar and sugar to the pot. Turn the slow cooker up to high and stir until the sugar has dissolved.

3 Re-cover and cook for 2 more hours, or until the fruit is very soft and the chutney fairly thick (it will thicken further as it cools). Stir in the lemon rind, mixed spice, coriander, cayenne pepper and salt. Cook, uncovered, for about 30 minutes, until little excess liquid remains.

4 Spoon the chutney into warmed sterilized jars, cover and seal. Store in a cool, dark place. Open within 10 months and, once opened, store in the refrigerator and use within 2 months.

> **Variation**
> *Pitted prunes can be substituted for the dates, and dried sour cherries for the dried cranberries.*

Mango Chutney

No Indian meal would be complete without this classic chutney, which is ideal for making in a slow cooker. Its gloriously sweet, tangy flavour is the perfect complement to warm spices.

Makes 450g/1lb

3 firm mangoes
120ml/4fl oz/½ cup cider vinegar
200g/7oz/scant 1 cup light muscovado (brown) sugar
1 small red finger chilli or jalapeño chilli, split
2.5cm/1in piece fresh root ginger, peeled and finely chopped
1 garlic clove, finely chopped
5 cardamom pods, bruised
1 bay leaf
2.5ml/½ tsp salt

1 Peel the mangoes and cut out the stone (pit), then cut the flesh into small chunks or thin wedges.

2 Put the chopped mangoes in the ceramic cooking pot of the slow cooker. Add the cider vinegar, stir briefly to combine, and cover the slow cooker with the lid. Switch the slow cooker to the high setting and cook for about 2 hours, stirring the chutney halfway through the cooking time.

3 Stir the sugar, chilli, ginger, garlic, bruised cardamom pods, bay leaf and salt into the mango mixture, until the sugar has dissolved completely.

4 Cover and cook for 2 hours, then uncover and let the mixture cook for a further 1 hour, or until the chutney is reduced to a thick consistency and no excess liquid remains. Stir the chutney every 15 minutes during the last hour.

5 Remove and discard the bay leaf and the chilli. Spoon the chutney into hot sterilized jars and seal. Store for 1 week before eating and use within 1 year.

> **Cook's Tip**
> *To make a more fiery chutney, seed and slice two green chillies and stir into the chutney mixture with the other spices.*

Mango Chutney Energy 1045kcal/4465kJ; Protein 4.1g; Carbohydrate 272.5g, of which sugars 271.1g; Fat 0.9g, of which saturates 0.5g; Cholesterol 0mg; Calcium 908mg; Fibre 11.7g; Sodium 1002mg.
Sweet Chutney Energy 2873kcal/12,248kJ; Protein 32g; Carbohydrate 714.3g, of which sugars 703.5g; Fat 6.8g, of which saturates 0.2g; Cholesterol 0mg; Calcium 1075mg; Fibre 52.1g; Sodium 2358mg.

Malay Vegetable Salad

This beansprout salad, known as kerabu, is deliciously crunchy and fresh, packed with crisp vegetables and lots of herbs. It is usually served as a side dish to accompany many of the highly spiced Malay curries.

Serves 4
115g/4oz fresh coconut, grated
30ml/2 tbsp dried prawns (shrimp), soaked in warm water for 1 hour or until soft
225g/8oz beansprouts, rinsed and drained
1 small cucumber, peeled, seeded and cut into julienne strips
2–3 spring onions (scallions), trimmed, cut into 2.5cm/1in pieces and halved lengthways
a handful of young, tender mangetouts (snow peas), halved diagonally
a handful of cooked green beans, halved lengthways
a handful of fresh chives, chopped into 2.5cm/1in pieces
a handful of fresh mint leaves, finely chopped
2–3 fresh red chillies, seeded and sliced finely along the length
juice of 2 limes
10ml/2 tsp sugar
salt and ground black pepper

1 Dry-roast the coconut in a heavy pan until it is lightly browned and emits a nutty aroma.

2 Using a mortar and pestle or a food processor, grind the roasted coconut to a coarse powder. Drain the soaked dried prawns and grind them coarsely too.

3 Put the vegetables, herbs and chillies into a bowl. Mix the lime juice with the sugar and pour it over the salad.

4 Season with salt and black pepper. Sprinkle the ground coconut and dried prawns over the salad, and toss well until thoroughly mixed. Serve immediately.

Cook's Tip
Try a mixture of other herbs in this salad, depending on what is available. Coriander (cilantro) and parsley both work well.

Sweet Cucumber Salad

This sweet dipping sauce is good served with Thai bites.

Makes 120ml/4fl oz/½ cup
¼ small cucumber, thinly sliced
75ml/5 tbsp water
30ml/2 tbsp sugar
2.5ml/½ tsp salt
15ml/1 tbsp rice or white wine vinegar
2 shallots or 1 small red onion, thinly sliced

1 With a sharp knife, cut the cucumber slices into quarters.

2 Put the water, sugar, salt and vinegar into a pan, bring to the boil and simmer until the sugar has dissolved. Leave to cool. Add the cucumber and shallots or onion. Serve immediately.

Pepper and Cucumber Salad

Fresh herbs transform familiar ingredients into a tasty side salad.

Serves 4
1 yellow or red (bell) pepper
1 large cucumber
4–5 tomatoes
1 bunch spring onions (scallions)
30ml/2 tbsp fresh parsley
30ml/2 tbsp fresh mint
30ml/2 tbsp fresh coriander (cilantro)
2 pitta breads, to serve

For the dressing
2 garlic cloves, crushed
75ml/5 tbsp olive oil
juice of 2 lemons
salt and ground black pepper

1 Halve, seed and core the pepper, then slice. Roughly chop the cucumber and tomatoes. Place in a large salad bowl.

2 Slice the spring onions and add to the cucumber, tomatoes and pepper. Finely chop the fresh herbs and add to the bowl.

3 To make the dressing, blend the garlic with the oil and lemon juice, then season to taste. Pour over the salad and toss.

4 Toast the pitta breads under a hot grill (broiler) and serve immediately while hot, alongside the salad.

Malay Salad Energy 230kcal/947kJ; Protein 12.6g; Carbohydrate 15.9g, of which sugars 13.9g; Fat 12.9g, of which saturates 10.2g; Cholesterol 0mg; Calcium 151mg; Fibre 7.8g; Sodium 24mg.
Sweet Cucumber Salad Energy 147kcal/624kJ; Protein 1.4g; Carbohydrate 37.2g, of which sugars 35.8g; Fat 0.2g, of which saturates 0g; Cholesterol 0mg; Calcium 44mg; Fibre 1.3g; Sodium 6mg.
Pepper Salad Energy 159kcal/656kJ; Protein 1.8g; Carbohydrate 5.8g, of which sugars 5.6g; Fat 14.4g, of which saturates 2.1g; Cholesterol 0mg; Calcium 46mg; Fibre 2.4g; Sodium 13mg.

Lentil and Spinach Salad

This wonderful, earthy salad is great for a curry or with spicy barbecued food.

Serves 6
225g/8oz/1 cup Puy lentils
1 fresh bay leaf
1 celery stick
fresh thyme sprig
30ml/2 tbsp olive oil
1 onion or 3–4 shallots, chopped
10ml/2 tsp crushed toasted
 cumin seeds
400g/14oz young spinach
salt and ground black pepper
30–45ml/2–3 tbsp chopped fresh
 parsley, plus a few extra sprigs
 to garnish

For the dressing
75ml/5 tbsp extra virgin olive oil
5ml/1 tsp Dijon mustard
15–25ml/3–5 tsp red or white
 wine vinegar
1 garlic clove, finely chopped
2.5ml/¹/₂ tsp grated lemon rind

1 Rinse the lentils and place them in a large pan. Add plenty of water to cover. Tie the bay leaf, celery and thyme into a bundle and add to the pan, then bring to the boil. Reduce the heat so that the water boils steadily. Cook the lentils for 30–45 minutes, until just tender. Do not add salt at this stage.

2 Meanwhile, to make the dressing, mix the oil, mustard, 15ml/3 tsp vinegar, the garlic and lemon rind, and season well.

3 Thoroughly drain the lentils, discarding the herbs and celery, and transfer them into a large bowl. Add most of the dressing and toss well, then set the lentils aside, stirring occasionally.

4 Heat the oil in a deep frying pan and cook the onion or shallots over low heat for about 4–5 minutes, until they are beginning to soften. Add the cumin and cook for 1 minute. Add the spinach and season to taste, cover and cook for about 2 minutes. Stir, then cook again briefly until wilted.

5 Stir the spinach into the lentils and leave the salad to cool. Bring back to room temperature if necessary. Stir in the remaining dressing and chopped parsley. Adjust the seasoning, adding extra salt and pepper or red wine vinegar if necessary. Turn the salad on to a serving platter and sprinkle over some fresh parsley sprigs before serving.

Pak Choi Salad with Lime Dressing

If you like your food hot and spicy, then this is the dish for you! The fiery flavours pack a punch.

Serves 4
30ml/2 tbsp oil
3 fresh red chillies, cut into
 thin strips
4 garlic cloves, thinly sliced
6 spring onions (scallions),
 sliced diagonally
2 pak choi (bok choy), shredded
15ml/1 tbsp crushed peanuts

For the dressing
30ml/2 tbsp fresh lime juice
15–30ml/1–2 tbsp Thai
 fish sauce
250ml/8fl oz/1 cup coconut milk

1 To make the dressing, put the lime juice and fish sauce in a bowl and mix well, then gradually whisk in the coconut milk until thoroughly combined.

2 Heat the oil in a wok and stir-fry the chillies for 2–3 minutes, until crisp. Transfer to a plate using a slotted spoon. Add the garlic to the wok and stir-fry for 30–60 seconds, until golden brown. Transfer to the plate.

3 Stir-fry the white parts of the spring onions for about 2–3 minutes, then add the green parts and stir-fry for 1 minute more. Transfer to the plate.

4 Bring a large pan of lightly salted water to the boil and add the pak choi. Stir twice, then drain immediately.

5 Place the pak choi in a large mixing bowl, pour over the dressing and toss to mix. Spoon into a large serving bowl and sprinkle with the crushed peanuts and the stir-fried chilli mixture. Serve immediately while still warm.

Variations
• *Thai fish sauce is traditionally used for this dressing, but if you are cooking for vegetarians, mushroom ketchup is a suitable vegetarian alternative.*
• *If pak choi is unavailable, use Chinese cabbage instead.*

Lentil Salad Energy 248kcal/1037kJ; Protein 11.2g; Carbohydrate 20.3g, of which sugars 2.1g; Fat 14.1g, of which saturates 2g; Cholesterol 0mg; Calcium 150mg; Fibre 5.1g; Sodium 102mg.
Pak Choi Salad Energy 104kcal/434kJ; Protein 3.3g; Carbohydrate 5.2g, of which sugars 4.8g; Fat 8g, of which saturates 1.2g; Cholesterol 0mg; Calcium 116mg; Fibre 1.5g; Sodium 408mg.

Potato Salad with Egg and Coronation Dressing

The connection between this recipe and traditional Indian cooking is tenuous, but coronation dressing is so popular that it would have been churlish to leave it out.

Serves 6
450g/1lb new potatoes
45ml/3 tbsp French dressing
3 spring onions (scallions), chopped
6 eggs, hard-boiled and halved
frilly lettuce leaves
¼ cucumber, cut into thin strips
6 large radishes, sliced
salad cress (optional)
salt and ground black pepper

For the coronation dressing
30ml/2 tbsp olive oil
1 small onion, chopped
15ml/1 tbsp mild curry powder or korma spice mix
10ml/2 tsp tomato purée (paste)
30ml/2 tbsp lemon juice
30ml/2 tbsp sherry
300ml/½ pint/1¼ cups mayonnaise
150ml/¼ pint/⅔ cup natural (plain) yogurt

1 Boil the potatoes in a pan of salted water until tender. Drain them, transfer to a large bowl and toss in the French dressing while they are still warm.

2 Stir the spring onions and the salt and pepper into the bowl with the potatoes, and leave to cool thoroughly.

3 Meanwhile, make the coronation dressing. Heat the oil in a small pan. Fry the onion for 3 minutes, until soft.

4 Stir in the curry powder or spice mix and fry for a further 1 minute, stirring constantly. Remove from the heat and mix in all the other dressing ingredients.

5 Pour the dressing over the potatoes and toss well. Add the eggs, then chill in the refrigerator.

6 Line a serving platter with the lettuce leaves and spoon the salad into the centre. Sprinkle over the cucumber and radishes with the cress, if using. Serve immediately.

Potato and Cellophane Noodle Salad

This tasty salad is an ideal side dish to serve at an Indian banquet or to take on a picnic. The recipe features gram flour, also known as besan, which is made from ground chickpeas.

Serves 4
2 medium potatoes, peeled and cut into eighths
175g/6oz cellophane noodles, soaked in hot water until soft
60ml/4 tbsp vegetable oil
1 onion, finely sliced
5ml/1 tsp ground turmeric
60ml/4 tbsp gram flour
5ml/1 tsp grated lemon rind
60–75ml/4–5 tbsp lemon juice
45ml/3 tbsp fish sauce
4 spring onions (scallions), finely sliced
salt and ground black pepper

1 Place the potatoes in a large pan. Add water to cover, bring to the boil and cook for about 15 minutes or until the potatoes are tender but still have a firmness to them. Drain the potatoes and set them aside to cool.

2 Meanwhile, cook the drained noodles in a pan of boiling water for 3 minutes or according to the packet instructions. Drain and rinse under cold running water. Drain well.

3 Heat the oil in a heavy frying pan. Add the onion and turmeric and fry for about 5–7 minutes until golden brown. Drain the onion, reserving the oil.

4 Heat a small frying pan. Add the gram flour and stir constantly for about 4–5 minutes until it turns light golden brown in colour. Take care to avoid it burning.

5 Mix the potatoes, noodles and fried onion in a large bowl. Add the reserved oil and the toasted gram flour with the lemon rind and juice, fish sauce and spring onions.

6 Mix all the ingredients together well and adjust the seasoning to taste with more salt and ground black pepper, if necessary. Serve the salad immediately.

Potato Salad Energy 590kcal/2443kJ; Protein 10.6g; Carbohydrate 18.1g, of which sugars 5.7g; Fat 51.9g, of which saturates 8.9g; Cholesterol 228mg; Calcium 114mg; Fibre 1.6g; Sodium 403mg.
Potato and Noodle Salad Energy 379kcal/1585kJ; Protein 8.2g; Carbohydrate 60g, of which sugars 3.2g; Fat 11.6g, of which saturates 1.7g; Cholesterol 0mg; Calcium 43mg; Fibre 1.4g; Sodium 558mg.

Curried Potato Salad with Mango

This sweet and spicy salad is a wonderful accompaniment to Indian feasts.

Serves 4–6
900g/2lb new potatoes
15ml/1 tbsp olive oil
1 onion, sliced into rings
1 garlic clove, crushed
5ml/1 tsp ground cumin
5ml/1 tsp ground coriander
1 mango, peeled, stoned (pitted) and diced
30ml/2 tbsp demerara (raw) sugar
30ml/2 tbsp lime juice
15ml/1 tbsp sesame seeds
salt and ground black pepper
deep fried coriander (cilantro) leaves, to garnish (optional)

1 Cut the potatoes in half, then cook them in their skins in boiling salted water until tender. Drain well.

2 Heat the oil in a large frying pan and fry the onion and garlic over a low heat for 8–10 minutes, stirring frequently, until they start to soften and turn brown.

3 Stir the ground cumin and coriander into the pan and fry for a few seconds. Stir in the diced mango and sugar and fry for a further 5 minutes, until soft.

4 Remove the pan from the heat and squeeze in the lime juice. Season with salt and pepper.

5 Place the potatoes in a large serving bowl and spoon the mango dressing over the top. Sprinkle with the sesame seeds and serve while the dressing is still warm. Garnish with the deep-fried coriander leaves, if using.

Cook's Tip
To prepare the mango, cut through the mango lengthwise on either side of the stone (pit) to slice off two sections. Leaving the skin on each section, cross hatch the flesh, then bend it back so that the cubes stand proud of the skin. Slice them off with a small knife. Peel the remaining central section of the mango, then cut off the remaining flesh in chunks and dice.

Sweet Potato and Carrot Salad

This simple salad has a delicious sweet-and-sour taste, and can be served warm as part of a light lunch or supper or eaten in a larger quantity as a main course.

Serves 4
1 medium sweet potato
2 carrots, cut into thick diagonal slices
3 medium tomatoes
8–10 iceberg lettuce leaves or Little Gem (Bibb) lettuce
75g/3oz/½ cup canned chickpeas, drained

For the dressing
15ml/1 tbsp clear honey
90ml/6 tbsp natural (plain) low-fat yogurt
2.5ml/½ tsp salt
2.5ml/1 tsp coarsely ground black pepper

For the garnish
15ml/1 tbsp walnuts, shelled and halved
15ml/1 tbsp sultanas (golden raisins)
1 small onion, cut into rings

1 Peel the sweet potato and roughly dice. Boil until soft but not mushy, cover the pan and set aside.

2 Boil the carrots for just a few minutes making sure they remain crunchy. Add the carrots to the sweet potato.

3 Drain all the water from the sweet potato and carrots and place them together in a bowl.

4 Slice the tops off the tomatoes, then scoop out and discard the seeds. Roughly chop the flesh.

5 Line a serving bowl with the lettuce leaves. Mix the sweet potato, carrots, chickpeas and tomatoes together and place in the bowl.

6 In a separate bowl, blend together all the ingredients for the dressing and beat using a fork or small whisk.

7 Garnish the salad with the walnuts, sultanas and onion rings. Pour the dressing over the salad or serve it in a separate bowl.

Curried Potato Salad Energy 174kcal/737kJ; Protein 3.3g; Carbohydrate 33.7g, of which sugars 11.2g; Fat 3.8g, of which saturates 0.7g; Cholesterol 0mg; Calcium 34mg; Fibre 2.5g; Sodium 18mg.
Sweet Potato Salad 153kcal/648kJ; Protein 4.7g; Carbohydrate 26.7g, of which sugars 15.4g; Fat 3.9g, of which saturates 0.6g; Cholesterol 0mg; Calcium 88mg; Fibre 3.9g; Sodium 95mg.

Nutty Bean Salad with Courgettes and Pasta Shells

Serve this delicious salad as an accompaniment or as an appetizer.

Serves 4
1 medium onion, cut into 12 rings
115g/4oz/½ cup canned red
   kidney beans, drained
1 medium green courgette
   (zucchini), sliced
1 medium yellow courgette, sliced
50g/2oz/⅔ cup pasta
   shells, cooked
50g/2oz/½ cup cashew nuts
25g/1oz/¼ cup peanuts

For the dressing
120ml/4fl oz/½ cup fromage
   frais or ricotta cheese
30ml/2 tbsp natural (plain) yogurt
1 fresh green chilli, seeded and
   finely chopped
15ml/1 tbsp chopped fresh
   coriander (cilantro)
2.5ml/½ tsp salt
2.5ml/½ tsp crushed black
   peppercorns
2.5ml/½ tsp crushed dried
   red chillies
15ml/1 tbsp lemon juice
lime wedges, to garnish

1 Arrange the onion rings, red kidney beans, courgette slices and pasta in a large salad dish and sprinkle the cashew nuts and peanuts over the top.

2 In a separate bowl, blend together the fromage frais or ricotta cheese, yogurt, chopped green chilli, fresh coriander and salt and beat it well using a fork.

3 Sprinkle the black pepper, crushed red chillies and lemon juice over the dressing in the bowl.

4 Garnish the salad with the lime wedges and serve immediately with the dressing either in a separate bowl or poured over the salad and gently tossed to combine.

Cook's Tip
If you cannot find a yellow courgette (zucchini), then simply use another of the green variety. The salad may not look quite as colourful but the flavour will not suffer as a result.

Vietnamese Table Salad

The Vietnamese table salad can vary from a bowl of fresh, leafy herbs to a more tropical combination of beansprouts, water chestnuts, mangoes, bananas, star fruit, peanuts and rice noodles. The arrangement of a salad is simple and attractive.

Serves 4–6
1 crunchy lettuce, individual
   leaves separated
half a cucumber, peeled and
   thinly sliced
2 carrots, peeled and
   finely sliced
200g/7oz/scant 1 cup
   beansprouts
2 unripe star fruit (carambola),
   finely sliced
2 green bananas, finely sliced
1 firm papaya, cut in half,
   seeds removed, peeled and
   finely sliced
1 bunch each fresh mint and
   basil, stalks removed
1 lime
dipping sauce, to serve

1 Arrange all the ingredients, except the lime and sauce, on a large serving plate, with the lettuce leaves placed on one side so that they can be used as wrappers.

2 Squeeze the lime and pour the juice all over the sliced fruits, particularly the bananas to help them retain their colour and avoid discoloration from contact with the air.

3 Place the salad on the serving plate in the middle of the table. Serve immediately with a dipping sauce in a separate bowl so that diners can help themselves.

Cook's Tips
• *When this Vietnamese table salad, known as sa lach dia, is served on its own, the vegetables and fruit are usually folded into little packets using lettuce leaves or rice wrappers, and then dipped in a sauce, or added bit by bit to bowls of plain boiled rice or noodles.*
• *Choose a lettuce with crisp, crunchy leaves such as iceberg, Little Gem (Bibb), cos or romaine.*

Nutty Bean Salad Energy 106kcal/444kJ; Protein 5.5g; Carbohydrate 11.9g, of which sugars 3.5g; Fat 4.4g, of which saturates 0.7g; Cholesterol 0mg; Calcium 62mg; Fibre 4.4g; Sodium 228mg.
Vietnamese Salad Energy 108kcal/455kJ; Protein 4g; Carbohydrate 21g, of which sugars 12g; Fat 1g, of which saturates 0g; Cholesterol 0mg; Calcium 110mg; Fibre 42g; Sodium 20mg.

Curried Red Cabbage Slaw

Quick and easy to make, this is a useful dish for a last-minute gathering.

Serves 4–6

1/2 red cabbage, thinly sliced
1 red (bell) pepper, chopped or very thinly sliced
1/2 red onion, chopped
60ml/4 tbsp red wine vinegar
60ml/4 tbsp sugar, or to taste
120ml/4fl oz/1/2 cup Greek (US strained plain) yogurt
120ml/4fl oz/1/2 cup mayonnaise, preferably home-made
1.5ml/1/4 tsp curry powder
2–3 handfuls of raisins
salt and ground black pepper

1 Put the cabbage, red pepper and red onions in a large mixing bowl and toss to combine thoroughly.

2 Heat the red wine vinegar and sugar in a small pan, stirring constantly until the sugar has dissolved, then pour over the vegetables. Leave to cool slightly.

3 Mix together the yogurt and mayonnaise, then stir into the cabbage mixture. Season to taste with curry powder, salt and ground black pepper, then mix in the raisins.

4 Chill the salad in the refrigerator for at least 2 hours before serving. Just before serving, drain off any excess liquid and briefly stir the slaw again.

Spiced Aubergine Salad

The delicate flavours of aubergine, tomatoes and cucumber are lightly spiced with cumin and coriander in this fresh-tasting salad.

Serves 4

2 small aubergines (eggplants) or 1 large aubergine, sliced
75ml/5 tbsp extra-virgin olive oil
50ml/2fl oz/1/4 cup red wine vinegar
2 garlic cloves, crushed
15ml/1 tbsp lemon juice
2.5ml/1/2 tsp ground cumin
2.5ml/1/2 tsp ground coriander
1/2 cucumber, thinly sliced
2 well-flavoured tomatoes, thinly sliced
30ml/2 tbsp natural (plain) yogurt
salt and ground black pepper
chopped fresh flat leaf parsley, to garnish

1 Preheat the grill (broiler). Lightly brush the aubergine slices with olive oil and cook under a high heat, turning once, until they are golden and tender.

2 When the aubergine slices are done, transfer them to a chopping board and cut them into quarters.

3 In a bowl, mix together the remaining oil, the vinegar, garlic, lemon juice, cumin and coriander. Season with salt and black pepper to taste and mix thoroughly.

4 Add the warm aubergines to the bowl, stir well and chill in the refrigerator for at least 2 hours. Add the sliced cucumber and tomatoes to the aubergine. Transfer to a serving dish and spoon the yogurt on top. Sprinkle with the chopped fresh parsley and serve immediately.

Fruit and Raw Vegetable Gado-Gado

Banana leaves are often used as wrappers in which to cook small parcels of food, but if you are serving this salad for a special occasion, you could use a large single banana leaf instead of the mixed salad leaves to line the platter.

Serves 6

1/2 cucumber
2 pears (not too ripe) or 175g/6oz wedge of yam bean
1–2 eating apples
juice of 1/2 lemon
mixed salad leaves or 1–2 banana leaves
6 tomatoes, seeded and cut into wedges
3 fresh pineapple slices, cored and cut into wedges
3 hard-boiled eggs, quartered
175g/6oz egg noodles, cooked, cooled and chopped
deep-fried onions, to garnish

For the peanut sauce

2–4 fresh red chillies, seeded and ground, or 15ml/1 tbsp hot tomato sambal
300ml/1/2 pint/1 1/4 cups coconut milk
350g/12oz/1 1/4 cups crunchy peanut butter
15ml/1 tbsp dark soy sauce or dark brown sugar
5ml/1 tsp tamarind pulp, soaked in 45ml/3 tbsp warm water
coarsely crushed peanuts
salt

1 Make the peanut sauce. Put the ground chillies or hot tomato sambal in a pan. Pour in the coconut milk, then stir in the peanut butter. Heat gently, stirring, until well blended.

2 Simmer the sauce gently until it begins to thicken, then stir in the soy sauce or sugar. Strain in the tamarind juice, discarding the seeds and pulp, add salt to taste and stir well. Spoon into a bowl and sprinkle with coarsely crushed peanuts.

3 To make the salad, core the cucumber and peel the pears or yam bean. Cut the flesh into fine matchsticks. Finely shred the apples and sprinkle them with the lemon juice. Spread a bed of mixed salad leaves on a flat platter and pile the cucumber, pears or yam bean, apples, tomatoes and pineapple on top.

4 Add the quartered eggs and the noodles and garnish with the deep-fried onions. Serve with the peanut sauce.

Curried Cabbage Slaw Energy 286kcal/1194kJ; Protein 3.5g; Carbohydrate 31.6g, of which sugars 31g; Fat 17g, of which saturates 2.6g; Cholesterol 17mg; Calcium 108mg; Fibre 3.1g; Sodium 134mg.
Aubergine Salad Energy 161kcal/669kJ; Protein 2.3g; Carbohydrate 5.8g, of which sugars 5.5g; Fat 14.6g, of which saturates 2.2g; Cholesterol 0mg; Calcium 37mg; Fibre 3.7g; Sodium 15mg.
Fruit Gado-Gado Energy 577kcal/2411kJ; Protein 21.2g; Carbohydrate 46.3g, of which sugars 21g; Fat 35.5g, of which saturates 8.4g; Cholesterol 95mg; Calcium 88mg; Fibre 6.8g; Sodium 482mg.

Green Mango Salad

Green mangoes have light green flesh and go well with prawns (shrimp) or beef.

Serves 4
450g/1lb green mangoes
rind and juice of 2 limes
30ml/2 tbsp sugar

30ml/2 tbsp nuoc cham
  (Vietnamese fish sauce)
2 green Thai chillies, seeded and
  finely sliced
1 small bunch fresh coriander
  (cilantro), stalks removed,
  finely chopped
salt

1 Peel, halve and stone (pit) the mangoes, then slice into strips.

2 In a bowl, mix together the lime juice and rind, sugar and nuoc cham. Add the mango strips with the chillies and coriander. Add salt to taste and set aside for 20 minutes before serving.

Mango, Tomato and Red Onion Salad

The firm texture of under-ripe mango blends perfectly with the tomato and gives this salad a delicious tropical touch. Serve this salad as a side dish to an Indian meal or as an appetizer.

Serves 4
1 firm under-ripe mango
2 large tomatoes or 1 beef
  tomato, sliced

½ red onion, sliced into rings
½ cucumber, peeled and
  thinly sliced

For the dressing
30ml/2 tbsp sunflower or
  vegetable oil
15ml/1 tbsp lemon juice
1 garlic clove, crushed
2.5ml/½ tsp hot pepper sauce
salt and ground black pepper
chopped fresh chives,
  to garnish

1 Halve the mango lengthwise, cutting either side of the stone (pit). Cut the flesh into slices and peel the skin away.

2 Arrange the mango slices, tomato, onion and cucumber on a large serving plate or in a shallow salad bowl.

3 To make the dressing, blend the sunflower or vegetable oil, lemon juice, garlic, pepper sauce and seasoning in a blender or food processor, or, if you prefer, place in a small screw-top jar and shake vigorously to combine.

4 Pour the dressing over the salad. Toss well with your hands or salad servers to ensure that the ingredients are all well coated in the dressing. Serve the salad immediately garnished with the chopped fresh chives.

Cook's Tip
You can adjust the quantity of hot pepper sauce in the dressing to suit your taste. Be careful as some varieties of hot pepper sauce are much hotter than others so always taste a tiny bit to check the heat levels.

Rocket and Coriander Salad

Rocket leaves have a wonderful, peppery flavour and, mixed with coriander, make a delicious salad. You may need extra spinach to pad this salad out unless you have a big supply of rocket.

Serves 4
115g/4oz or more rocket
  (arugula) leaves

115g/4oz young spinach leaves
1 large bunch (about 25g/1oz)
  fresh coriander
2–3 fresh parsley sprigs
1 garlic clove, crushed
45ml/3 tbsp olive oil
10ml/2 tsp white wine vinegar
pinch of paprika
salt
cayenne pepper

1 Wash the rocket and spinach, pat dry, then place in a salad bowl. Chop the herbs and add to the salad.

2 In a small jug (pitcher), blend together the garlic, olive oil, vinegar, paprika, salt and cayenne pepper.

3 Pour the dressing over the salad in the bowl. Toss with your hands to coat the salad in the dressing and serve immediately.

Mango Salad Energy 89kcal/369kJ; Protein 1.1g; Carbohydrate 8.6g, of which sugars 7.9g; Fat 5.8g, of which saturates 0.8g; Cholesterol 0mg; Calcium 17mg; Fibre 1.9g; Sodium 7mg.
Green Mango Salad Energy 92kcal/391kJ; Protein 1g; Carbohydrate 22g, of which sugars 15g; Fat 0g, of which saturates 0g; Cholesterol 0mg; Calcium 32mg; Fibre 33g; Sodium 0.5mg.
Rocket Salad Energy 68kcal/280kJ; Protein 2g; Carbohydrate 1.3g, of which sugars 1.2g; Fat 6.1g, of which saturates 0.9g; Cholesterol 0mg; Calcium 123mg; Fibre 1.8g; Sodium 85mg.

Cambodian Soya Beansprout Salad

Unlike mung beansprouts, soya beansprouts are slightly poisonous raw and need to be par-boiled before using. Tossed in a salad and served with noodles and rice they make a perfect light meal.

Serves 4
450g/1lb fresh soya beansprouts
2 spring onions (scallions),
    finely sliced

1 small bunch fresh coriander
    (cilantro), stalks removed

For the dressing
15ml/1 tbsp sesame oil
30ml/2 tbsp light soy sauce
15ml/1 tbsp white rice vinegar
10ml/2 tsp palm sugar (jaggery)
1 fresh red chilli, seeded and
    finely sliced
15g/½oz fresh young root ginger,
    finely shredded

1 To make the dressing, in a bowl, beat the sesame oil, soy sauce and rice vinegar with the palm sugar, until it dissolves. Stir in the sliced red chilli and ginger and set the bowl aside for about 30 minutes to let the flavours develop.

2 Bring a pan of salted water to the boil. Drop in the beansprouts and blanch for a minute only. Drain and refresh under cold water until cool. Drain again and put them into a clean dish towel. Shake out the excess water.

3 Put the beansprouts into a bowl with the spring onions. Pour over the dressing and toss well. Garnish with the coriander leaves and serve immediately.

Fennel Coleslaw

Another variation on traditional coleslaw in which the flavour of fennel plays a major role in creating this delectable salad.

Serves 4
175g/6oz fennel
2 spring onions (scallions)
175g/6oz white cabbage
115g/4oz celery

175g/6oz carrots
50g/2oz/scant ½ cup sultanas
    (golden raisins)
2.5ml/½ tsp caraway
    seeds (optional)
15ml/1 tbsp chopped
    fresh parsley
45ml/3 tbsp extra-virgin olive oil
5ml/1 tsp lemon juice
strips of spring onion (scallion),
    to garnish

1 Using a sharp knife, cut the fennel and spring onions into thin slices. Place in a serving bowl.

2 Slice the cabbage and celery finely and cut the carrots into fine strips. Add to the fennel and spring onions in the serving bowl. Add the sultanas and caraway seeds to the bowl, if using, and toss lightly to mix through.

3 Stir the chopped parsley, olive oil and lemon juice into the bowl and mix all the ingredients very thoroughly.

4 Cover the bowl with clear film (plastic wrap) and chill in the refrigerator for about 3 hours to allow all the flavours of the coleslaw to mingle together. Serve the coleslaw immediately, garnished with strips of spring onion.

Korean Cucumber Namul

This sautéed dish retains the natural succulence of the cucumber, while also infusing the recipe with a pleasantly refreshing hint of garlic and fresh chilli.

Serves 2
200g/7oz cucumber
15ml/1 tbsp vegetable oil

5ml/1 tsp spring onion (scallion),
    finely chopped
1 garlic clove, crushed
5ml/1 tsp sesame oil or
    groundnut (peanut) oil
sesame seeds, and seeded
    and shredded red chilli,
    to garnish
salt

1 Thinly slice the cucumber and place in a colander over a bowl. Sprinkle with about 5ml/1 tsp salt, then leave to stand in a cool place for at least 10 minutes.

2 Drain off any excess liquid from the cucumber slices and transfer them to a clean bowl.

3 Coat a frying pan or wok with the vegetable oil, and heat it over a medium heat. Add the spring onion, garlic and cucumber to the pan, and quickly stir-fry together for about 2–3 minutes.

4 Remove the pan from the heat, add the sesame or groundnut oil and toss lightly to blend all the ingredients. Place the salad in a shallow serving dish and garnish with the sesame seeds and shredded red chilli before serving.

Cook's Tip
Take care when handling chillies that you don't touch other sensitive parts of your body afterwards otherwise the chilli oil from your fingers will cause irritation. Wash your hands well.

Variation
Replace the chilli with thin strips of shredded red (bell) pepper if you prefer a version with less heat.

Cambodian Salad Energy 95kcal/396kJ; Protein 4.5g; Carbohydrate 8.4g, of which sugars 5.6g; Fat 5.6g, of which saturates 0.5g; Cholesterol 3mg; Calcium 54mg; Fibre 2.4g; Sodium 79mg.
Fennel Coleslaw Energy 145kcal/604kJ; Protein 1.9g; Carbohydrate 15.6g, of which sugars 15.3g; Fat 8.7g, of which saturates 1.2g; Cholesterol 0mg; Calcium 70mg; Fibre 3.8g; Sodium 46mg.
Korean Namul Energy 74kcal/304kJ; Protein 0.8g; Carbohydrate 1.7g, of which sugars 1.6g; Fat 7.1g, of which saturates 0.9g; Cholesterol 0mg; Calcium 20mg; Fibre 0.7g; Sodium 4mg.

Bamboo Shoot Salad

This hot, sharp-flavoured salad originated in north-eastern Thailand. Serve with noodles and stir-fried vegetables, or as a side dish with a green or red curry.

Serves 4

400g/14oz canned bamboo
   shoots, in large pieces
25g/1oz/about 3 tbsp
   glutinous rice
30ml/2 tbsp chopped shallots
15ml/1 tbsp chopped garlic
45ml/3 tbsp chopped spring
   onions (scallions)
30ml/2 tbsp light soy sauce
30ml/2 tbsp fresh lime juice
5ml/1 tsp sugar
2.5ml/½ tsp dried chilli flakes
20–25 small fresh mint leaves
15ml/1 tbsp toasted
   sesame seeds

1 Rinse the bamboo shoots under cold running water, then drain them and pat them thoroughly dry with kitchen paper and set them aside.

2 Dry-roast the rice in a frying pan until it is golden brown. Leave to cool slightly, then turn into a mortar and grind to fine crumbs with a pestle.

3 Transfer the rice to a bowl and add the shallots, garlic, spring onions, soy sauce, lime juice, sugar, chillies and half the mint leaves. Mix well.

4 Add the bamboo shoots to the bowl and toss well to ensure they are evenly coated in all the other ingredients.

5 Sprinkle the salad with the toasted sesame seeds and the remaining fresh mint leaves and serve immediately.

> **Cook's Tips**
> • Glutinous rice does not, in fact, contain any gluten – it's just sticky. It is very popular in South-east Asian cooking.
> • This recipe works best with canned whole bamboo shoots, if you can find them – they have more flavour than the more common sliced variety.

Cucumber and Shallot Salad

In Malaysia and Singapore, this light, refreshing salad is served with Indian food almost as often as the cooling mint-flavoured cucumber raita. The Malays also enjoy this salad with many of their spicy fish and grilled meat dishes. It can be made ahead of time and kept in the refrigerator. Serve it as a salad, or a relish.

Serves 4

1 cucumber, peeled, halved
   lengthways and seeded
4 shallots, halved lengthways and
   sliced finely along the grain
1–2 green chillies, seeded and
   sliced finely lengthways
60ml/4 tbsp coconut milk
5–10ml/1–2 tsp cumin seeds,
   dry-roasted and ground to
   a powder
salt
1 lime, quartered, to serve

1 Slice the cucumber halves finely and sprinkle with a little salt. Set aside for about 10–15 minutes to draw out any excess moisture. Rinse well and drain off any excess water.

2 Put the cucumber, shallots and chillies in a salad serving bowl. Pour in the coconut milk and toss well. Sprinkle most of the roasted cumin seeds over the top.

3 Just before serving, toss the salad again, season with salt, and sprinkle the rest of the roasted cumin seeds over the top. Serve with lime wedges to squeeze over the salad.

Orange and Red Onion Salad

Cumin and mint give this refreshing, quick-to-prepare salad a very Middle Eastern flavour. Small, seedless oranges are most suitable, if available.

Serves 6

6 oranges
2 red onions
15ml/1 tbsp cumin seeds
5ml/1 tsp coarsely ground
   black pepper
15ml/1 tbsp chopped
   fresh mint
90ml/6 tbsp olive oil
salt
fresh mint sprigs and black
   olives, to garnish

1 Slice the oranges thinly, catching any juices. Holding each orange slice in turn over a bowl, cut round with scissors to remove the peel and pith. Reserve the juice.

2 Slice the red onions thinly and as evenly as possible. Separate each of the slices into rings.

3 Arrange the orange and onion slices in layers in a shallow dish, sprinkling each layer with cumin seeds, ground black pepper, chopped mint, olive oil and salt to taste. Pour over the reserved orange juice.

4 Leave the salad in a cool place or in the refrigerator for a minimum of 2 hours but no longer than about 4 hours.

5 Sprinkle over the fresh mint sprigs and black olives to garnish, and serve immediately.

Bamboo Shoot Salad Energy 72kcal/305kJ; Protein 3.9g; Carbohydrate 13g, of which sugars 6.2g; Fat 0.7g, of which saturates 0.1g; Cholesterol 0mg; Calcium 31mg; Fibre 1.9g; Sodium 185mg.
Cucumber Salad Energy 17kcal/68kJ; Protein 0.7g; Carbohydrate 3.3g, of which sugars 2.7g; Fat 0.1g, of which saturates 0g; Cholesterol 0mg; Calcium 19mg; Fibre 0.7g; Sodium 15mg.
Orange Salad Energy 199kcal/825kJ; Protein 1.6g; Carbohydrate 11.5g, of which sugars 11.3g; Fat 16.6g, of which saturates 2.4g; Cholesterol 0mg; Calcium 68mg; Fibre 2.3g; Sodium 7mg.

Raw Vegetable Yam

In Thai cooking, 'yam' dishes are salads made with raw or lightly cooked vegetables. Serve with a fiery curry to appreciate the cooling effect.

Serves 4

50g/2oz watercress or baby
   spinach, chopped
½ cucumber, finely diced
2 celery sticks, finely diced
2 carrots, finely diced
1 red (bell) pepper, seeded
   and finely diced
2 tomatoes, seeded and
   finely diced
small bunch fresh mint,
   finely chopped
90g/3½oz cellophane noodles

For the yam

2 small fresh red chillies, seeded
   and finely chopped
60ml/4 tbsp light soy sauce
45ml/3 tbsp lemon juice
5ml/1 tsp palm sugar (jaggery)
   or light muscovado
   (brown) sugar
60ml/4 tbsp water
1 head pickled garlic, finely
   chopped, plus 15ml/1 tbsp
   vinegar from the jar
50g/2oz/scant ½ cup peanuts,
   roasted and chopped
90g/3½oz fried tofu,
   finely chopped
15ml/1 tbsp sesame
   seeds, toasted

1 Place the watercress or spinach, cucumber, celery, carrots, red pepper and tomatoes in a large serving bowl. Add the chopped fresh mint and toss together.

2 Soak the noodles in boiling water for about 3 minutes, or according to the packet instructions, rinse in cold water.

3 Drain the noodles well and snip with a pair of scissors into shorter lengths. Add them to the vegetables in the bowl.

4 To make the yam, put the chopped chillies in a pan and add the soy sauce, lemon juice, sugar and water. Place over a medium heat and stir until the sugar has dissolved.

5 Add the garlic, with the pickling vinegar from the jar, then mix in the chopped nuts, tofu and toasted sesame seeds.

6 Pour the yam over the vegetables and noodles, toss together until well mixed, and serve immediately.

Green Papaya Salad

This salad appears in many guises in South-east Asia. As green papaya is not easy to get hold of, finely grated carrots, cucumber or even crisp green apple can be used instead. Alternatively, use very thinly sliced white cabbage.

Serves 4

1 green papaya
4 garlic cloves, coarsely chopped
15ml/1 tbsp chopped shallots

3–4 fresh red chillies, seeded
   and sliced
2.5ml/½ tsp salt
2–3 yard-long beans or
   6 green beans, cut into
   2cm/¾in lengths
2 tomatoes, cut into thin wedges
45ml/3 tbsp Thai fish sauce
15ml/1 tbsp caster
   (superfine) sugar
juice of 1 lime
30ml/2 tbsp crushed roasted
   peanuts
sliced fresh red chillies, to garnish

1 Cut the papaya in half lengthways. Scrape out the seeds with a spoon and discard, then peel, using a swivel vegetable peeler or a small sharp knife. Shred the papaya flesh finely in a food processor or by using a grater.

2 Put the garlic, shallots, red chillies and salt in a large mortar and grind to a paste with a pestle.

3 Add the shredded papaya to the mortar, a small amount at a time, pounding with the pestle until it becomes slightly limp.

4 Add the sliced yard-long or green beans and wedges of tomato to the mortar and crush them lightly with the pestle until they are incorporated.

5 Season the mixture with the fish sauce, sugar and lime juice. Transfer to a serving dish and sprinkle with the crushed roasted peanuts. Garnish with the red chillies and serve immediately.

Cook's Tip
When ripe, papayas have a vivid golden-yellow skin and juicy, silky flesh. The seeds are edible, with a peppery taste.

Raw Vegetable Yam Energy 276kcal/1152kJ; Protein 12.1g; Carbohydrate 28.8g, of which sugars 9g; Fat 12.4g, of which saturates 1.5g; Cholesterol 0mg; Calcium 415mg; Fibre 3.1g; Sodium 1101mg.
Green Papaya Salad Energy 63kcal/263kJ; Protein 2.5g; Carbohydrate 6.2g, of which sugars 5.6g; Fat 3.3g, of which saturates 0.6g; Cholesterol 0mg; Calcium 19mg; Fibre 1.8g; Sodium 835mg.

Index